REAL VEGETARIAN THAI

REAL VEGETARIAN THAI

by Nancie McDermott

Illustrations by Jennie Oppenheimer

CHRONICLE BOOKS

SAN FRANCISCO

Library of Congress Cataloging–in–Publication Data:

McDermott, Nancie.
   Real vegetarian Thai/by Nancie McDermott; illustrations
by Jennie Oppenheimer.
      p. cm.
   Includes bibliographical references and index.
   ISBN 0–8118–1151–4 (pbk.)
   1. Cookery, Thai. 2. Vegetarian cookery. I. Title.
TX724.5 T5M3423 1997
641.5'636–dc21   96–37096
                                        CIP

Printed in the United States of America.

Book and cover design: Studio Pepin, Tokyo
Cover and interior illustrations:
Jennie Oppenheimer, Studio Zocolo

Distributed in Canada by Raincoast Books
8680 Cambie Street
Vancouver, British Columbia V6P 6M9

10 9 8 7 6 5 4 3 2 1

Chronicle Books
85 Second Street
San Francisco, California 94105

Web Site: www.chronbooks.com

This book is dedicated to my friends and fellow Peace Corps volunteers Kathy Judd, Mary Claire Peceny, Kay Strong, and Sandi and Dudley Younkin, with gratitude for the humor, adventure, insight, generosity, and good company with which they provided me during the years we spent in Thailand.

ACKNOWLEDGMENTS

My thanks to Phillis Carey, Jill O'Connor, and Fiona Urquhart for their excellent work in bringing this book to life, both in the kitchen and on the page. Their efforts have made the book indescribably better and the process a lot more fun. I am grateful to my husband, Will Lee, and our beloved daughters, Camellia and Isabelle, for cheering me on and for making life sweet while I worked on this book.

I would be delighted to hear what you think of this book and its recipes. You can contact me at the address below:

Nancie McDermott, Author
c/o Chronicle Books
85 Second Street
San Francisco, CA 94105

TABLE OF CONTENTS

INTRODUCTION

INTRODUCTION

ᏬᏣ This is a book about the remarkable food of the remarkable kingdom where I had the good fortune to spend three years of my life. I went to Thailand not to explore an extraordinary cuisine in its vibrant context, but to teach English as a second language to Thai adolescents in an upcountry junior high. In fact, I did both during my stay, as well as receiving an education in eating, laughing, shopping, linguistics, friendship, art, agriculture, cooking, economics, conversation, and enjoying life.

ᏬᏣ Had I foreseen that I would turn to writing cookbooks and teaching Thai cooking classes, I would have asked questions, sought out experts, and made notes about the innumerable feasts, everyday suppers, and snacks I savored during my stay in Thailand. When I set out to write my first cookbook, *Real Thai: The Best of Thailand's Regional Cooking*, I longed to turn back the clock and relive my time in Thailand as an official student of its cuisine. I regretted that my culinary concerns had run no further than finding a dynamite version of *paht Thai, som tum,* or *tome yum* soup, and making brownies on a bucket-shaped charcoal stove. But now I consider this a blessing, because I absorbed the foundation of my knowledge of Thai food and culture like a child, soaking up a whole world along with the plain jasmine rice I ate morning, noon, and night.

ᏬᏣ Although I am not a vegetarian, I wanted to write a cookbook for people who love Thai food but who do not eat meat. It was a great pleasure to create these recipes, coming up with delicious versions of traditional Thai dishes while respecting the commitments of the vegetarian kitchen. To do so I quickly found I had to veer away from the framework of authenticity within which I love to explore Thai cooking, for unlike India, China, and Japan, Thailand lacks a strong indigenous vegetarian tradition.

ᏬᏣ Despite the fact that the majority of Thais are devoted to the teachings of Theravada Buddhism, vegetarian practice is rare. Even the Theravada Buddhist monks may be unable to follow a vegetarian diet, since they vow to live simply, subsisting on whatever the people provide for them. The people establish merit toward future incarnations by making daily offerings of food and other necessities of life to the monks.

ᏬᏣ Fresh from the river or preserved in countless forms, fish is a profoundly important part of the traditional diet, along with prodigious amounts of the quintessential Thai dish, plain rice. Next in importance are abundant vegetables, raw and cooked, followed by noodles, fruit, and the universe of sweets and snacks known as *kanome*. Then comes meat, often appearing in small amounts as a seasoning in a soup, curry, or stir-fry, rather than as a separate dish. Often the quantity of meat and the frequency with which it appears are a function of expense rather than principle.

෴ Seafood is an even greater luxury than meat, even in the seaside villages and coastal towns dotting the Gulf of Siam. Thai fishermen who troll the warm gulf waters before dawn rarely feast on the day's catch at home, since most of it is iced down and hustled off to Bangkok by sunrise, for sale to fancy restaurants and specialty markets at a hefty price.

෴ Although vegetarianism is not widespread in Thailand, there are those who refrain from eating flesh. Followers of *ahahn mahng-saha-wiraht*, a religious practice with origins in the traditions of ayurvedic medicine and the teachings of Hinduism, forsake the eating of meat, although they may find eggs and dairy foods acceptable. They generally do not consider it necessary to maintain separate utensils to prepare and serve food.

෴ A more common tradition of vegetarianism in Thailand is *ahahn jay*. The first word means "food," and the second refers to Chinese vegetarian practice. The Thai phrase *Kin jay* conveys that you do not eat meat. Chinese vegetarianism is rooted in Mahayana Buddhist practice, and around it has sprung up a highly developed cuisine of tofu, wheat gluten, and other protein-rich foods that are created to resemble meat in shape and texture. Within *ahahn mahng-saha-wiraht*, the emphasis is on eating vegetables for their own sake, while within the tradition of *ahahn jay*, cooks use meatlike foods to "vegetarianize" beloved dishes that are traditionally made with meat.

෴ While they may not embrace vegetarianism as a way of life, each year many Thai-Chinese people abstain from eating meat for a period of time. These Mahayana Buddhists see vegetarianism as a means of purification, a route to mindfulness through temporary abstinence and sacrifice, much like the Christian observance of Lent. Believers forego meat and animal products in any form, and food must be prepared and served using special pans, plates, and utensils. This ten-day celebration is most prominent in southern Thai cities, particularly Phuket, where a large Thai-Chinese population has kept numerous Chinese cultural practices thriving for generations. In Bangkok and other large cities where the Chinese influence is strong, you will find a few Chinese vegetarian cafés, and even street vendors who specialize in snacks made of tofu and gluten, sold in charming little cups fashioned from banana and bamboo leaves.

✧ Within the last decade or so, a small number of Thais have adopted vegetarianism and have begun reinventing Thai cuisine without the use of meat or fish. Enthusiasm for this approach is growing, for health as well as religious reasons. Visitors to Thailand can sample this vegetarian work in progress at a few restaurants in Bangkok and in the fabled northern Thai city of Chiang Mai.

✧ I created these recipes using no meat, fish, seafood, or any condiments containing them. This meant omitting the fish sauce that seasons virtually every savory dish prepared in a Thai kitchen. Simply substituting an equal amount of soy sauce did not do the job: Soy sauce is heavy and rich by comparison and it takes over a dish. To replace the fish sauce, I arrived at a simple formula of increasing the salt while adding vegetable broth and a little soy sauce. In some cases, where an especially pungent, over-the-top saltiness is required, a touch of Asian bean sauce can be included. I also played with the scrumptious French mushroom creation called *duxelles*, to invent an alternative to the minced pork mixture flavored with cilantro, garlic, and pepper that is used extensively in Thai food. The result is Mushroom Mince (page 206), and it is used in savory dishes througout this book. These adaptations worked beautifully, enabling me to create a vegetarian way of cooking within the traditions of Thai cuisine.

✧ For vegans, Thai food is easy to enjoy, since dairy products are virtually unknown in the traditional cuisine of almost every Asian country except India, where yogurt and ghee are widely used. Eggs are quite popular and not limited to breakfast, but in most cases they are left whole; consequently, substitutions and omissions are easy to make. In most of the recipes that use eggs, I have given adaptations for vegan readers in the notes that follow the recipes.

❖ ❖ ❖

✧ During my time in Thailand, I lived in Thatoom, a town of ten thousand people on the Mun River in the northeastern Thai province of Surin. Like the Thai provinces of Buriram and Sri Saket, its neighbors to the east and west, Surin was part of Cambodia through the centuries during which the Khmer empire dominated the region. By the fifteenth century, Thailand had taken control of these three provinces. Today, they make up a small portion of Pahk

Issahn, Thailand's large northeastern region, which retains cultural and linguistic ties to neighboring Laos. Strong traces of Cambodian influence endure in Surin and its neighbors, particularly in the form of traditional silk weaving and in the Khmer dialect spoken in upcountry homes.

വ I shared a house with several students from our school, whose villages were too far from Thatoom to permit them a daily commute. In a traditional Thai arrangement, I provided room and board while my students took care of household chores and kept a huge, barrel-shaped jar in my kitchen supplied with jasmine rice from their family larders. The house I rented was a spacious wooden structure in the typical Thai style, with the living quarters raised one story off the ground on sturdy posts, and the kitchen and bathroom down below. This keeps everyone high and dry during the monsoon season, when flooding of up to a foot or so is common. Upstairs, a long sitting room ran the length of the house, with three bedrooms taking up the remaining space. The room opened onto a porch lined with benches, with wide steps leading down to the cement patio beneath the house.

വ This sheltered space under the house is where country people can park their plows and shelter their water buffalo, oxen, ducks, and chickens through the night. Here we parked bicycles and shoes, lawn chairs, low tables, and straw mats lined with pillows. In this shady oasis, we often waited out the melting heat of a weekend afternoon, sustained by oscillating fans, conversation, the BBC World Service, and Thai iced tea. One-third of this downstairs patio was enclosed to form a small bathroom and a simple but spacious kitchen, with huge wooden shutters over windows and doors. These were sealed up tight each night and flung open again each morning, creating an almost alfresco room in which to cook and eat. A picket fence enclosed our small yard, which contained two beautiful mango trees, big plump jars to catch rainwater for drinking and cooking, and a well that provided water for household use.

വ Rising at dawn is standard operating procedure all over Thailand. I quickly grew fond of the cool, soft ambience of those morning hours, and an early start helped me take it slow in the harsh light and heat of afternoon. It also pays to show up at the market as early as possible. In a modest market like ours, cabbage, cucumbers, cauliflower, and chilies were always available, but laggards were sure to miss out on sweet, crunchy snow peas, ears of baby corn in diminutive husks, small piles of fresh straw mushrooms, and any unusually good batches of curry.

ᴄᴏ I pedaled my bicycle to the market each morning, never in the first wave of shoppers but always early enough to merit only modest teasing from passing neighbors on their way home. I picked up some curry and a little soup or chili sauce to supplement our breakfast rice, along with whatever we needed to cook supper. I topped off my tote bag with *kanome*, delicious Thai snacks made by enterprising townsfolk who had risen to cook them a good bit earlier than dawn. My personal favorite was *dao suan*, a warm, sweet mung bean pudding made with palm sugar and coconut milk, but banana leaf packets of coconut sticky rice with custard could turn my head, and it was almost impossible to walk by the fried banana lady without trading a few *baht* for a cluster of warm, crunchy *gluay kaek*. This would keep us patient till the morning's rice was ready.

ᴄᴏ In my absence, my students had risen, bathed, and dressed and then turned to morning chores. The boys drew water, the girls lit the charcoal stoves, put on the rice pot, and got breakfast started, and everyone pitched in on the sweeping and on washing down the wooden floors upstairs. While I got ready for school, the two girls, Onjan and Titimah, finished cooking and set out our morning meal, spreading out thick straw mats to transform the kitchen floor into the scene of a homey feast. When five plates heaped with steaming jasmine rice ringed the circle of half-a-dozen savory dishes, we gathered for a quick meal before heading off, striving to be in our appointed places at school in time for the playing of the national anthem and the raising of the flag.

ᴄᴏ Left behind in our quiet kitchen were the simple appointments of Thai home cooking. A pair of bucket-shaped charcoal stoves stood on a low platform that raised them to the perfect height for cooking. A handy straw fan helped us crank up the heat as needed, and a covered bucket stood by with tongs, accepting deposits of live coals when we wanted to turn it down. A worktable held two mortars, one a tall, deep clay cone with a wooden pestle for green papaya salad, and the other a squat, sturdy bowl of blue-green granite for curry pastes. Beside it were the cutting board, a thick pale round of hardwood cut from a sturdy tamarind tree, and a no-nonsense cleaver and assorted paring knives. A stack of enameled-tin dinner plates stood by, along with a basket of silverware. This consisted of the forks and large spoons Thais use for eating. Diners scoop up rice and its accompaniments onto the spoon, using the fork to direct the tidbits of food. The basket also contained chopsticks, both long ones for cooking and regular ones for eating, on those occa-

sions when we brought home noodle dishes from the corner noodle shop.
ᴄʌ Pots, pans, and a shallow, lightweight Thai-style wok hung on the wall,
along with two steamers— a large, metal Chinese-style steamer and a cone-
shaped, woven bamboo steamer for Laotian-style sticky rice. Nearby hung
various utensils along with market bags and copious supplies of the ubiquitous twin elements of Thai cooking, listed in recipes simply as *hohm-gratiem*,
"garlic and shallots." Both are tiny compared to their Western cousins,
flavor-packed and tinged with a deep, lovely shade of pink.

ᴄʌ On the far wall stood our *thoo*, a dead ringer for my Granny Suitt's pie
safe, but with screenwire lining the doors rather than embossed tin. Here we
kept condiments and food screened away from pesky flies, and cordoned off
from tenacious ants by a quartet of ceramic cups in which the four legs of the
cabinet stood. Each cup provided a little moat filled with water. This fended
off creatures with a mind to crawl up the *thoo* leg for a picnic without immers-
ing the cabinet's wooden legs in water, which would rot them over time. In
the two far corners stood waist-high glazed jars, one filled with rainwater
for cooking and drinking, and the other holding about fifty pounds of
jasmine rice.

ᴄʌ My kitchen was simple and sensible, and most of its equipment, or a good
substitute, is easily found in the West. Thai ingredients are a bigger challenge
to find, although the availability of excellent condiments and fresh, gorgeous
Southeast Asian herbs increases every year. I have offered suggestions on substitutions whenever possible, and I salute your efforts to work out your version of a dish with whatever you have available if you cannot find choices A
and B. Check the Mail-Order Sources section in the back of this book for some
excellent purveyors of Asian ingredients and equipment. Thailand's cuisine
owes much to that of India and China, and any acquaintance you make with
Chinese and Indian cooking will serve you well as you cook Thai food.

❖ ❖ ❖

ᴄʌ To organize this book in a truly Thai culinary spirit, I would need only
four chapters, defined by the respectful relationship Thais automatically create
between rice and everything else they eat. Rice and Noodles would be Chapter
One, Good Stuff to Set Our Rice Aglow would be Chapter Two, Snacks and
Sweets to Enjoy between Rice-Centered Meals would be Chapter Three, and
Basic Recipes would be Chapter Four.

ᴄʌ Of these four chapters, Chapter Two would be the largest, encompassing the range of what Thais call *gahp kao*, *gahp* meaning "with" and kao meaning "rice." I have broken this category Western-style into Soups, Salads, Curries, and Other Main Dishes to make it easier to find favorite dishes and to put a vegetarian Thai menu together. Chapter One, the Rice and Noodles chapter, might not even exist, since every Thai person old enough to light an upcountry charcoal stove learns how to cook a pot of rice, and since noodles are savored in noodle shops rather than cooked at home.

℘ Instead, this book is organized into eight chapters, beginning with Appetizers and Snacks, followed by Salads, and then Soups. In these three chapters you will find dishes that are light in spirit, often appropriate for a first course, a nibble with which to welcome guests, or a simple lunch or supper for one or two people. Next comes Curries, with a roundup of saucy, spectacular dishes, each with a Thai-style curry paste as its flavorful base. Other Main Dishes offers grilled vegetables and an array of stir-fries. As with curries, you will want to serve these dishes along with lots of unseasoned rice, either jasmine rice or Laotian-style sticky rice. Both serve as a pleasing foil for the array of intense flavors that compose a Thai meal.

℘ Next comes a savory chapter on Rice and Noodles. Here you will find basic rice recipes, seasoned rice dishes such as fried rice and coconut rice, and a delicious array of noodle dishes. You can enjoy *paht Thai* and Thai-style fried rice as one-dish meals, or serve them along with other dishes as is often done in Thai restaurants in the West. Sweets and Drinks follows, where you will find classics such as Cool, Crisp Rubies in Coconut Milk and Thai Iced Tea, as well as irresistible East-West creations, including Thai Coffee Ice Cream, Coconut Rice Pudding, and Fresh Lemongrass Lemonade. The final chapter, Basic Recipes, is a compendium of condiments and other dishes called for in recipes throughout the book. Here you will find instructions for dipping sauces, curry pastes, Roasted Rice Powder, and Tamarind Liquid, as well as advice for those of you who want to make coconut milk from scratch and grow lemongrass in your home garden.

℘ Following this final chapter of recipes are four appendices: a bibliography of useful books on Thailand and Thai food; suggested vegetarian menus; a mail-order section, where you will find information on culinary newsletters, booksellers, and vendors who can supply you with herbs, spices, and utensils; and a glossary containing information about the ingredients you will encounter in this book.

℘ For a traditional Thai approach to a vegetarian menu, try to think in terms of a few principles rather than a list of specific dishes. Think of a typical home-style Thai meal as an edible solar system, with lots of delicious little planets revolving around the sun. The latter, for our purposes, is an abundance of naturally fragrant unseasoned jasmine rice. The planets must not only nourish us and taste good, they must also delight us in their variety, orbiting in a harmonious vegetarian dance, which we are free to choreograph in a number of ways.

Foremost is variety of flavors. You have probably heard that Thai people love chilies, but even a Thai with the proverbial asbestos palate wants only one or two incendiary dishes to set the meal aflame, not a tableful, because then the balance is gone. Pick a chili-hot curry as your centerpiece dish, and add contrasting planets to your universe, with something sour such as Lemongrass Soup with Rice and Basil Chez Sovan, something sweet such as Son-in-Law Eggs, and something salty such as Dao Jiow Lone Dipping Sauce with a rainbow of vegetables.

Another way to ensure variety is to avoid repetition of ingredients. Do not make tofu or mushrooms, for example, a major player in more than one dish. Also, you will want to vary textures and cooking methods. Rather than preparing several stir-fries, pick one and round out the menu with something deep-fried for a rich, crispy note, something liquid such as clear soup for a simple resonance, and perhaps a salad for a cool hit and a raw vegetable crunch.

Finally, I add my personal mission to achieve variety in the amount of effort I must expend to put forth the meal. If I am making labor-intensive Sweet Potato Wonton Soup with Crispy Garlic and frying delicious Mung Bean Fritters to welcome my guests, I will take every possible shortcut for the rest of the meal, from assigning someone else to bring a salad and drinks, to serving a fruit tart or brownies from my favorite bakery for dessert.

Keep in mind that these are guidelines and not commandments. If you take anxiety into the kitchen, it will get in the food. Thai people make a national pastime out of surrendering to the universe and following their hearts. Just pick a recipe, start cooking, and you will be doing it right.

My goal is to put words about Thai food on paper in such a way that you will long to taste it, and thus be driven to cook it to life. I hope these recipes will create delicious vegetarian Thai food for you and for those who share your table. May this book bring you pleasure, and pass along to you some of the magic I have found in the world of food, cooking, and all things Thai.

1
·
APPETIZERS AND SNACKS

APPETIZERS AND SNACKS

೧ Early in my three-year sojourn in Thailand, I made the common observation that Thai people seem to eat all the time. This custom pleased me enormously, since food has always been of great interest to me. I also wanted to make up for time lost in growing to adulthood in a world without the blessing of Thai food.

೧ From the bluish hour before sunrise until the bullfrogs and cicadas serenade the last night owls off to sleep, the people of Thailand are cooking, buying provisions at the market, eating square meals, snacking on an endless array of tidbits, toting food to someone else for sharing, or talking about food. Many of the dishes that comprise these rituals fit into the category of *ahahn wahng,* with *ahahn* meaning "food" and *wahng* meaning "free," alluding to leisure, free time, and the appeal of passing a little time nibbling and chatting with friends and family.

೧ On returning to my desk in the teacher's room after a seventh-grade English class, I was certain to find edible reinforcements on the conference table: cool, juicy chunks of ripe pineapple for dipping in a tiny mountain of salt laced with dried red chilies, silver dollar–sized pancakes of freshly grated coconut known as *kanome ping,* crispy fried bananas called *gluay kaek.* The teachers enjoying the treats would quickly beckon, calling out an invitation to each returning colleague to take a moment to visit and enjoy a bite. If I were the one heading out on my break to bicycle to the post office or the bank, I kept an eye out for something sweet or savory to bring back, lest I return empty-handed. I loved this custom and still do, for the company as well as the food. During our training, we greenhorn Peace Corps volunteers learned that eating while strolling down the street was considered poor manners. I imagine the rationale is not the incongruous prissy attitude I surmised at the time, but a respect for food and an appreciation of its intrinsic pleasure and the benefits of eating with people one enjoys.

೧ Most of the recipes in this chapter are for street food, the appealing, portable snacks that fuel Thai people between their three daily meals centered on rice. The custom of ordering a first course in a restaurant or serving one as part of a special meal at home is more Western than Thai. Certainly you will be offered food within minutes of arriving at someone's home, but this hospitality would be shown whether or not a meal was soon to follow. These dishes work well as informal appetizers before a meal, or as snacks any time the urge strikes you for the taste of Thai food. Have *miang kum*–Lettuce Bites–ready when guests arrive, for nibbling while you command the grill and pour tempting tumblers of Thai Iced Tea. Fry up a sizzling saucer of Two-Potato Curry Pot Stickers to go with the popcorn while you watch the playoff games, or present delectable and lovely Pineapple Bites for a sparkling note at the next potluck.

↻ All but two of the recipes in this chapter are my vegetarian versions of traditional Thai dishes. I created the Garlicky Mushroom Turnovers to showcase Mushroom Mince, the scrumptious filling found in the Basic Recipes chapter that you will use many times in the course of cooking recipes from this book. The other, Sweet and Spicy Nuts, was inspired by peanut brittle and honey-roasted nuts and carried to Thai heights with the addition of red curry paste, roasted cumin, and toasted shredded coconut. You will need to make these in advance, and you may need to do as I do and have an un-bribable family member hide them so that some remain to serve to your guests. The pot stickers, Sweet Potato Shiao Mai, Fried Peanuts with Green Onions and Chilies, and Crispy Spring Rolls with Sweet and Hot Garlic Sauce are Thai-Chinese dishes that entered Thailand's culinary landscape centuries ago as part of the great Chinese legacy to Thai cuisine.

↻ The amount of time and the degree of skill required to prepare the recipes vary widely. The two dipping sauces, Roasted Eggplant Dip with Thai Flavors and Dao Jiow Lone Dipping Sauce, are simple to make, as are Pineapple Bites and Sweet and Spicy Nuts. Curried Corncakes, Mung Bean Fritters, and Fried Peanuts with Green Onions and Chilies are straightforward but require the care and effort demanded by deep-frying. The *shiao mai*, pot stickers, and spring rolls involve the challenge of filling, rolling, and shaping each piece, and then steaming or frying the result, but the rewards will be great. Keep in mind as you try your hand at making these "greatest hits" of the world of Thai street food that you are venturing where Thai home cooks seldom go, since these good things are commonly purchased from vendors, experts for whom making spring rolls or dumplings is a daily task.

❧ PINEAPPLE BITES ❧

This classic Thai snack goes by the mysterious name *mah haw*. The first word means "horse" and the second refers to the Haw people, who migrated to northern Thailand from the southwestern Chinese province of Yunnan centuries ago. While I am still working out the connection to horses, Haw people, and a royal–style Thai snack, I can say with certainty that almost everyone loves these. Fresh pineapple is lovely, canned pineapple is easy, and using either one produces a great taste. If you choose fresh pineapple, reserve the leafy top, place it on the serving platter as a garnish, and surround it with a flotilla of tiny Pineapple Bites.

*1 small ripe pineapple or 1 can
    (14 ounces) pineapple rings or
    chunks, drained*
1 cup Mushroom Mince (page 206)

*1 tablespoon finely chopped salted,
    dry-roasted peanuts*
½ red sweet pepper
½ bunch fresh cilantro

Carefully peel the pineapple and cut it crosswise into slices about ¼ inch thick. Cut each slice in half and then remove and discard its tough core. Cut each slice into little tiles or wedge–shaped bite-sized pieces. Cut canned pineapple rings in the same way.

In a small bowl, combine the Mushroom Mince and peanuts and stir well. Cut the red pepper into slivers ½ inch long. Tear off a handful of small whole cilantro leaves.

Carefully top a pineapple piece with about ½ teaspoon of the Mushroom Mince mixture, then garnish with a cilantro leaf and a piece or two of red pepper. Place on a serving platter and repeat until all the ingredients are used. Serve at room temperature.

MAKES ABOUT 36 BITES.

NOTE • *You will need only ½ recipe Mushroom Mince for this dish, but I usually make a full recipe and enjoy the rest tossed with pasta or rice, in an omelet, or spread on a grilled vegetable sandwich.* ❖ *The classic presentation for this dish is to arrange 2 small slivers of pepper in an X over the filling. But as long as you have the splash of red and green you will have an appealing appetizer.*

✧ MUNG BEAN FRITTERS ✧

These crunchy golden tidbits are delicious, appealing, and simple to make. Yellow mung beans are the hulled and split yellow centers of round green mung beans. They are sold in cellophane packages in Asian and Indian markets, and are usually labeled mung beans, just like their unhulled twins, so look for tiny, oval butter–yellow pellets rather than the khaki–green hull–on kind. Soaking them for 3 hours and then steaming them is the standard preparation method for this classic snack, but if you are pressed for time, you can bring unsoaked yellow mung beans to a boil, reduce the heat to low, and simmer until tender enough to mash, 5 to 10 minutes. Serve these fritters with one of the Thai sauces I have suggested, or with any favorite tangy dipping sauce.

1 cup dried yellow mung beans
½ cup all-purpose flour
1 tablespoon curry powder
1 teaspoon salt
4 green onions, thinly sliced crosswise

Vegetable oil for deep-frying
A handful of fresh cilantro sprigs
Tangy Tamarind Sauce (page 225)
* or Sweet and Hot Garlic Sauce*
* (page 224)*

Place the mung beans in a bowl and add warm water to cover by about 2 inches. Let soak for 3 hours and then drain well. Meanwhile, combine the flour, curry powder, and salt in a bowl, mix well with a fork, and set aside.

Place the soaked mung beans on a steamer basket and steam until soft enough to mash with a spoon, about 15 minutes. Transfer to the bowl holding the flour mixture and mix well, stirring, scraping, and mashing to combine everything into a fairly smooth paste. Stir in the green onions and mix well.

To cook the fritters, form the thick batter into walnut–sized lumps, and then pinch each lump into a football shape. You should have about 48 balls; set them near the stove. Pour vegetable oil into a large, deep, heavy skillet or wok to a depth of 3 inches. Place over medium heat for 5 to 10 minutes. Meanwhile, line a baking sheet with paper towels and have a slotted spoon or Asian–style wire strainer ready for scooping the cooked fritters from the oil.

The oil is ready when a bit of batter dropped into the pan sizzles and floats at once. (The oil should register 360 to 375 degrees F on a cooking thermometer.) Gently lower about 6 fritters into the oil and cook until they are beautifully browned and crisp, 1 to 2 minutes. Using the wire strainer, remove the fritters, holding them briefly over the pan to drain, and then set them aside on the towel-lined baking sheet while you cook the remaining fritters in the same way.

When all the fritters are done, transfer to a serving platter. Garnish with the cilantro and serve at once with a small bowl of Tangy Tamarind Sauce or Sweet and Hot Garlic Sauce.

MAKES ABOUT 48 FRITTERS.

NOTE • *You can prepare the batter up to 1 day in advance, cover, and refrigerate until cooking time.* ❖ *If you need to cook the fritters in advance, you can keep them warm for 30 minutes or so in a 250 degree F oven. Or set them aside to cool to room temperature, transfer to an airtight container until serving time, and then loosely wrap them in aluminum foil and reheat in a 250 degree F oven until heated through, 10 to 15 minutes.*

∽ CURRIED CORNCAKES WITH SWEET AND HOT GARLIC SAUCE ∽

Like most Asian people, Thais seldom eat corn, and when they do it tends to be sturdy roasting ears grilled over charcoal, or plump kernels floating in coconut milk–based sweets. But this vegetarian version of the popular Thai fritter of ground fish called *tod mun* is wildly popular throughout the kingdom. In this *tod mun kao pode*, fresh corn is ideal, but frozen kernels work fine, if given time to thaw before cooking. Rice flour is sold in health–food stores and Asian markets and makes the fritters crispier, but you can omit it and use 5 tablespoons all–purpose flour instead.

2 cups fresh or thawed frozen corn kernels
3 tablespoons rice flour
2 tablespoons all-purpose flour
2 teaspoons Red Curry Paste (page 198)
½ teaspoon soy sauce
½ teaspoon salt

1 egg, lightly beaten
Vegetable oil for deep-frying
Sweet-and-Sour Cucumber Salad (page 66)
Sweet and Hot Garlic Sauce (page 224) or
*   Tangy Tamarind Sauce (page 225)*

In a bowl, combine the corn, flours, curry paste, soy sauce, salt, and egg and stir to mix well. The batter will be thick, wet, and nubby. Set it aside while you heat the oil for frying.

Pour vegetable oil into a large, heavy, deep skillet or wok to a depth of 3 inches. Place over medium heat for 5 to 10 minutes. Meanwhile, line a baking sheet with paper towels and have a slotted spoon or Asian-style wire strainer ready for scooping the fritters from the oil.

The oil is ready when a bit of batter dropped into it sizzles and floats at once. (The oil should register 360 to 375 degrees F on a cooking thermometer.) Using a large spoon, scoop up about 1 tablespoon of the batter and carefully slip it into the hot oil. Add 2 or 3 more spoonfuls and cook until the cakes are nicely browned on the bottom, about 2 minutes. Carefully turn them to brown the top, about 1 minute. Using the wire strainer, remove each fritter, holding it briefly over the pan to drain, and then set it on the towel-lined baking sheet. Cook the remaining fritters in the same way.

When all the fritters are done, transfer to a serving platter. Serve at once with small bowls of Sweet-and-Sour Cucumber Salad and Sweet and Hot Garlic Sauce or Tangy Tamarind Sauce on the side.

MAKES ABOUT 24 CORNCAKES.

∾ VEGETABLE CURRY PUFFS ∾

Thais depend on complex curry pastes for most of their curry dishes, but they also often make use of curry powder, known as *pong kah-ree*. It probably entered the Thai pantry via the Chinese– and British–influenced kitchens of neighboring Malaysia and Singapore, and its familiar golden hue appears in savory snacks such as these delicious turnovers. They are traditionally made with a double–layered lard–based pastry, but here I use the shortcut of frozen puff pastry dough, widely available in Western supermarkets. You could also use a homemade samosa–type dough.

1 large baking potato	*1 teaspoon soy sauce*
1 carrot	*1 teaspoon salt*
1 yellow onion	*½ cup Vegetable Stock (pages 204 and 205)*
10 green beans	*1 package (17¼ ounces; 2 sheets) frozen*
2 large cloves garlic	*puff pastry, thawed*
2 tablespoons vegetable oil	*¼ cup finely chopped fresh cilantro*
2 tablespoons curry powder	*1 egg mixed with 1 tablespoon water*
1 tablespoon sugar	*Sweet and Hot Garlic Sauce (page 224)*

Peel the potato and carrot and cut into ¼-inch cubes. Finely chop the onion, and trim and cut the green beans crosswise into thin slices. Mince the garlic. Place all the vegetables near the stove.

In a skillet with a tight–fitting lid, heat the vegetable oil over medium heat until a bit of garlic added to the pan sizzles at once. Add all the vegetables and sprinkle them with the curry powder. Cook for 2 minutes, tossing often. Add the sugar, soy sauce, salt, and stock and bring to a gentle boil. Reduce the heat to low, cover, and cook until the vegetables are tender, about 5 minutes.

Uncover the pan, raise the heat to medium, and continue to cook, tossing often, until all the liquid has evaporated, 3 to 4 minutes. Turn the vegetable mixture out onto a plate and spread it out to cool to room temperature.

Meanwhile, roll out 1 sheet of the puff pastry on a lightly floured board, shaping it into a 12–by–15–inch rectangle ¼ inch thick. Cut the pastry into twenty 3–inch squares.

When you are ready to fill the curry puffs, preheat an oven to 400 degrees F. Add the cilantro to the cooled vegetable mixture and toss well. Line a baking sheet with baking parchment paper and place it next to your work space. Spoon about 2 teaspoons of the curry filling onto each pastry square. Brush 2 adjacent sides of the square with the egg mixture and fold the square to form a triangle, enclosing the filling. Pinch and stretch the dough as needed to seal it tightly. Crimp the edges of the triangle with a fork and place on the parchment-lined baking sheet. Repeat with the remaining pastry squares, curry filling, and puff pastry sheet until all the ingredients are used.

Brush the tops of the curry puffs with the remaining egg mixture and place in the oven. Bake until a rich, golden brown, 15 to 20 minutes. Serve hot or warm with Sweet and Hot Garlic Sauce.

MAKES ABOUT 60 PUFFS.

ᘓ GARLICKY MUSHROOM TURNOVERS ᘓ

Here are plump little pockets filled with a savory mixture of tofu and mushrooms, seasoned with the traditional Thai flavor combination of garlic, cilantro root, and peppercorns. Make the dough first and then make the filling while it rests. If you have time to fill these tiny pastries a day ahead of serving, you can refrigerate the unbaked turnovers and then bake them just before the festivities begin.

Pastry:
2 ½ cups all-purpose flour
1 teaspoon salt
⅔ cup vegetable oil
⅓ cup water

Filling:
2 cups Mushroom Mince (page 206)
2 tablespoons minced green onions
2 tablespoons minced fresh cilantro

A handful of fresh cilantro sprigs
Sweet and Hot Garlic Sauce (page 224)

To make the pastry, combine the flour and salt in a large bowl and stir to mix well. Combine the oil and the water in a measuring cup and pour over the flour and salt. Using a fork, stir until the mixture comes together. Continue working the dough with the fork or with your fingers until it can be gathered into a ball.

Divide the dough in half and form each half into a flat disk. Wrap each disk in plastic wrap and let stand at room temperature for 20 minutes.

To make the filling, combine the Mushroom Mince, green onions, and cilantro in a small bowl and stir to mix well. Cover and refrigerate until you are ready to form the turnovers.

Preheat the oven to 400 degrees F. Line a baking sheet with baking parchment paper or lightly grease with vegetable oil. Place 1 pastry disk between 2 large sheets of plastic wrap. Roll out the pastry about ⅛-inch thick. Using a round cutter about 2½ inches in diameter, cut the dough into rounds. Repeat with the remaining disk. You should have about 36 rounds in all.

Place about 1 teaspoon filling on a pastry round. Fold it in half to form a half-moon and pinch the edges together firmly to seal. Crimp the sealed edge with the tines of a fork and place on the prepared baking sheet. Repeat with the remaining pastry rounds and filling.

Bake until lightly browned, about 20 minutes. Transfer to a serving platter. Garnish with cilantro and serve warm with Sweet and Hot Garlic Sauce.

MAKES ABOUT 36 TURNOVERS.

ᦉ CHEWY "PEARL" DUMPLINGS WITH MUSHROOM MINCE AND CRISPY GARLIC ᦉ

Inside these chewy little dumplings is a garlicky mushroom filling studded with chopped peanuts for crunch. Known in Thai as *saku sai heht*, they are placed on a leaf of lettuce, topped with crispy garlic, a few leaves of fresh cilantro, and a burst of fresh green chili heat, and then enjoyed in one or two glorious bites. Tiny tapioca pearls, a traditional Thai ingredient found in even the smallest market town, are used in sweets as well as savory dishes such as this one. During its bath of steam, the chalky white tapioca dough is transformed into a silvery noodlelike covering. These irresistible treats are best when freshly made, so if you need to prepare them in advance, shape the balls, chill for a few hours, and then steam briefly an hour or so before serving, so they will be at room temperature.

Filling:
2 tablespoons finely chopped salted, dry-
    roasted peanuts
About ¾ cup Mushroom Mince (page 206)

Dough:
2 cups small tapioca pearls
1½ cups warm water

32 leaf lettuce cups or small lettuce leaves
½ cup loosely packed fresh cilantro leaves
1 fresh green serrano chili, thinly sliced
    crosswise, or 10 tiny Thai bird chilies
    (optional)
¼ cup Crispy Garlic in Oil (page 221)

To make the filling, stir the peanuts into the Mushroom Mince, combining well; set aside.

To make the dough, place the tapioca pearls in a medium bowl. Slowly add the warm water while kneading the tapioca pearls with your hands for several minutes to soften them and coax them to absorb the water. You should end up with a thick, sticky, chalk-white paste. Let stand for 5 minutes, and then knead until the dough is a soft, malleable clay that comes together and "wipes" the bowl clean, about 1 minute longer. Shape the dough into a log and cut it into 32 equal pieces; they should be about a tablespoon each. Roll each piece into a ball, moistening your hands as needed to work and shape the dough.

To fill each ball, hold it in the palm of one hand and poke the thumb of your other hand into its center to hollow out a tiny chamber. Add about ½ teaspoon of the mushroom mixture and then carefully pinch and press the dough back over the filling to seal it up and smooth it off. Moisten your fingers lightly if needed to ease this task, and use bits of moistened dough to seal any broken patches. Try to keep the dough an even thickness all around, although it will be somewhat thicker at the seam. Set aside on a platter while you continue forming the remaining dough and filling into balls.

To cook the balls, fill the bottom of a steamer or a heavy saucepan with several inches of water and bring it to a rolling boil over medium heat. Meanwhile, place the balls on a lightly oiled steamer basket or tray, taking care that they do not touch one another or the sides of the basket. When the steam is steady and strong, place the balls over the steam, cover, and adjust the heat to maintain a steady head of steam. Cook until the balls turn from small, dry golf balls into plump, tender, voluptuous, translucent dumplings, 12 to 15 minutes. Check the water level and add very hot water as needed, increasing the cooking time to cover any time lost while the water returns to a steamy boil. Test for doneness by cutting open a dumpling; the wrapping should be chewy and the filling heated through. Remove the steaming basket from the heat and set aside to rest for about 5 minutes.

Lightly grease a platter (or moisten it with cold water) and transfer the dumplings to it, placing them an inch or so apart. Let cool to room temperature.

To serve, mound the dumplings on a platter along with the lettuce cups, cilantro leaves, and the chilies, if using, and pour the Crispy Garlic in Oil over the dumplings. To eat, place a lettuce cup in your palm, top with a dumpling and sprinkle on a little cilantro and some chilies, if you like. Fold the leaf into a packet and enjoy it in a bite or two. Alternatively, arrange the small lettuce leaves on 1 or 2 platters and place a dumpling on each leaf. Spoon a little Crispy Garlic in Oil over each dumpling and top with a few cilantro leaves. Set out the chilies for diners to add to taste.

MAKES 32 BALLS.

NOTE • *When the dumplings are hot, stickiness can be a problem. If they stick when you try to remove them from the steamer, dip your utensils in water or lightly grease any surface they touch.* ❖ *You can mask the steaming rack with a banana leaf or leaves of cabbage or sturdy lettuce if you like; the leaves may lessen the stickiness. If you have a small basket steamer, simply cook the dumplings in batches.* ❖ *If you have trouble filling the balls as directed, try flattening each ball into a little pancake on your palm. Place the filling in the center and then pinch the edges together to enclose it, taking care to keep the center of the pancake thick enough to cover the filling without splitting once it is sealed.*

ᏨᏍ LETTUCE BITES ᏨᏍ

Known as *miang kum*—*miang* means "leaf" and *kum* means "a small mouthful"—this unique dish provides a beautiful centerpiece and a delectable nibble that can be prepared hours in advance. In Thailand, each guest prepares his or her own portions, but you may want to assemble several lettuce bites to start. That way your guests will have an idea of how they go together before they begin making their own. Make 1 cup of the Toasted Coconut, since it is used for both the sauce and the treats. The sauce needs time to cool to room temperature, and it keeps well for several days, so you may want to make it in advance and then assemble the treats just before serving.

Sauce:
½ cup Toasted Coconut (page 217)
3 tablespoons peeled and coarsely chopped
    fresh ginger
2 tablespoons coarsely chopped shallots
1 tablespoon Asian bean sauce
¾ cup Vegetable Stock (pages 204 and 205)
1 cup palm sugar or brown sugar
¼ cup Tamarind Liquid (page 212)
1 teaspoon soy sauce
1 teaspoon salt

Treats:
½ cup Toasted Coconut (page 217)
½ cup cut-up peeled fresh ginger
    (¼-inch chunks)
½ cup cut-up limes, including peel
    (¼-inch chunks)
½ cup cut-up shallots or purple onions
    (¼ inch chunks)
2 tablespoons thinly sliced fresh green
    chilies such as Thai bird, serrano, or
    jalapeño
½ cup salted, dry-roasted peanuts
½ cup salted sunflower seeds
1 head lettuce with cup-shaped leaves
    (see note)

To make the sauce, in a mini processor or a blender, combine the coconut, ginger, shallots, and Asian bean sauce and grind to a fairly smooth paste. Use on-off pulses, and scrape down the sides as you work, adding a little of the vegetable stock as needed to move the blades.

   In a saucepan, combine the coconut–ginger paste, vegetable stock, sugar, tamarind, soy sauce, and salt. Stir well and bring to a rolling boil over medium heat, stirring often. Boil for 2 minutes, stirring and adjusting the heat as needed to be sure the sauce does not boil over. Reduce the heat to maintain a gentle boil and simmer, stirring and scraping the sides down now and then, until the sauce is dark brown, thickened to a medium syrup, and well combined, about 10 minutes.

When the sauce reaches room temperature it should be a little thicker than real maple syrup and a good bit thinner than honey. Transfer to a bowl and set aside, uncovered, to cool to room temperature; you should have about 1¼ cups. (At this point the sauce can be tightly covered and refrigerated for 3 or 4 days.)

To ready the treats, arrange all the ingredients except the lettuce in separate heaps on a platter or in small separate bowls. Separate the lettuce leaves and arrange a platter of pretty, cup-shaped leaves nearby. Place the sauce in a small, deep serving bowl and provide a small serving spoon.

To eat, take a lettuce leaf, add small amounts of each treat to it, and then top with a dollop of sauce. Fold into a small packet, pop it into your mouth, and chew, chew, chew! It's a mouthful, but biting it daintily tends to spill the whole business all over you, and the idea is to get the extraordinary flavor combination in one grand explosion.

SERVES 10.

NOTE • *If you have a large, heavy mortar and pestle and would like to use a traditional method to prepare the sauce, here is what to do: In the bowl of the mortar, pound the ginger with the pestle to soften it and break down its fibers. Add the Asian bean sauce and pound and grind to combine well, scraping down the sides as you work. Add the toasted coconut and continue to grind and pound until you have a well combined, fairly smooth paste, scraping down the sides with a spoon as you work to incorporate everything well.* ❖ *Some traditional versions of this sauce call for fresh galanga rather than fresh ginger, and roast both the galanga and the shallots before grinding them with the coconut and bean sauce. A spoonful of finely ground peanuts is also sometimes added. Try these variations if you have the ingredients and the time.* ❖ *Ideal lettuce varieties include Boston, butter, limestone, or iceberg lettuce. Large fresh spinach leaves can also be used. You want diminutive cup-shaped leaves, or palm-sized leaves that can be folded into large bite-sized packets. Belgian endive spears make a chic, practical substitute for the lettuce.* ❖ *You can also serve these with the ingredients already portioned out into the leaves. You can leave the sauce on the side, or dollop the sauce in first before adding the other ingredients.*

ɘ ROASTED EGGPLANT DIP WITH THAI FLAVORS ɘ

Lime, cilantro, and chili paste impart a Thai sizzle to the natural richness of roasted eggplant. Enjoy this as a dip for thick strips of cucumber, green sweet pepper, carrots, or blanched broccoli, asparagus or green beans. Or serve it as a spread for Crispy Rice Cakes (page 46).

1 large eggplant, about 1¼ pounds
1 tablespoon palm sugar or brown sugar
1 teaspoon soy sauce
½ teaspoon salt
2 tablespoons Roasted Chili Paste (page 222)

2 tablespoons freshly squeezed lime or
    lemon juice
¼ cup finely chopped fresh cilantro leaves
2 green onions, thinly sliced crosswise
A small handful of fresh cilantro leaves

Preheat the oven to 400 degrees F. Lightly grease a baking sheet. Cut the eggplant in half lengthwise, stem and all, and place it on the prepared baking sheet, cut side down. Bake until the flesh is soft and the purple skin is a dark, burnished brown, about 30 minutes. Remove from the oven and set aside to cool to room temperature.

Scoop out the flesh and transfer it to a food processor fitted with the metal blade. Add the sugar, soy sauce, salt, Roasted Chili Paste, and lime or lemon juice. Using on-off pulses, process to a thick, coarse purée, stopping to scrape down the sides as needed to grind evenly.

Transfer to a bowl and stir in the chopped cilantro and green onions. Serve at room temperature, garnished with the cilantro leaves.

MAKES ABOUT 1½ CUPS.

NOTE • *If you do not have a food processor, place the flesh of the roasted eggplant on your cutting board and chop it to a fine, moist, fairly smooth mush. Transfer to a bowl and add the sugar, soy sauce, salt, Roasted Chili Paste, and lime or lemon juice. Stir to dissolve the sugar and combine everything well, then mix in the chopped cilantro and green onions.*

❧ DAO JIOW LONE DIPPING SAUCE WITH VEGETABLES ❧

The word *lone* identifies this sauce as one of the rich, pungent dipping sauces made with coconut milk that are typical of the cuisine of central Thailand. *Lone* dishes are elegant members of the larger family of *nahm prik* dishes, intensely flavored dipping sauces generally fiery with chilies and uncushioned by the coconut sweetness found in a *lone*. All these spunky sauces exist to flavor fresh vegetables and plain jasmine or sticky rice. This *lone* stars the super-salty bean sauce Thais inherited from the kitchens of China.

Sauce:
¾ cup coarsely chopped tofu
1 tablespoon Asian bean sauce
⅓ cup Vegetable Stock (pages 204 and 205)
½ cup minced shallots
1 tablespoon vegetable oil
2 tablespoons coarsely chopped garlic
½ cup finely chopped purple onion
⅔ cup unsweetened coconut milk
2 tablespoons palm sugar or brown sugar
1 teaspoon soy sauce
¼ teaspoon salt
2 tablespoons Tamarind Liquid (page 212), or as needed

Vegetables:
3 small cucumbers or 1 large hothouse cucumber, peeled, halved lengthwise, and cut into thick slices
3 wedges green cabbage, about 2 inches wide at their widest point
15 green beans, cut into 3-inch lengths, or whole snow peas
½ red sweet pepper, cut into long, thin strips
10 carrot sticks
5 large radishes, trimmed and halved lengthwise

To make the sauce, combine the tofu, Asian bean sauce, vegetable stock, and half of the shallots in a mini processor or blender. Using on–off pulses, grind to a fairly smooth paste, stopping to scrape down the sides as needed to grind evenly. Transfer to a small bowl and set aside.

In a small skillet over medium heat, warm the oil until a bit of garlic added to the pan sizzles at once. Add the garlic and onion and cook, tossing often, until fragrant, shiny, and tender, about 2 minutes. Stir in the coconut milk and bring to a gentle boil. Adjust the heat to maintain an active simmer and cook until the coconut milk thickens slightly and releases its sweet fragrance, 5 to 7 minutes.

When the coconut milk is ready, add the tofu paste and cook, stirring occasionally, for 3 minutes. Add the remaining shallots, sugar, soy sauce, and salt. Cook, stirring occasionally, for 2 minutes longer, and then remove from the heat. Stir in the tamarind. Taste the sauce. Seeking a pleasing balance of salty, sour, and sweet, adjust to your liking with a little more salt, tamarind, or sugar, if needed. You should have about 1¼ cups.

Let the sauce cool until slightly warm or to room temperature. Transfer to a small bowl and place on a serving platter. Arrange the vegetables around the bowl of sauce and serve. Store any extra sauce in an airtight jar in the refrigerator for up to 2 days.

SERVES 10 TO 12.

NOTE • *Although* lone *and* nahm prik *dishes are always presented with raw vegetables for dipping, there is usually rice as well.* ❖ *Lime juice sweetened with a little brown sugar can replace the tamarind liquid in a pinch*

❧ CRISPY SPRING ROLLS WITH SWEET AND HOT GARLIC SAUCE ❧

You are in for some work when you make these spring rolls, as you will need to stir-fry the noodle filling, shape the rolls, and then deep-fry them shortly before serving. Believe me when I tell you that they are worth every bit of the effort, however, that they are worlds better than the ho–hum spring rolls many Asian restaurants serve. In Thailand, spring rolls are street food, made up and peddled by specialty vendors who sell them in the market and at noodle and dim sum cafés. They are seldom available in restaurants and almost never made at home. Their Thai name, *boh biah tote*, comes from the Teochew Chinese dialect and, because these delectable snacks are a culinary legacy of Chinese migration throughout the region, you will find the same word used in neighboring Southeast Asian countries. To lighten the load of preparing them, follow the Thai tradition of recruiting a friend or two to help you. The effort becomes entertainment when you have good company, and once you become famous for your Thai spring rolls, you will have volunteers. If you roll them up in advance and then deep-fry them just before your guests arrive, you will have time to enjoy the party.

4 ounces bean thread noodles

6 dried shiitake mushrooms or Chinese
    mushrooms (about ½ ounce)

Vegetable oil for sautéing and deep-frying

2 eggs, lightly beaten

8 ounces fresh button mushrooms, thinly
    sliced

1 tablespoon soy sauce

1 teaspoon sugar

½ teaspoon salt

½ teaspoon freshly ground pepper

1 tablespoon coarsely chopped garlic (4 to
    6 cloves)

¼ cup finely chopped shallots or yellow
    onion

1 cup shredded carrots

½ cup minced green onions

1 package (1 pound) frozen spring roll
    wrappers (25 to 30 wrappers)

¼ cup minced fresh cilantro

A handful of fresh cilantro as garnish

Sweet and Hot Garlic Sauce (page 224)

Place the bean thread noodles in a large bowl, add warm water to cover, and soak until tender, about 30 minutes. Place the dried mushrooms in another bowl, add warm water to cover, and soak until softened, about 30 minutes.

    Meanwhile, heat 1 teaspoon vegetable oil in a nonstick skillet, and place a plate next to the stove. Add half of the beaten egg to the pan and swirl it so the egg covers the bottom in a thin sheet. Cook until set and opaque, about 30 seconds. Turn out egg sheet onto the plate and repeat with another 1 teaspoon oil and the remaining egg. When the egg sheets have cooled, roll them up, slice them into thin shreds, and set aside.

    Drain the bean thread noodles and mound them on your cutting board in a plump log, horizontal to you. Cut the noodles crosswise into 2-inch lengths. Do not fret about precision here, as the point is to make these extremely long noodles more manageable for stir-frying. Transfer the noodles to a bowl, toss to separate them, and set them aside with the egg strips.

    Drain the softened dried mushrooms, and cut away and discard their tough stem ends. Slice into long, thin shreds and set aside along with the sliced button mushrooms. In a small bowl, combine the soy sauce, sugar, salt, and pepper and stir well. Set it next to the stove, along with the garlic, shallots or onion, dried and fresh mushrooms, and the carrots. Have ready a large platter to hold the cooked filling.

Heat a wok or large, deep skillet over medium–high heat. Add 1 tablespoon vegetable oil and swirl to coat the surface. When a bit of garlic added to the pan sizzles at once, add the garlic and shallots and stir and toss for 1 minute. Add dried and fresh mushrooms and stir-fry until shiny and softened, about 3 minutes. Add the carrots and cook for 1 minute more, tossing once. Give the soy sauce mixture a stir and add it to the pan, tossing to coat everything well.

Add the noodles and egg strips to the pan and cook, tumbling and turning everything to combine well, until the noodles are transformed from stiff, white, wiry threads into transparent, soft, curly strands, about 2 minutes. Once the noodles are tender and evenly coated with the sauce, turn off the heat, add the green onions and minced cilantro, and toss well. Transfer the filling to the platter, spread it out in an even layer, and set it aside to cool.

To wrap the spring rolls, remove the spring roll wrappers from the freezer and set them out to thaw for about 30 minutes. Set out a baking sheet on which to place the finished spring rolls and a small bowl of water to use for sealing the filled rolls. Gently separate the stack of wrappers into 3 or 4 piles and cover them with a damp kitchen towel or plastic wrap while you work. Carefully peel off 1 wrapper and place it on a clean, dry work surface, smooth side down. Position the wrapper like a diamond, with one point toward you.

Place about 3 tablespoons of the filling on the wrapper, centering it on the half of the diamond closest to you. Use your fingers to shape it into a log about 3 inches long. Fold the point closest to you up, over, and around the filling, and then tightly roll the wrapper over once to the center of the diamond. Fold the right and left points in toward the middle, completely enclosing the filling, and then continue rolling. When you reach the topmost point, moisten its edges with water and seal the roll like an envelope. Set the roll aside on the baking sheet, seam side down. Continue filling and rolling until you have used all the filling mixture. Space the rolls so that they do not touch, and separate the layers with plastic wrap if you stack them. Seal any unused wrappers airtight and return them to the freezer at once.

To fry the spring rolls, pour vegetable oil into a wok or large, deep, heavy skillet to a depth of 3 inches. Place over medium–high heat for 5 to 10 minutes. Meanwhile, line a baking sheet with paper towels and have a slotted spoon or Asian–style wire strainer ready for scooping the rolls from the oil.

The oil is ready when a bit of spring roll wrapper dropped into it sizzles and floats at once. (The oil should register 350 to 365 degrees F on a cooking thermometer.) Carefully add a spring roll by sliding it gently down the curved side of the wok or lowering it carefully into the skillet. Add 2 or 3 more rolls, but do not crowd the pan. Cook, turning the rolls occasionally to brown them evenly, until golden brown, about 3 minutes.

Using the slotted spoon or wire strainer, remove each spring roll, holding it briefly over the pan to drain, and set it on the towel–lined baking sheet. Cook the remaining rolls in the same way. When all the spring rolls are done, arrange them on a serving platter. Garnish with cilantro and serve with indi-vidual bowls of the Sweet and Hot Garlic Sauce.

MAKES ABOUT 24 SPRING ROLLS.

NOTE • *To prepare the spring rolls in advance, cook the filling, cover it, and store in the refrigerator for up to 2 days. Or you can store the uncooked spring rolls, covered airtight, in the refrigerator for up to 2 days, providing that you have just made the filling. You can also freeze the uncooked spring rolls for up to 1 month. To cook frozen spring rolls, do not thaw them, but allow an extra minute or two in the oil.* ❖ *You can use cloud ear mushrooms instead of or in addition to the dried mushrooms, soaking and draining them as directed and cutting away any hard little navels you may find as you examine them with your fingers. These are the points at which the mushrooms were attached to their host trees, and they are tough to chew. Then slice into thin strips and use as directed for the dried mushrooms.*

ᔷ TWO-POTATO CURRY POT STICKERS ᔷ

Pot stickers appear in Thailand among the array of dim sum goodies offered in upcountry Chinese cafés and as part of the Chinese menus offered in hotels. Make up these tasty bites in advance and then fry them up after your guests arrive for a hot starter that will get you back to the party quickly.

1 cup Mushroom Mince (page 206)
¾ cup mashed cooked white potatoes
¾ cup mashed cooked sweet potatoes
½ cup bread crumbs (see note)
1 egg, lightly beaten
1 teaspoon soy sauce
½ teaspoon curry powder
¼ teaspoon sugar
¼ teaspoon salt
2 green onions, finely chopped

¼ cup finely chopped sturdy greens such
   as bok choy, napa cabbage, or green
   head cabbage
⅓ cup coarsely chopped fresh cilantro
1 package (10 ounces) gyoza wrappers
   (about 42 wrappers)
Sweet and Hot Garlic Sauce (page 224)
1 to 2 tablespoons vegetable oil for every
   12 pot stickers you cook
¼ cup Vegetable Stock (pages 204 and 205)
   for every 12 pot stickers
Chopped fresh cilantro for garnish

In a bowl, combine the Mushroom Mince, white and sweet potatoes, bread crumbs, egg, soy sauce, curry powder, sugar, salt, green onions, greens, and cilantro. Stir until all the ingredients are evenly distributed. Set up a work space with a clean, dry cutting board, a baking sheet, a small bowl of water, the gyoza wrappers, and the two–potato filling.

    Place a gyoza wrapper before you on the cutting board and place about 2 teaspoons filling in its center. Dip your finger in the water and moisten the edges of the wrapper. Fold it in half to form a half circle, enclosing the filling, and pinch together the top center point to seal it. Now form 2 pleats in the left side of the wrapper close to you and press to seal closed. Form 2 pleats in the right side of the wrapper and press to seal closed. Now tap the pot sticker on the cutting board to flatten its base and help it stand upright with its sealed, pleated edge pointing skyward. You can also shape the gyoza by simply fold-ing them into half circles, sealing without the pleats, and then standing them up and tapping them on the cutting board to form a sturdy base with the fold standing straight up like a crest. Place on the baking sheet. Fill and shape the remaining pot stickers in the same way. Place them without touching on the baking sheet.

To cook the pot stickers, place a small bowl of Sweet and Hot Garlic Sauce on a serving platter and position it by the stove to hold the pot stickers when they are done. In a medium skillet with a tight–fitting lid, heat 1 or 2 tablespoons oil over medium–high heat for about 1 minute. Add the pot stickers, placing them with their flattened base down, tucking them close together, and fitting about 12 into the pan. Cook until the bottoms are golden brown, 1 to 2 minutes. Add ¼ cup vegetable stock, cover, and cook until most of the liquid evaporates and the wrapper is translucent, tender, and ready to eat, 2 to 3 minutes. Flip the pot stickers out onto the platter, sprinkle with some of the cilantro, and serve at once with the dipping sauce. Cook the remaining pot stickers in batches in the same way, using additional oil and vegetable stock as needed.

MAKES ABOUT 40 POT STICKERS.

NOTE • *Vegan readers can omit the egg and add an additional 2 tablespoons bread crumbs to the sweet potato mixture. The filling will be quite soft, so handle the dumplings carefully.* ❖ *To make bread crumbs, break or cut a piece or two of stale bread into small pieces and then grind them to crumbs in a mini processor or blender, using on-off pulses to keep the bread on the blades. Or create dry, stale bread by toasting a slice or two to a handsome golden brown and then cutting into small pieces. Let cool and then grind them to a pile of crumbs. If you are using a blender, you may need to do a larger quantity of bread in order to get the machine to do its best job. Stop grinding while you have a somewhat coarse texture, before the bread turns to powder. Seal airtight and store away from heat and light for up to 1 month.* ❖ *Gyoza are the Japanese version of pot stickers. Gyoza wrappers are thicker than wonton wrappers, and are round rather than square. If gyoza wrappers are unavailable, trim the corners from a package of wonton wrappers and use them in the same way, handling carefully as they are more likely to tear.*

❦ SWEET POTATO SHIAO MAI ❦

These delicious Chinese tidbits are a familiar feature in Thailand, both as street food and at dim sum feasts. Thais call them *kanome jeep*, enjoying them when they find them, but never bothering to make them at home. They look fabulous standing at attention on a plate and garnished with a bouquet of cilantro leaves. Accompany them with a small saucer of soy sauce kissed with a little vinegar and sugar and sprinkled with minced green onions.

1 cup Mushroom Mince (page 206)
1 cup mashed cooked sweet potato
½ cup bread crumbs (see note, page 40)
1 egg, lightly beaten
1 teaspoon soy sauce
¼ teaspoon sugar
¼ teaspoon salt

2 green onions, finely chopped
2 tablespoons minced fresh mint
1 package (12 ounces) wonton wrappers
Soy sauce, seasoned to taste with white
*   vinegar, sugar, and green onions,*
*   for dipping*

In a bowl, combine the Mushroom Mince, sweet potato, bread crumbs, egg, soy sauce, sugar, salt, green onions, and mint. Mix very well. Set up a work space with a clean, dry cutting board, a baking sheet, a small bowl of water, the wonton wrappers, and the sweet potato filling.

Divide the stack of wonton wrappers into thirds and trim away the four corners of each stack, reserving the little pasta triangles to toss into your next pot of boiling soup. Place 3 of the now-octagonal wrappers before you on the cutting board. Place about 2 teaspoons filling in the center of each wrapper. Now, your job is to coax each wrapper into a tiny, slender version of a paper baking cup filled with cupcake batter. Begin by using a table knife to spread out the filling on each wrapper as if it were peanut butter on bread. Stop just short of the edge, leaving a thin border of pasta all the way around. Then place one wrapper in your palm and, using the fingers of your other hand, pinch its sides up into a cup. Tap its base on the cutting board to firm it up. Next, work your way around the exterior, pressing the dull side of the table knife into the sides to even up the little folds and give the dumpling an upright shape, like a column holding up a roof. Tap the base again and set the tall but diminutive "cupcake" aside on the baking sheet. Fill and shape the remaining dumplings in the same way. Place them without touching on the baking sheet. At this point, you can seal the dumplings airtight and refrigerate them for 1 to 2 days, or freeze for up to 1 month. They can be steamed directly from the refrigerator or freezer.

To steam the dumplings, fill the bottom of a steamer or a heavy saucepan with several inches of water and bring it to a rolling boil over medium heat. Meanwhile, place a batch of the dumplings on a steamer basket or tray. When the steam is steady and strong, place the dumplings over the steam, cover, and adjust the heat to maintain a steady head of steam. Cook until the filling firms up and the wrappers are tender and cooked, about 15 minutes. Transfer carefully to a serving platter. Serve warm with seasoned soy sauce.

MAKES ABOUT 48 DUMPLINGS.

NOTE • *Vegan readers can omit the egg and add an extra 2 tablespoons of bread crumbs to the sweet potato mixture. The filling will be quite soft, so take care when handling the dumplings. ❖ You can mask the steaming rack with a banana leaf or leaves of cabbage or sturdy lettuce if you like; the leaves may lessen the stickiness. If you have a small basket steamer, simply cook the dumplings in batches.*

❧ SATAY PEANUT SAUCE WITH GRILLED VEGETABLES, FRIED TOFU, AND TOAST ❧

Thais learned this sauce from Malaysian cooks, and while the dish has southern Thai roots, it has spread to every corner of the kingdom. Street vendors make up their signature sauces in the morning and then travel to every gathering place. There they set up shop, fan charcoal into hellish flames to grill skewered foods, and dish out little saucers of peanut sauce and piquant cucumber salad to garnish each platter. Serving grilled vegetables and fried tofu with peanut sauce is my vegetarian adaptation for the usual skewers of meat, but the toast is 100 percent Thai. You will find this West–meets–East touch in upcountry Thailand, where it is offered alongside standard meat kebabs as a traditional means of soaking up every last bit of scrumptious sauce. Put the zucchini and other vegetables in their marinade while you prepare the peanut sauce and cucumber salad. The sauce can cool to room temperature and the salad can develop its tangy flavors while you grill foods to enjoy along with them.

Satay Peanut Sauce:
½ cup unsweetened coconut milk
2 tablespoons Red Curry Paste (page 198)
¾ cup Vegetable Stock (pages 204 and 205)
2 tablespoons palm sugar or brown sugar
¼ cup freshly ground salted, dry-roasted peanuts or peanut butter
2 tablespoons Tamarind Liquid (page 212) or freshly squeezed lime or lemon juice
½ teaspoon salt

Vegetables and Tofu:
6 zucchini
6 Japanese eggplants
3 red sweet peppers
20 small fresh button mushrooms
⅓ cup vegetable oil, plus additional oil for deep-frying
2 teaspoons curry powder
1 teaspoon soy sauce
½ teaspoon salt
6 white bread slices
8 ounces firm tofu

Sweet-and-Sour Cucumber Salad (page 66)

To make the sauce, warm the coconut milk in a saucepan over medium heat until it comes to a gentle boil. Simmer, stirring now and then, until it releases its sweet fragrance and thickens a bit, about 5 minutes. Add the curry paste and cook for 3 to 4 minutes longer, mashing and scraping to dissolve the paste and mix everything well. Add the vegetable stock and sugar and simmer for 5 minutes, stirring once or twice. Add the peanuts or peanut butter and cook for 3 minutes more, stirring as needed to dissolve the peanut butter into the sauce. Remove from the heat and season with the tamarind or citrus juice and salt, stirring to mix well. Set aside to cool to room temperature. At this point, the sauce can be covered and refrigerated for up to 2 days; reheat gently and thin with a little vegetable stock before serving.

Make the cucumber salad and set it aside to allow the flavors to blend.

To prepare the vegetables, trim the ends from the zucchini and Japanese eggplants and cut in half lengthwise. Stem and seed the sweet peppers and cut them into 2-inch squares. Trim the base of each mushroom stem but leave whole.

In a medium bowl, combine the ⅓ cup vegetable oil, curry powder, soy sauce, and salt and mix well. Add the zucchini, eggplants, sweet peppers, and mushrooms and toss to coat well. Set aside for 30 minutes. (They can also be covered and refrigerated as long as overnight, tossing now and then.)

When you are ready to cook the vegetables, prepare a very hot fire in a grill. Thread the sweet peppers and mushrooms on bamboo skewers and place them on the grill rack, along with the zucchini and eggplant halves, cut side down. Cook until tender and nicely charred, turning often to cook them evenly, about 5 minutes. Transfer to a platter and let cool until warm or at room temperature, 5 minutes or longer.

Meanwhile, place the bread slices on the grill rack and toast them on both sides to a handsome, golden crunchy state. Remove from the grill and cut each twice on the diagonal into 4 triangles. Remove the crusts first if you want the most traditional look, and leave them on if you like the crust as I do. Set aside near the cooling vegetables.

Meanwhile, in a skillet, pour in vegetable oil to a depth of several inches and place over medium-high heat for about 10 minutes. While it heats, cut the tofu in half horizontally to form 2 blocks. Cut each block lengthwise into thirds and then crosswise in half. This will give you 12 thick rods of tofu. Blot them dry on a clean kitchen towel and set aside. Line a plate with paper towels and place near the stove along with a slotted spoon or long–handled Asian–style wire strainer.

When the oil is hot, 350 to 365 degrees F, gently slide 3 rods of tofu into the oil and cook, turning once or twice to brown evenly, until crispy and golden brown, about 3 minutes. Using the slotted spoon or wire strainer, remove from the oil, draining briefly over the pan, and transfer to the towel–lined plate to drain well. Continue cooking the remaining tofu in the same way.

To serve, make up two or more platters, putting a small bowl of peanut sauce, a small bowl of cucumber salad, and a beautiful assortment of grilled vegetables, fried tofu, and toast triangles on each. The vegetables, tofu, and toast are all delicious dipped in the sauce.

SERVES 6 TO 8.

NOTE • *You can also serve the peanut sauce with the Mixed Grill (page 114), or you can toss it with hot cooked pasta and cucumbers and a little of the marinade from the Sweet-and-Sour Cucumber Salad.* ❖ *Bamboo skewers come in several lengths, with 6-inch ones and foot-long ones the most common. Long ones are more traditional, but use whatever is easiest and appeals to you. Cover them completely with food, embedding the tip in something and leaving the handle end exposed. If you want to be fancy, you can stem the zucchini and eggplants, slice them lengthwise into thin strips, and then thread the marinated strips onto skewers in S-shaped ribbons.* ❖ *You can soak the bamboo skewers for an hour or so if you like, to discourage them from catching fire. Since vegetables cook quickly and my grill is not given to pyrotechnic displays, I generally do not. You can also use the professional satay vendor's method of shielding the skewers from the charcoal fire by placing them at the edge of the grill surface, so that the food rests on the grill while the skewers extend out toward you into thin air and can be easily grasped and turned as needed. Finally, if the skewers need to be close to the center of the grill to cook well, you can mask the area where the skewers rest with aluminum foil before you heat the grill.*

CRISPY RICE CAKES

This old-time treat traveled across the Mekong River and into Thailand from her cultural first-cousin and neighboring kingdom, Laos. The puffy white rafts of crunchy rice are crowned with a palm sugar spiral for a homey, satisfying snack. Thais call them *kao taen* in the northern region, where they are particularly popular, and *nahng leht* elsewhere in the kingdom. For a savory treat, leave off the palm sugar adornment and use the cakes as edible platforms for scrumptious Thai sauces. Spread them with Roasted Chili Paste (page 222), or serve them with Roasted Eggplant Dip with Thai Flavors (page 33), Satay Peanut Sauce (page 43), or Tangy Tamarind Sauce (page 225).

1½ cups long-grain white sticky rice *1 cup palm sugar or brown sugar*
Vegetable oil for deep-frying

Cook the rice as directed on page 150 and turn the hot rice out onto a large tray or baking sheet. Quickly and gently spread it into a shallow layer to release some of the steam and moisture. As soon as the rice is cool enough to touch, shape it into several dozen small thin disks, each 2 to 3 inches in diameter and only 3 or 4 grains thick. Wet your hands with water as needed to ward off stickiness and make the disks as thin as you can. Resist the urge to press them too firmly into submission or they will be very hard. Work fast, knowing that your cakes need not be perfectly round; a raggedy edge is fine.

Place your shaped disks on cooling racks or trays to air-dry as you work. When all the disks are formed, set them out in the full sun until they are brittle and very dry, turning them over several times to dry them evenly, 6 to 8 hours. (See the note at the end of this recipe for two easy, practical substitutes if this extended sunbath is not workable for you.)

To fry the cakes, in a large, deep skillet pour in vegetable oil to a depth of about 3 inches. Place over medium heat for 5 to 10 minutes. Meanwhile, line a baking sheet with paper towels and have a slotted spoon or Asian-style wire strainer ready for scooping the cakes from the oil.

The oil is ready when a small piece of rice cake dropped into it sinks and then immediately floats to the top. (The oil should register 350 to 365 degrees F on a cooking thermometer.) Gently slide 3 cakes into the oil and tend them as they float and swell into thick, white rice crackers. When they stop swelling on the first side, turn them and cook until they are fully puffed, 1 to 3 minutes in all. Do not let them brown. Using the slotted spoon or strainer, remove each cake, holding it briefly over the pan to drain, and set it on the towel–lined baking sheet. Cook the remaining disks in the same way.

Place the sugar in a small, heavy saucepan and bring to a gentle boil over medium heat. Simmer, stirring occasionally, until the sugar melts into a syrup and turns a rich caramel color (somewhere in color and texture between real maple syrup and honey), 5 to 10 minutes. When ready, the syrup should fall in a shiny ribbon when the spoon is lifted.

Quickly drizzle some of the syrup in a spiral design onto each rice cake, starting at the center and twirling it out to the edge. Let the rice cakes dry at room temperature until the syrup sets. Store in an airtight container for up to 1 week.

MAKES 24 TO 36 RICE CAKES.

NOTE • *If an all-day sunbath is too slow or otherwise not practical for you, simply dry your rice disks in a 150 degree F oven for about 3 hours. Check them every hour and remove them as soon as they are dry. They should not brown at all. You can also leave them out on your kitchen counter for 1 or 2 days, turning them occasionally.* ❖ *You may want to try a method many Thai cooks use for decorating the cakes: Form a piece of banana leaf into a cone, with a small hole at the pointed tip. Fill this Thai-style pastry bag with a nice dose of the warm, caramelized sugar syrup and let it ooze out over each rice cake in a spiral design.* ❖ *This recipe is for the kind of rice cakes that vendors fry up in quantity to sell in the upcountry markets. Home cooks would make them as a way to use up the brown, crispy crust of rice that often forms when rice is cooked the old-fashioned way, on a stove rather than in an electric rice cooker. This can happen over charcoal, gas, or electric heat. In Thailand, these rice crusts are always in demand by one family member or another, to enjoy along with supper. If you find yourself with a layer of rice stuck but not burned onto the bottom of your cooking pot, scrape out all the soft rice to leave a shell of browned, hardened rice in the pot. Place the pot over low heat so that the crust can dry out and shrink a little, which helps it separate from the cooking pot, then carefully remove the shell and set it aside at room temperature for a day or two, until it is brittle and completely dry. Break it into pieces of 3 to 4 inches each, and fry them as directed in the recipe. You can also collect these natural rice crusts over time, combine them in a lock-top bag, and store in the freezer for a month or so before frying them.*

ೞ FRIED PEANUTS WITH GREEN ONIONS AND CHILIES ೞ

Yes, these are rich, but they are spectacularly good and worth the culinary splurge. Look for raw peanuts in Asian markets and health-food stores. Remove the red husks by rubbing the peanuts between your hands. You can substitute raw cashews here with terrific results. Make yourself a pitcher of lemonade or limeade while this delicious snack cools down, stirring a little salt into the pitcher if you want to enjoy it Thai style.

Peanut oil or other vegetable oil for	*20 small dried red chilies*
deep-frying	*1 teaspoon salt*
8 ounces raw whole peanuts	*3 green onions, thinly sliced crosswise*

Line a large bowl or a baking sheet with paper towels and place it near the stove along with a small plate for the chilies and a long-handled Asian-style wire strainer or a slotted spoon. In a wok or deep, heavy skillet, pour in peanut or vegetable oil to a depth of about 3 inches. Place over medium-low heat for 5 to 10 minutes. The oil is ready when a bit of green onion dropped into it sizzles at once. (The oil should register 300 to 325 degrees F on a cooking thermometer.)

Carefully add the peanuts to the oil and stir them gently. Cook for about 5 minutes, stirring and lifting them up out of the oil now and then with the scoop or spoon. When the peanuts are a rich, deep, reddish gold, scoop them out, holding them over the oil briefly to drain. Then transfer to the towel-lined bowl or baking sheet to drain well.

Meanwhile, place the chilies in the strainer or slotted spoon, lower them into the oil for about 30 seconds, and then lift them out. Repeat this process, giving the chilies short baths, until they darken a bit and have a rich, roasted aroma. If they burn, discard them and try again with a new batch. When they are ready, turn off the heat, lift them out, and set aside on a small plate to cool.

Transfer the hot, drained peanuts to a clean bowl and sprinkle them with the salt, tossing at the same time to mix well. Toss in the chilies and set aside to cool for about 5 minutes, then transfer to a serving plate. Sprinkle with the green onions and serve at once.

SERVES 4.

NOTE • *If you deep-fry food now and then, treat yourself to a long-handled Asian-style wire-mesh strainer. The bamboo handle and beautiful golden mesh bowl are perfect for handling hot food in quantity deftly and quickly. You can find these in Asian markets and through many of the mail-order sources listed on page 232.*

✂ SWEET AND SPICY NUTS ✂

This nontraditional dish is a delectable combination of Thai spices and nuts—scrumptious and simple to make. It is a dandy gift for friends and neighbors, if you can resist eating too many as you pack them up. You can use all almonds, all cashews, or all pecans if you are nuts about a particular nut.

1 cup sugar

1 cup water

2 teaspoons ground ginger

1 teaspoon ground cardamom

1 teaspoon ground cinnamon

1 teaspoon ground cumin, toasted in a
    small dry skillet over medium heat
    until fragrant and a little darkened,
    about 1 minute

½ teaspoon ground nutmeg

½ teaspoon ground cloves

2 teaspoons or more Red Curry Paste
    (page 198)

½ teaspoon chili garlic sauce or Red Chili
    Purée (page 227)

1 cup unsalted whole cashews

1 cup unsalted whole pecans

1 cup unsalted whole almonds

3 tablespoons butter or margarine

1 cup Toasted Coconut (page 217)

Preheat an oven to 400 degrees F. Lightly grease a baking sheet and set aside.

In a large, heavy saucepan, combine the sugar and water, ginger, cardamom, cinnamon, toasted cumin, nutmeg, cloves, curry paste, and chili garlic sauce or Red Chili purée. Bring to a gentle boil over medium heat and cook, stirring occasionally, until a thin syrup forms, about 3 minutes.

Add all the nuts and cook over medium heat, stirring almost constantly, until the nuts have absorbed most of the syrup and are beginning to clump together, about 5 minutes. Add the butter or margarine and stir until it melts, about 1 minute. Remove from the heat and turn out the nuts onto the prepared baking sheet. Spread them out so that they are in a single layer but still touching.

Bake until fragrant and the coating is bubbly, about 15 minutes. Remove from the oven and sprinkle with the Toasted Coconut. Set the nuts aside on the baking sheet to cool to room temperature, about 30 minutes. Store airtight at room temperature for 2 to 3 weeks.

MAKES ABOUT 3 CUPS.

NOTE • *These delectable tidbits will leave behind a dusting of their crunchy coating on the baking sheet. I like to scrape it into a small bowl and set it aside to enjoy over ice cream.* ❖ *You can use raw or roasted nuts in this recipe.*

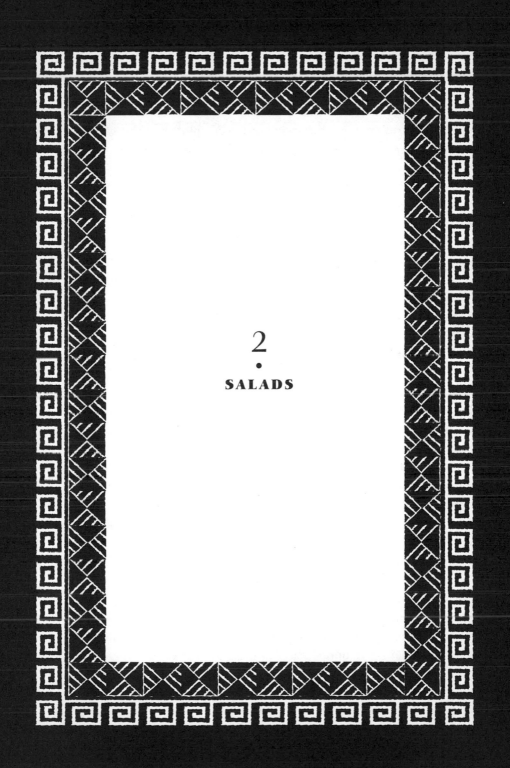

2
·
SALADS

SALADS

℘ Thais relish raw vegetables and fruits, including them often as an accompaniment to rice-centered meals. The dishes that would be considered salads in Western terms are *yums*. These are hearty and substantial combinations of meat or seafood served with a tangy lime juice dressing liberally anointed with red chili pepper flakes. Lots of greens—for nibbling as well as for presentation—cradle a typical *yum*, and it is generally garnished with cucumber rounds, cherry tomatoes, and cabbage wedges.

℘ *Yum* is actually a verb, and it describes the action of taking an array of seasonings, including the chilies mentioned above, plus sugar and lime juice, and mashing and mixing them all up by hand into an explosion of hot, sweet, and tangy flavors. The classic Thai soup *tome yum* is the same culinary concept in liquid form, with *tome* meaning "boiled."

℘ In Thailand, *yums* are often served as stand-alone dishes, as snacks enjoyed by a group. They are often accompanied with Thai whiskey, beer, or home brew, while diners contemplate whether or not to progress to a proper meal. I like to serve them just as I would a salad in a Western meal.

℘ For vegetarians it is a simple task to place tofu, sautéed tempeh, or wheat gluten in a salad's starring role and treat it to the typical *yum* flavors. You can also serve countless vegetables in this same way with delicious results.

℘ This chapter begins with my favorite vegetarian *yum*, Oyster Mushroom Salad with Chilies and Lime. The mushrooms are cooked briefly to make them tender before their immersion in a sparkling dressing laced with herbs. This is followed by *soop naw mai*, a unique toss of bamboo shoots with garlic, shallots, and a shower of fresh mint. Both these dishes share a *yum* trademark—Roasted Rice Powder. Thai cooks dry-fry whole raw grains of rice in a hot skillet to a rich, wheaty brown. The grains are pounded to a coarse powder, and tossed into *yum* dishes to provide a sandy crunch and a rustic flavor on the pleasurable side of burnt.

℘ Both the bamboo shoot salad and Green Papaya Salad are trademark dishes of the northeastern region of Thailand known as Pahk Issahn. Green refers to the hard, raw, unripe state of the papayas used for this dish. Home cooks and street vendors keep a steady drumbeat going throughout the kingdom from dawn until nightfall, pounding up pale, sturdy shreds of green papaya and seasonings with mighty pestles in tall, heavy mortars designed specifically for this job. The details vary around a basic formula of garlic, chilies, sugar, tomato, green beans, and a burst of lime. You will want to serve these traditional Thai salads with their typical companion, sticky rice. It is finger food and the classic foil for both bamboo and green papaya salads on their home turf, the Lao- and Cambodian-influenced region of northeastern Thailand.

Salaht kaek, a dish of Indian origin beloved in southern Thailand, packs well for a picnic, as it is essentially raw vegetables and a peanut dressing for dipping. Sweet-and-Sour Cucumber Salad is the classic accompaniment to satay and peanut sauce, and it is a satisfying partner for grilled or fried dishes. Winding up this chapter are two Thai-inspired fruit salads that can be made in advance and enjoyed along with volcanic dishes or as desserts when you want sweetness without a heavy note.

You may want to add a Thai touch to your Western green salads by using one of the sauces in my Basic Recipes chapter to boost the flavor of your favorite dressings. Try a dollop of Tangy Tamarind Sauce in your favorite vinaigrette, or fire up a bowlful of baby lettuce and halved cherry tomatoes with a little Sweet and Hot Garlic Sauce and a squeeze of lime.

You can also create a salad course in the style of the Thai dishes called *nahm prik*, an array of hot and pungent chili dipping sauces served with raw or blanched vegetables and usually eaten with rice. Check the Appetizers and Snacks chapter for Roasted Eggplant Dip with Thai Flavors or Dao Jiow Lone Dipping Sauce, and present a bowl of either dip along with the traditional Thai accompaniments of cucumber rounds, green beans, and wedges of cabbage, or with a rainbow of radishes, carrot sticks, sweet peppers, and blanched broccoli, asparagus, or snow peas.

✑ OYSTER MUSHROOM SALAD WITH CHILIES AND LIME ✑

This is my mushroom version of the salads that fall under the single Thai umbrella of *yum*. Here, sautéed mushrooms, onions, fresh herbs, chilies, sugar, and lime juice are coaxed into an explosion of delicious contrasts of sweet and sour, salty, and spicy hot. Enjoy it as a dynamite starter, or serve it alongside other dishes on a menu anchored with rice. This salad is terrific even if you substitute additional button mushrooms for the oyster mushrooms.

2 tablespoons vegetable oil
1 tablespoon coarsely chopped garlic
   (4 to 6 cloves)
½ cup coarsely chopped yellow onions
½ teaspoon salt
8 ounces fresh button mushrooms, thickly
   sliced
9 ounces fresh oyster mushrooms
⅓ cup Vegetable Stock (pages 204 and 205)
3 tablespoons freshly squeezed lime juice

2 green onions, thinly sliced crosswise
2 tablespoons finely chopped fresh mint
1 tablespoon finely chopped shallots
1 tablespoon Roasted Rice Powder (page
   216)
2 teaspoons sugar
½ teaspoon soy sauce
½ teaspoon red chili pepper flakes, or
   more to taste
Lettuce leaves to line serving plate

In a medium skillet over medium–high heat, warm the vegetable oil until a bit of garlic dropped into it sizzles at once. Add the yellow onions and cook, tossing often, until fragrant, shiny, and beginning to brown, about 2 minutes. Add the garlic and ¼ teaspoon of the salt, toss well, and add the button mushrooms. Cook for 2 minutes, tossing often. Add the oyster mushrooms and continue cooking, tossing often, until the mushrooms are tender, shiny, nicely browned, and reduced in volume, about 3 minutes longer. Transfer to a plate and set aside to cool to room temperature.

To complete the salad, in a saucepan, bring the stock to a gentle boil over medium heat. Add the mushrooms, toss for about 1 minute to warm and season them, and remove from the heat. Add the lime juice, green onions, mint, shallots, rice powder, sugar, soy sauce, red chili pepper flakes, and the remaining ¼ teaspoon salt. Mix well, using your fingers or a large spoon.

Transfer to a bed of lettuce and serve at once.

SERVES 4.

NOTE • *I like to serve these sprightly salads Thai style, that is, right after they are tossed together with their seasonings. If you would like to prepare the salad in advance, you can toss everything together, cover, and refrigerate for up to 1 day. You can then serve it chilled or at room temperature. Or you can cook the mushrooms, let them cool completely, and then cover and refrigerate them for up to 1 day. To serve, heat the vegetable stock and proceed as directed. In this case, the completed salad can be covered and refrigerated for an additional day. To get the most crunchy, toasty pleasure from the rice powder, toss it in just before you serve the salad.*

∽ SHREDDED BAMBOO SALAD, ISSAHN-STYLE ∽

This traditional dish marries the cool, country crunch of rice powder and bamboo shoots with the hot, sharp sizzle of chilies, lime, and mint. Its Thai name is *soop naw mai*. The result is a bracing little platter of summery flavors, and it is especially suited to toting along on picnics and serving on buffets, as it comes together quickly and keeps well for several hours at room temperature. Thais enjoy it with grilled foods and Sticky Rice (page 150), the classic fare of the country's northeastern Pahk Issahn region. Roasted Rice Powder imparts a traditional rustic texture, but the salad will still be tasty if it is omitted.

1 can (14 ounces) whole or sliced bamboo
   shoots
2 tablespoons finely chopped shallots
1 tablespoon finely chopped garlic
   (4 to 6 cloves)
2 green onions, thinly sliced crosswise
2 tablespoons Vegetable Stock
   (pages 204 and 205)
2 tablespoons freshly squeezed lime juice
1 tablespoon Roasted Rice Powder (page
   216)

2 teaspoons sugar
½ teaspoon salt
½ teaspoon red chili pepper flakes, or
   more to taste
A handful of fresh mint sprigs
2 wedges green cabbage, each about
   2 inches wide at the widest point
9 green beans, trimmed and halved crosswise

Drain the bamboo shoots, rinse, and drain again. Shred or cut them lengthwise into very thin strips about 2 inches long. Place in a bowl and add the shallots, garlic, green onions, vegetable stock, lime juice, rice powder, sugar, salt, and chili pepper flakes and toss well. Reserve a few beautiful mint sprigs for garnish; remove the leaves from the remainder and shred them crosswise into thin strips. Add to the bowl and toss well. Taste and adjust with more lime juice, sugar, or salt, if you wish.

Transfer the salad to a small, deep serving plate and arrange the cabbage wedges and green beans on one side. Garnish with the reserved mint sprigs. Serve at room temperature, or cover and chill for up to 1 day.

SERVES 4 TO 6.

NOTE • *If you want to make this Thai-style salad in advance and have the time to fuss, combine the bamboo, shallots, garlic, green onions, and mint and set aside. In a small container, combine the vegetable stock, lime juice, sugar, salt, and red chili pepper flakes and mix well to make the dressing. Keep the rice powder separate. Close to serving time, give the dressing a good stir and then combine it with the bamboo mixture and the rice powder and toss well. If you do not have time to fuss, simply toss everything together and cover and chill until serving time, and the salad will still taste great. ❖ You can use the ubiquitous canned sliced bamboo shoots sold in the Asian section of major supermarkets. If you have the time, check out Asian markets for a wider selection of varieties and forms of this beloved Asian vegetable, which is generally sold loose in the refrigerated section or in cans on the shelf. In my upcountry town of Thatoom, Thailand, we occasionally made this salad with fresh bamboo shoots, but since they were not always available and take ages of slow stewing to become tender, we were quite happy with the bamboo shoots that someone else brought to market in a ready-to-eat form. ❖ This dish is traditionally hot stuff. Crank up the amount of chili flakes if you love fiery food, or cut it to ¼ teaspoon if you want pleasing sparks with only a mild flame.*

✂ GREEN PAPAYA SALAD ✂

This sparkling tangle of shredded unripe papaya, juicy tomatoes, shallots, and garlic is infused with an incendiary combination of lime juice, palm sugar, and chilies. Known by its Laotian name, *som tum*, this rustic, intensely flavored dish is made from simple ingredients that epitomize the cuisine and spirit of northeastern Thailand. The classic companion is Laotian–style Sticky Rice (page 150) or Coconut Rice with Cilantro and Fresh Ginger (page 157). If an unripe papaya is hard to come by, use a mix of shredded green and purple cabbage (a total of 2 cups) spiked with a good sprinkling of shredded carrot.

2 fresh green serrano chilies or 1 fresh green jalapeño chili

1 tablespoon coarsely chopped garlic (4 to 6 cloves)

1 tablespoon coarsely chopped shallots

1 small hard, green unripe papaya, peeled and finely shredded (about 2 cups)

9 green beans, trimmed and cut into 2-inch lengths

2 teaspoons palm sugar or brown sugar

½ teaspoon salt

2 tablespoons Vegetable Stock (pages 204 and 205)

½ lime, quartered lengthwise

9 cherry tomatoes, quartered

In a large, heavy mortar, combine the chilies, garlic, and shallots. Grind and pound with a pestle until everything is broken down but not completely mushy. Use a spoon to scrape down the sides now and then and mix everything in well.

Add the papaya and pound until the stiff shreds become limp and soft, about 3 minutes. Use the spoon to scrape and turn the mixture over as you work.

Add the green beans and pound to bruise them. One at a time, add the sugar, salt, and vegetable stock, pounding a little after each addition. Squeeze in the juice from each piece of lime, and then add the pieces of squeezed lime to the mortar as well. Add the tomatoes and pound another minute, turning as before as the tomatoes release some of their liquid. Pound more gently so that you do not get splashed.

Taste the sauce in the bottom of the mortar and adjust the seasonings; there should be an interesting balance of sour, hot, salty, and sweet. Using a slotted spoon, transfer the salad to a small serving platter. Drizzle on some of the sauce remaining in the mortar and serve at once.

SERVES 4.

NOTE • *If you do not have a heavy Thai-style mortar and pestle, here is a shortcut version: To crush and bruise the shredded papaya, place it in a big plastic bag on your cutting board, leaving the bag open. Pound it with a cooking mallet or rolling pin, working it until all the shreds are limp and bruised. Transfer to a bowl. Combine the garlic, shallots, sugar, salt, and vegetable stock in a blender or mini processor and blend until fairly smooth. Toss with the papaya. Add the tomatoes and squeeze the juice from lime quarters over the salad, tossing in the lime pieces when you are done. Using your hands, toss again, squeezing the salad to crush the tomatoes so they will release some of their juice as you mix in the lime. Transfer to a deep serving platter and serve at once.*

∾ MUSLIM-STYLE SALAD WITH PEANUT DRESSING ∾

In Thailand, this dish is called *salaht kaek*, the first word being the Thai pro-
nunciation of salad and the second word meaning either "Indian" or "Muslim."
Southern Thailand has a clear Indian influence due to centuries of seagoing
trade with the subcontinent, and to a significant number of Thais who follow
the religion of Islam. Peanuts figure in most of the dishes considered *ah-hahn
kaek*, or "Indian–Muslim food," by Thais. Examples are satay, Indian noodles,
and mussamun curry. This southern Thai salad is satisfying enough to be a
one–dish meal, and it can also add a fresh note to a meal of rice and an array
of savory dishes. You can vary the ingredients to suit yourself. Potatoes are
widely available in Thailand, but they still remain a bit exotic to Thai cooks.
The potato chips called for here were once freshly fried potato strips, but
when potato chips came on the scene, Thai cooks spotted a shortcut to the
rich, salty crunch called for here. Vegans can omit the hard–boiled eggs and
add chunks of firm tofu fried to a crisp, golden brown.

Dressing:

¾ cup unsweetened coconut milk

1½ teaspoons Red Curry Paste (page 198)

½ cup Vegetable Stock (pages 204 and 205)

2 tablespoons palm sugar or brown sugar

2 tablespoons finely ground salted, dry-
  roasted peanuts or peanut butter

½ teaspoon salt

1 tablespoon freshly squeezed lime juice or
  lemon juice or vinegar

Composed Salad:

About 8 ounces leaf lettuce, torn in bite-
  sized pieces

1 small red onion or yellow onion, sliced
  crosswise into thin rings

1 cup bean sprouts

About 2 cups potato chips

1 hothouse cucumber or about 8 ounces
  any variety cucumber, peeled and cut
  crosswise into thick rounds

3 hard-boiled eggs, quartered lengthwise

2 tomatoes, cut lengthwise into wedges, or
  12 cherry tomatoes, halved lengthwise

To make the dressing, in a saucepan over medium heat, warm the coconut
milk until it comes to a gentle boil. Cook, stirring occasionally, until it releases
its sweet fragrance and thickens a bit, 2 to 3 minutes. Add the curry paste and
cook for 2 to 3 minutes longer, mashing and scraping to dissolve the curry

paste and mix everything well. Add the vegetable stock, sugar, peanuts or peanut butter, and salt and stir well. Cook until the sauce comes together and is thick and smooth, 3 to 5 minutes longer. Remove from the heat, add the citrus juice or vinegar, and stir to mix well. Taste and add more lime juice, sugar, or salt if you need it for a pleasing balance of sour, sweet, and salty flavors. Set aside to cool to room temperature.

To prepare the salad, line a platter with the lettuce leaves and sprinkle the onion rings over the lettuce. Place the bean sprouts and potato chips in little mounds on one end of the platter, along with a small bowl containing the peanut sauce. Arrange the cucumber rounds, eggs, and tomatoes on and around the lettuce. Serve at once. Guests take portions of all the ingredients and a dollop or two of peanut sauce to use as a dip.

SERVES 4 TO 6.

NOTE • *The dressing is thick and is usually enjoyed more as a dipping sauce than as a mixture for tossing with ingredients. If you want a tossed salad, thin the dressing with a little vegetable stock or water to the consistency you like. ❖ The dressing will keep well for 2 to 3 days. It thickens as it stands and chills, so bring it to room temperature and thin it with vegetable stock or water if needed before serving.*

✑ KAO YUM RICE SALAD, SOUTHERN STYLE ✑

This salad is a crazy quilt of Thai flavors, with explosions of herbal freshness and sweet–sour crunch in every bite. I first tasted this terrific dish in the cool shadows of the marketplace in Nakorn Sri Thammaraht, an old city that is rich with Buddhist history and the natural beauty of Thailand's enchanting southern provinces. The salad is a lunchtime standard in the cool, shaded corners of the marketplace near the main Buddhist temple. It is offered as a plate of room temperature rice and a rainbow of traditional accompaniments that you pile on as you like before giving it all a toss. I persuaded the smiling food vendor to fix mine up for me the way she liked it, as I was a greenhorn and wanted to try the standard version. You may want to toss it for your guests to keep things simple, or offer everything a la carte and let folks put together their own combinations. Make the rice and the dressing ahead of time so they will have time to cool to room temperature. Do not let the list of ingredients intimidate you. Use what you can find at the market, omitting the lemongrass or lime leaves or sataw beans if need be, and adding whatever strikes you as being in the spirit of the dish.

Dressing:

5 stalks lemongrass

12 quarter-sized slices fresh galanga or ginger or a handful of dried galanga pieces

10 wild lime leaves

2½ cups Vegetable Stock (pages 204 and 205)

1 cup water

1 cup palm sugar or brown sugar

1 teaspoon Asian bean sauce

1 teaspoon salt

Salad:

6 cups cooked Jasmine Rice (page 149), at room temperature

2 stalks lemongrass

25 wild lime leaves or 2 tablespoons finely chopped lime zest

1 cup Toasted Coconut (page 217)

¼ cup red chili pepper flakes

1 cup thinly sliced winged beans or green beans, sliced crosswise

1 cup sataw beans or barely cooked fresh fava beans, snow peas, or green peas

3 small cucumbers or 1 hothouse cucumber, peeled, quartered lengthwise, and cut crosswise into small triangles

1 cup bean sprouts

1 cup peeled and coarsely chopped pomelo, grapefruit, or orange pulp

1 cup peeled and slivered green, unripe mango; chopped unpeeled green apple; or chopped fresh or canned pineapple

To make the dressing, prepare the lemongrass by trimming away and discarding any hard, dried root portions, leaving a smooth, flat base just below the bulb. Trim away the tops, including any dried brown leaf portions; you should have handsome stalks about 6 inches long, including the bulbous base. Slice these crosswise into paper–thin rounds. Place the lemongrass into a saucepan along with the galanga or ginger.

Cut the lime leaves crosswise into strips and add them to the pot along with the vegetable stock, water, sugar, Asian bean sauce, and salt. Bring to a rolling boil over high heat. Reduce the heat to maintain a gentle boil and simmer, stirring occasionally, until the sauce is dark and thickened, about 20 minutes. It should be as thick as real maple syrup, but thinner than pancake syrup or honey.

Remove from the heat and let cool to room temperature. Strain, discarding the solids, and transfer to a jar; seal airtight. Set aside at room temperature until ready to serve. (The sauce will keep a day or two at room temperature, or about 5 days in the refrigerator.)

To make the salad, place the rice in a large bowl. Prepare the lemongrass as directed for the dressing. Set aside in a small bowl.

Shred the lime leaves crosswise into hair-fine threads: Stack a few at a time and use a sawing motion to stay on the edge of the leaves. If you can figure out how to strip away the central vein of each leaf before you shred it, do so; if not, simply leave them intact. Set aside in a small bowl.

Prepare the remaining ingredients as directed, putting them in small bowls or arranging them in heaps on a platter surrounding the rice.

To serve, toss the rice in its bowl with all the ingredients. Add the dressing a few tablespoons at a time, using only enough dressing to season everything lightly; do not soak the ingredients. Serve at once.

Alternatively, mound the rice on a platter and surround it with the accompaniments in small bowls or little heaps; place dressing in a bowl on the side. Guests can serve themselves about 1 cup of the rice and several spoonfuls of each accompaniment, top it off with a dollop of dressing, and then give everything a good toss.

SERVES 6.

NOTE • *Look for sataw beans in the freezer case in Asian markets. Simply let them thaw before adding them to the salad, as they would be used raw in Thailand.* ❖ *Whatever citrus fruit you use, you want only the juicy pulp with none of the stringy membranes attached.* ❖ *Use rice made the same day for this dish. If you absolutely must use rice that has been refrigerated, warm it gently in the microwave or on the stove with a little water and then let it cool down again.*

∾ SWEET-AND-SOUR CUCUMBER SALAD ∾

Like the chutneys of India, this simple relish is a ideal counterpoint to the richness and fire of coconut milk–based curries. It is also always present alongside skewers of curry-kissed satay and spicy peanut sauce. Like the refrigerator pickles of my Southern childhood, these cool cucumbers are a good thing to have on hand, no matter what is on the menu.

½ cup distilled white vinegar
½ cup water
½ cup sugar
1 teaspoon salt
1 large hothouse cucumber or other
   cucumber variety, about 12 ounces

¼ cup coarsely chopped red onion
⅓ cup finely chopped salted dry-roasted
   peanuts
3 tablespoons coarsely chopped fresh
   cilantro
A handful of cilantro leaves

In a small saucepan over medium heat, combine the vinegar, water, sugar, and salt and bring to a gentle boil, stirring occasionally to dissolve the sugar and salt. When the syrup is clear and slightly thickened, after about 2 minutes, remove from the heat. Let cool to room temperature.

Peel the cucumber and quarter it lengthwise to make 4 long strips. Slice the strips crosswise into little triangles about ¼ inch thick. In a bowl, combine the cucumber, the cooled vinegar mixture, the onion, and chopped cilantro and stir well.

To serve, using a slotted spoon, scoop the salad out of the dressing into several small serving bowls. For a traditional presentation, add a little dressing to each bowl, and then divide the peanuts and cilantro leaves among the bowls. Sprinkle the garnishes over about half of each bowl, so that guests can see lots of cucumber with a burst of peanuts and cilantro leaves adorning one side. Or simply sprinkle them evenly over the top. Either way, everything gets tossed together before eating.

MAKES ABOUT 1¼ CUPS; SERVES 4 TO 6.

NOTE • *If you have tender cucumbers from the garden or hothouse cucumbers with nice unwaxed skin, leave some of the skin on. If you are using a large cucumber with lots of seeds, halve it lengthwise, scoop out and discard the seeds with a spoon, and then cut each half* *crosswise into crescent-moon slices.* ❖ *I prefer these pickles crisp, so when preparing them in advance, I chill the dressing and mix it with the cucumbers about an hour before serving. Then I add the peanut and cilantro garnishes just before putting it on the table. But it is fine to mix them together in advance, stirring in the peanuts and cilantro leaves, and to cover and refrigerate for 2 to 3 days.*

℘ PICKLED CABBAGE ℘

This simple pickle goes beautifully with the sweet and spicy heat of Thailand's delicious coconut–milk curries. Add shredded or julienned carrots or thinly sliced green onions for a dash of color.

1 small head green cabbage	*½ cup sugar*
¾ cup distilled white vinegar	*2 teaspoons salt*

Fill a saucepan with water and bring to a rolling boil over high heat. Meanwhile, core the cabbage and chop into large pieces about 2 inches by 1 inch. You will need about 4 cups. Reserve remaining cabbage for another use. Place a colander in the sink.

When the water is boiling, add cabbage and press to submerge all the leaves. Cook for 30 seconds, then drain into the colander. Let cool to room temperature. When cool enough to handle, squeeze leaves to soften them and release some water.

Meanwhile, make the pickling brine: Combine the vinegar, sugar, and salt in a saucepan and bring to a rolling boil over medium heat, stirring to dissolve the sugar and salt. Remove from the heat, pour into a bowl large enough to accommodate the cabbage, and let cool to room temperature.

Add the cabbage to the brine and toss to coat well. Transfer the cabbage and brine to a jar and seal with a tight–fitting lid. Refrigerate for 2 days, turning the jar occasionally to coat all the leaves with the brine.

Serve cold or at room temperature. The cabbage will keep refrigerated for about 3 weeks.

MAKES ABOUT 3 CUPS.

✂ GREEN SALAD WITH SPICY THAI CITRUS DRESSING ✂

Here, Thai flavors jazz up a Western-style salad dressing that is bright in flavor and light in texture. If you want a hotter dressing, add more chilies; if you want a thicker dressing, add a little more oil. You can highlight the dressing's fruitiness by adding grapes, mandarin orange sections, toasted walnuts, chunks of apple, or fresh strawberries to the salad. The dressing recipe yields 1 cup, enough for three salads of the size given here. Store the remaining dressing in the refrigerator for up to 3 days.

Dressing:
½ cup freshly squeezed orange juice
½ cup freshly squeeze lime juice
¼ cup palm sugar or brown sugar
1 teaspoon soy sauce
¼ teaspoon freshly ground pepper
1 tablespoon minced fresh green serrano
   or jalapeño chilies
1 teaspoon minced garlic
3 tablespoons vegetable oil

Salad:
About 6 ounces lettuce, torn into bite-
   sized pieces
1 ripe tomato or 3 plum tomatoes, cut
   into bite-sized chunks
3 small cucumbers or 1 hothouse cucumber, peeled and cut crosswise into thick
   rounds
2 green onions, thinly sliced crosswise
A handful of fresh cilantro leaves,
   coarsely chopped

To make the dressing, in a jar with a tight-fitting lid, combine the orange juice, lime juice, palm sugar, soy sauce, and ground pepper. Cover and shake well until the sugar is dissolved. Add the chilies, garlic, and vegetable oil and shake again to combine well. You should have about 1 cup.

To make the salad, in a large bowl, combine the lettuce, tomatoes, cucumbers, green onions, and cilantro. Drizzle on about ⅓ cup of the dressing. Toss well and serve at once.

SERVES 4.

✃ THAI FRUIT SALAD ✃

A platter of fresh fruit is the only traditional Thai dessert there is, so this beautiful cool salad would be right at home among the desserts at the end of this book. An ice–cold combo of plain ripe pineapple and watermelon is my sentimental favorite, but here I have expanded the palette with other fruits and a citrus dressing. This Thai–inspired fruit salad is at its best within a few hours of preparation, but it keeps surprisingly well in the refrigerator for a day or two.

1 pineapple, about 3½ pounds, peeled and cut into bite-sized chunks (about 4 cups)

3 large mangoes, peeled, pitted, and cut into bite-sized chunks (about 2 cups)

1 piece watermelon, about 1½ pounds, seeded and cut into bite-sized chunks (about 3 cups)

3 bananas, peeled and cut into 1-inch chunks

¼ cup freshly squeezed lime or lemon juice

3 tablespoons sugar

Combine the pineapple, mangoes, watermelon, and bananas in a large bowl. In a small bowl, combine the lime or lemon juice and sugar and stir well until the sugar dissolves. Pour over the fruit and toss gently to coat the fruit well. Cover and refrigerate for at least 30 minutes before serving. Serve ice cold.

SERVES 6.

NOTE • *You can substitute other ripe fruits cut into bite-sized chunks for those suggested here, planning on 10 cups in all. Good candidates include honeydew melon, cantaloupe, orange sections, papaya, apple, peaches, nectarines, and plums. You can also use berries. Add them closer to serving time if you are making the salad well in advance, however, so they keep their texture and shape.*

✌ ORANGE SALAD IN GINGER SYRUP WITH FRESH MINT ✌

Like the Thai Fruit Salad on page 69, this simple dish would be enjoyed as a sweet snack in Thailand rather than as a salad. I like to serve it along with the carousel of sour, salty, sweet, and fiery flavors that light up a traditional Thai menu. It can also round out a dessert course, served with an array of dainty cookies and a round of coffee or tea.

1 cup sugar
1 cup water
1 piece fresh ginger, about 3 inches long, peeled and sliced crosswise into ¼-inch-thick coins

8 sweet oranges
A handful of small fresh mint sprigs

In a heavy saucepan, combine the sugar, water, and ginger and bring them to a boil over high heat. Cook, stirring occasionally to dissolve the sugar, until the mixture becomes a medium syrup, 2 to 3 minutes. Remove from the heat, pour into a bowl, and let cool. Cover and chill until very cold.

Meanwhile, section the oranges: Working with 1 orange at a time, place it on a cutting board and cut a thick slice off the top and bottom to expose the flesh. Stand the orange on the cutting board and use a sharp knife to cut off the peel and all the white pith in thick strips, cutting downward and following the curve of the fruit. Repeat with the remaining oranges. Then hold a peeled orange in the palm of one hand positioned over a bowl. Loosen the meat by running a knife between the segments and let them fall into the bowl as you work around the membrane. After you have removed all the segments, squeeze the core of membranes into the bowl to extract any remaining juice before you discard it and continue with the remaining peeled oranges.

Strain the ginger coins from the chilled syrup and pour the syrup into the bowl of orange sections. Toss gently to combine well, and cover and chill until serving time. Reserve a few mint sprigs for garnish; remove the remaining mint leaves from the sprigs and shred the leaves, cutting them crosswise into thin ribbons. Stir them into the oranges.

Serve the salad very cold in small bowls. Garnish with mint sprigs.

SERVES 4 TO 6.

NOTE • *To chill the ginger syrup quickly, fill a large bowl with ice and nestle the syrup bowl in the ice. You can make the syrup in advance and hold it for several days before you combine it with the fruit and mint. You can also toss together oranges, room-temperature syrup, and shredded mint, chill the lot for an hour or so, and serve whenever you are ready.*
❖ *If you do not have fresh mint, do not despair. In Thailand, this dish is* som loy gaew, *or "orange jewels afloat," and it comes without mint or ginger and with a handful of crushed ice on top to cool it down on the spot.* ❖ *For an express-lane version of this dish, toss the dressing with chunks of banana and well-drained mandarin oranges from a can.*

3
·
SOUPS

SOUPS

～ In Thailand, soup is an essential component of almost every meal, served and savored along with rice and its accompanying dishes. In keeping with Thailand's Chinese culinary ancestry, soup functions as a beverage, a liquid refreshment that cleanses the palate between bites and makes way for further rides on the roller coaster of tastes that make up a classic Thai meal. Drinks come either before or after the rice, so soup gives diners something hot and delicious to sip throughout the meal. These soups work their magic in two ways, as a hot beverage and as another dish to spoon onto one's rice.

～ Many Thai restaurants in the West bow to Western habits and bring soup first, in tiny individual bowls and without a grain of rice, much less the remaining dishes that will make up the meal. This works with the co-queens of the Thai soup repertoire, *tome yum* and *tome kha*, because these classic soups are strongly flavored and spectacular enough to stand alone. But other soups, such as the less flashy representatives of the *gaeng jeute* category, never earn favor because they are what their name implies— plain soups created to support more dazzling dishes and contribute a nice, salty note to the sweet, sour, and hot flavors on the Thai table.

～ Soup is woven into the heart of the Thai meal and is usually the last dish set before you. Most dishes, including curries, stews, and stir-frys, are considered tastier when they have cooled off a little after removal from the heat. Soup is the exception, served steaming hot and right off the heat. I remember my Thai students calling our household to eat. We settled in on the straw mats covering the concrete kitchen floor where the meal had been laid out dish by dish as each one came off the two small charcoal stoves that fueled our cooking. One student piled our individual plates with rice, while another put finishing touches on the soup, fanning the charcoal to bring it to a boil, transferring it to a serving bowl, and then finishing it off with a flourish of cilantro or a squeeze of lime. If company came, we passed out individual bowls, but if it was just us, we spooned the soup from the serving bowl onto our rice a few bites at a time, just as we did the other dishes.

～ However you eat your soup, you will find much pleasure in the recipes that make up this chapter. It opens with the aforementioned co-queens of Thai soup, *tome kha* and *tome yum*. *Tome* means "boiled," or "cooked in broth," and the former is a luxurious concoction of coconut milk, mushrooms, and tofu infused with galanga, ginger's Siamese cousin known in Thailand as *kha*. The latter soup is a clear broth set on fire with chili paste and sharpened to a glorious edge with a final burst of freshly squeezed lime juice. If you like your food volcanic, add a few Thai chilies after bruising each one with the flat side of a chef's knife or cleaver to expose its fiery interior while leaving the chili intact.

C/ɔ Next come two versions of *gaeng jeute*, the plain soups. Incongruous as it may seem in a cuisine famed for fireworks and fancy presentation, Thai food has a cherished place for the chorus as well as the stars. A meal needs one or two hot and spicy dishes but not four or five, as that would be monotonous, albeit in a histrionic way. *Gaeng jeute* is comforting and satisfying, a boon companion to rice enjoyed with a rich coconut curry, a sweet-sour stir-fry, and a saladlike dish with a sharp citrus tang.

C/ɔ The remaining soups in this chapter would be one-dish meals in Thailand, although you can serve them along with other dishes or as a warm, inviting option on a buffet. Jasmine Rice Soup is Thai comfort food made from yesterday's rice, and is the classic cure for what ails you, simmered up for invalids, those with hangovers, and the very old and the very young. The lemongrass soup is an herb-laced variation shared with me by my friend Sovan Bounthuy, from her terrific Cambodian restaurant Chez Sovan in San Jose, California. Rice Noodles with Spinach in Shiitake Mushroom Soup is chopstick food, unlike most Thai dishes, although a soup spoon is always included so the tasty broth can be enjoyed.

C/ɔ Finally, there is my favorite, Sweet Potato Wonton Soup with Cilantro and Crispy Garlic. There is some work to making this, but what a fine feast when you are done. Try it with regular potatoes, pumpkin, or any other winter squash, and make enough wontons to tuck away in the freezer for a return engagement on a night when you need a treat. These last four dishes come to Thailand direct from her culinary godmother, China. In each case, however, the Thai touches are transcendant, creating dishes you will hunger for later and cook many times.

TOME YUM SOUP WITH MUSHROOMS AND TOFU

This classic soup is a one-bowl celebration of Thailand's sparkling cuisine. Spicy hot with Roasted Chili Paste and sharply fragrant with lemongrass, wild lime leaves, and a squeeze of lime, *tome yum* sounds an inviting reveille to your senses. Entice your guests with a glance at its gorgeous flame-colored broth studded with brilliant green herbs, and then treat them to a whiff of its exotic citrus perfume as you serve it up Thai style, along with other dishes and a plate of jasmine rice. Thais value fresh lemongrass as a healing herb with particular power over fever and colds. If you are caring for an ailing friend who enjoys the chili-pepper heat, this clear, sharp soup would be good medicine.

4 cups Vegetable Stock (pages 204 and 205)

3 large stalks lemongrass

12 wild lime leaves (optional)

2½ tablespoons freshly squeezed lime juice

3 green onions, cut crosswise into 1-inch lengths

1 fresh green jalapeño chili

8 ounces firm tofu, cut into 1-inch chunks

1 cup well-drained canned whole straw mushrooms or sliced fresh button mushrooms

2 tablespoons Roasted Chili Paste (page 222)

2 teaspoons sugar

½ teaspoon soy sauce

½ teaspoon salt

In a large saucepan, bring the vegetable stock to a boil over medium heat. Meanwhile, trim the lemongrass stalks: Cut away and discard any hard, dried root portions, leaving a smooth, flat base just below the bulb. Trim away the tops, including any dried brown leaf portions; you should have handsome stalks about 6 inches long, including the bulbous base. Using the blunt edge of a cleaver blade or heavy knife or the side of an unopened can, bruise each stalk, whacking it firmly at 2-inch intervals and rolling it over to bruise on all sides. Cut into 2-inch lengths.

When the stock is boiling, add the bruised lemongrass stalks and half of the lime leaves (if using), and reduce the heat to maintain a simmer. Cook until the stock is fragrant and the lemongrass has faded from bright green to a dull khaki, about 5 minutes.

While the soup simmers, combine the lime juice, the remaining lime leaves (if using), and the green onions in a serving bowl large enough to accommodate the soup. Remove the stem from the jalapeño and cut the chili crosswise into thick rounds; add 2 or more of the rounds to the serving bowl; the amount depends on your love of chili heat. Reserve any leftover chili for another use and set aside.

Scoop out the lemongrass from the stock and discard it. Raise the heat to high and add the tofu, straw or button mushrooms, chili paste, sugar, soy sauce, and salt and stir well. When the soup boils again, remove it from the heat and quickly pour it into the serving bowl. Stir to combine the lime juice and herbs with the soup and serve at once.

SERVES 4 TO 6.

NOTE • *This soup should be intensely and wonderfully sour, salty, and spicy hot. If you like, check the seasoning just before serving and fine-tune it to your liking with a little more lime juice, chili paste, sugar, and/or salt.* ❖ *To make this soup in advance, hold the lime juice mixture aside until serving time and then gently reheat the soup, combine it with the lime juice mixture, and serve at once.* ❖ *Except at banquets, Thai cooks serve soup along with rice and all the other dishes that make up a meal. If you prefer soup as a first course, you may want to offer small bowls of rice with it, so that your guests can savor it as Asian people traditionally do, both straight from the bowl and spooned over plain rice.*

✑ COCONUT SOUP WITH GALANGA AND BUTTERNUT SQUASH ✑

This is my vegetarian version of the classic Thai soup *tome kha, kha* meaning "galanga." Use shiitake, portobello, or other exotic mushrooms in this extraordinary soup if you like, or add a rainbow of bell peppers to the pot just before removing it from the heat.

4 stalks lemongrass

2 cans (14 ounces each) unsweetened coconut milk

1½ cups Vegetable Stock (pages 204 and 205)

20 quarter-sized slices fresh galanga or ginger or 10 large pieces dried galanga

10 peppercorns

20 wild lime leaves, or 12 strips lime zest, each about 2 inches long by ½ inch wide

1 butternut squash, about 1½ pounds

1 can (15 ounces) straw mushrooms, rinsed and drained, or 6 ounces fresh mushrooms, sliced (about 1¼ cups)

8 ounces firm tofu, cut into bite-sized chunks

1 tablespoon soy sauce

1 teaspoon salt

2 tablespoons freshly squeezed lime juice

½ cup coarsely chopped fresh cilantro

3 green onions, thinly sliced crosswise

Trim the lemongrass stalks: Cut away and discard any hard, dried root portions, leaving a smooth, flat base just below the bulb. Trim away the tops, including any dried, brown leaf portions; you should have handsome stalks about 6 inches long, including the bulbous base. Using the blunt edge of a cleaver blade or heavy knife or the side of an unopened can, bruise each stalk, whacking it firmly at 2-inch intervals and rolling it over to bruise on all sides. Cut into 2-inch lengths.

In a 3-quart saucepan, combine the coconut milk and vegetable stock, and bring to a gentle boil over medium-high heat. Stir in the lemongrass, galanga or ginger, peppercorns, and half of the lime leaves or all of the lime zest; adjust the heat to maintain an active simmer.

Meanwhile, cut the butternut squash in half lengthwise. Scoop out and discard seeds, cut the squash into large chunks, and, using a paring knife, peel the chunks carefully. Cut the peeled squash into generous bite-sized pieces; you should have 3 to 4 cups. Add to the simmering soup along with the mushrooms. Increase the heat to medium-high and bring soup back to a gentle boil. Cook for 10 minutes.

Add the tofu and cook until the squash is tender but still firm and the tofu is heated through, about 5 minutes longer.

Remove the soup from the heat and use tongs to remove and discard the lemongrass, galanga or ginger, and lime leaves or lime zest. Stir in the soy sauce, salt, lime juice, cilantro, green onions, and the remaining lime leaves. Taste and add more salt, soy sauce, or lime juice if you like. Transfer to a serving bowl and serve hot.

SERVES 6 TO 8.

NOTE • *The lemongrass, galanga or ginger, and lime leaves add flavor, but are too big and too tough to eat. Thais leave them in and eat around them, but if you prefer to remove them, use tongs as directed in the recipe. Or strain the soup into a large bowl, pick out and discard the flavorings, and return the cooked squash and mushrooms to the soup.* ❖ *Dried galanga works well in this dish, imparting lots of flavor and aroma. It keeps indefinitely on your pantry shelf, a plus since fresh galanga is not always available, even in Asian markets. Dried galanga does swell into enormous woody chunks as it cooks, so be sure to remove it prior to serving.* ❖ *Use any winter squash or pumpkin instead of butternut, such as kabocha pumpkin or acorn squash, or use chunks of peeled sweet potato, which will cook a bit more quickly than the squash.*

✂ CLEAR SOUP WITH SPINACH AND TOFU ✂

This is the classic *gaeng jeute*, or "plain soup." Despite the usual Thai affection for over-the-top flavors, a bland soup is often welcomed as a soothing foil to the appealing cacaphony of seasonings found in a traditional Thai meal. In upcountry kitchens, Thai families keep alive the Chinese culinary legacy of serving soup as the sole beverage accompanying each meal. While many city-dwelling Thais have taken up the Western practice of sipping a cool beverage throughout the meal, the love of soup remains, and the question that arises when putting a Thai menu together is not whether to serve soup, but which soup to serve. Choose this one when you want satisfaction, simple and swift. Serve with rice and pass a little hot sauce around if your guests crave a little drama.

4 cups Vegetable Stock (pages 204 and 205)
8 ounces firm tofu, cut into 1-inch chunks
½ teaspoon freshly ground pepper
½ teaspoon soy sauce
¼ teaspoon sugar

A handful of small spinach leaves, stemmed and left whole, or large leaves torn into big bite-sized pieces
3 green onions, thinly sliced crosswise
Salt to taste
2 tablespoons Crispy Garlic in Oil (page 221)

In a saucepan, bring the stock to a gentle boil over medium heat. Add the tofu, pepper, soy sauce, and sugar and simmer until the tofu is heated through, about 2 minutes. Stir in the spinach and green onions and remove from the heat.

Taste and add a little salt, if you like. Transfer to a serving bowl and top with the Crispy Garlic in Oil.

SERVES 4 TO 6.

೧౨ CLEAR SOUP WITH ROASTED PORTOBELLO MUSHROOMS AND BEAN THREAD NOODLES ೧౨

Here, a clear and shiny tangle of bean thread noodles and strips of roasted mushroom float in a garlic-and-pepper-laced broth. It is the perfect companion to a plate of jasmine rice, a fiesty coconut milk curry, and a plate of garlicky sautéed greens. If you do not have Roasted Chili Paste on hand, marinate the mushrooms in a little vegetable oil seasoned with minced garlic, a dash of soy sauce, and a generous pinch of sugar.

2 ounces bean thread noodles

6 ounces portobello mushrooms

3 tablespoons Roasted Chili Paste (page 222)

4 cups Vegetable Stock (pages 204 and 205)

1 tablespoon finely chopped garlic

¾ teaspoon freshly ground pepper

½ teaspoon soy sauce

¼ teaspoon sugar

3 green onions, thinly sliced crosswise

A handful of fresh cilantro leaves, coarsely
chopped

Place the bean thread noodles in a bowl, add warm water to cover, and soak until softened, flexible, and easily separated into threads, 15 to 20 minutes.

Meanwhile, trim away the stems from the mushrooms and cut them lengthwise into strips about ¾ inch thick. Place in a bowl. Add the chili paste and toss to coat evenly. Set the mushrooms aside while you fire up a gas grill or broiler, or preheat an oven to 450 degrees F for cooking them. Grill or roast the mushrooms, turning as needed, until tender and handsomely browned, 5 to 7 minutes. Set aside until cool enough to touch.

Pour the stock into a saucepan, place over medium heat, and bring to a rolling boil. Meanwhile, drain the noodles and dump the tangle onto your cutting board. Cut through the pile of noodles lengthwise and then crosswise. Cut the cooled roasted mushrooms into big bite-sized chunks and set them aside with the noodles.

When the stock boils, add the noodles, mushrooms, garlic, ½ teaspoon of the pepper, the soy sauce, and sugar and stir well. As soon as the noodles are clear and curling into tendrils, add the green onions and remove the soup from the heat. Transfer to a serving bowl, spoon on the remaining ¼ teaspoon ground pepper and sprinkle with the cilantro leaves. Serve at once.

SERVES 4 TO 6.

NOTE • *This dish is a soup on its first serving, but if you should have some left over, it may well transform itself into a tasty noodle dish, with the bean thread noodles absorbing most of the broth. Covered and refrigerated, it will keep a day or so. Reheat it gently and serve it with forks and chopsticks instead of a spoon.* ❖ *You can leave the mushrooms to marinate in the Roasted Chili Paste for up to 1 hour, or for 4 to 6 hours if you cover and refrigerate them first.* ❖ *Although this soup is filled with noodles, Thais consider it more a soup than a noodle dish, to be portioned out in small individual bowls and enjoyed with rice and other dishes. If you love Asian-style soup noodle dishes, served in gigantic individual bowls as a one-dish meal, try Rice Noodles with Spinach in Shiitake Mushroom Soup (page 82) and Sweet Potato Wonton Soup with Cilantro and Crispy Garlic (page 87).*

⋙ RICE NOODLES WITH SPINACH IN SHIITAKE MUSHROOM SOUP ⋘

This is a meal in a bowl, perfect for a hearty supper. Thais have adopted the Chinese tradition of noodle soup, although since it is easy to find a noodle shop in even the tiniest Thai town, they seldom cook noodle dishes at home. If you enjoy soup noodles, invest in some large, deep Chinese-style soup bowls, which are widely available in Asian markets. Each guest needs his or her own bowl large enough to hold an entire serving and both chopsticks and a large spoon with which to eat. Use fresh, soft rice noodles (see note) if you have access to an Asian market, or use dried rice noodles or any cooked noodle with delicious results. If you have Crispy Garlic in Oil made up in advance, this is a quick dish to put together. If you do not have it on hand, you can leave it out, or increase the amount of garlic you sauté along with the mushrooms.

3 ounces dried shiitake mushrooms or
    Chinese mushrooms
8 ounces dried rice noodles, preferably
    wide, flat ones, or 1 pound fresh fet-
    tuccine or linguine
2 tablespoons vegetable oil
1 tablespoon coarsely chopped garlic
12 ounces fresh button mushrooms, sliced
½ teaspoon salt

6 cups Vegetable Stock (pages 204 and 205)
6 ounces spinach leaves (7 to 8 cups)
6 green onions, thinly sliced crosswise
2 teaspoons freshly ground pepper
½ cup chopped fresh cilantro, including
    some stems
6 tablespoons Crispy Garlic in Oil (page
    221)

Place the dried shiitake mushrooms in a small bowl and add hot water to cover them. Let them soften for 30 minutes, pressing occasionally to submerge them all, while you prepare other ingredients.

Meanwhile, prepare the noodles. For dried rice noodles, place them in a large bowl. add warm water to cover, and soak until white and pliable, 15 to 20 minutes. To cook, bring a large pot of water to a rolling boil. Drain the softened noodles, add them to the pot, and cook, using chopsticks or forks to separate them as they boil, until tender but still firm, about 3 minutes. If you are using fresh fettuccine or linguine, cook it in the same way, then drain and set aside.

In a large skillet over high heat, warm the vegetable oil until a bit of garlic dropped into the pan sizzles at once. Add the garlic and the fresh mushrooms and sprinkle them with the salt. Cook, tossing often, until shiny, softened, and nicely browned, 4 to 5 minutes. Transfer to a bowl and set aside.

In a saucepan over medium heat, bring the vegetable stock to a rolling boil. Meanwhile, remove softened mushrooms from their soaking liquid; strain them through a fine-mesh sieve or a coffee filter, and add to the stock. Slice the shiitakes into long, thin strips and set aside.

When the stock is hot, divide the noodles among 6 large bowls, one for each guest. Divide the spinach as well, remembering that its volume will reduce greatly once it wilts in the hot soup. Garnish each serving with an equal portion of shiitake mushrooms, sautéed mushrooms, and green onions. Ladle about 1 cup of hot stock into each bowl, sprinkle with ground pepper and cilantro leaves, and top with a generous tablespoon of Crispy Garlic in Oil. Serve at once.

SERVES 6.

NOTE • *You can streamline this recipe by omitting the dried mushrooms and Crispy Garlic in Oil. You can enhance it by adding shredded carrots, bean sprouts, chunks of tofu, strips of omelet, slices of hard-boiled egg, or any cooked vegetable.* ❖ *You can use dried rice noodles of any size, from wire-thin vermicelli to medium linguinelike threads to wide, flat fettuccine-like ribbons. You can also use fresh soft rice noodles if you live in a community large enough to support an Asian shop that carries the delicate product. Fresh rice noodle sheets are highly perishable, and in Asia they are sold and used on the same day. Here you may find them refrigerated or even frozen. If you find a fresh source, buy either precut noodles, which are in wide ribbons, or a flat rectangular packet, which is a gigantic noodle sheet folded into a 1-pound pad the size of a book. Cut the noodle pad lengthwise into strips about 1 inch wide, and then gently separate the strips into noodles. Some will break apart and this is fine, but strive to keep the noodles intact as long as possible. Taste one, and if it is pleasingly tender, use the noodles as they are, adding them to the serving bowls to be bathed in hot soup. If they are a little dry, stiff, or firm, they are old enough to have needed refrigeration, so refresh them with a quick dip in boiling water before serving them. You can also use dried rice flakes, which are found with other dried noodles in Asian markets, and look like white but translucent tortilla chips. Add them to boiling water, stir well, and watch them turn white and curl into little scrolls.*

✑ JASMINE RICE SOUP WITH MUSHROOMS, GREEN ONIONS, AND CRISPY GARLIC ✑

Rice soup is comfort food in Thailand, simmered up from leftover rice to nourish a family member who is ill. It is also popular as a hearty breakfast or midnight snack. Colds, fevers, aches, hangovers, and heartbreaks all seem to soften their edge just a little when a generous steaming bowl of *kao tome* appears. I can not make medical claims here, but I know this soup can boost your spirits, and I love it even when all is well, especially on a blustery winter evening when I am hungry for a satisfying one–dish meal. Thais serve this with flavorful condiments to jumpstart its mild flavor. Try Pickled Cabbage (page 67) or pickled garlic from an Asian market, sliced hard–boiled egg, chunks of cooked Salty Eggs (page 220), thinly sliced celery and celery leaves, chopped fresh or dried chilies, soy sauce, and Asian sesame oil.

2 tablespoons coarsely chopped garlic
½ teaspoon freshly ground pepper
¼ cup coarsely chopped fresh cilantro roots
*   or stems*
5 cups Vegetable Stock (pages 204 and 205)
1 tablespoon vegetable oil
1 cup thinly sliced fresh mushrooms (about
*   6 ounces)*
1 ¼ teaspoons salt

½ recipe Wheatballs (page 207) or 1 can
*   (8 ounces) wheat gluten, drained*
*   (about 1 cup)*
½ cup shredded carrots
½ teaspoon sugar
1½ cups cooked Jasmine Rice (page 149)
2 green onions, thinly sliced crosswise
¼ cup coarsely chopped fresh cilantro leaves
¼ cup Crispy Garlic in Oil (page 221)

In a blender, combine the garlic, pepper, cilantro roots, and ½ cup of the vegetable stock and blend until fairly smooth, about 1 minute. In a saucepan, combine the remaining 4½ cups vegetable stock with this garlic–cilantro purée and bring to a boil over medium heat. Reduce the heat to maintain a simmer.

Meanwhile, in a skillet over medium–high heat, warm the vegetable oil for 1 minute. Add the mushrooms and cook, tossing often, until darkened, shiny, and tender, about 5 minutes. Remove from the heat and season with ¼ teaspoon of the salt.

Stir the sautéed mushrooms, Wheatballs or wheat gluten, carrots, the remaining 1 teaspoon salt, and sugar into the stock and cook for 5 minutes.

Add the rice and cook, stirring occasionally, for 5 minutes. Stir in the green onions and remove from the heat.

Serve hot or warm. Garnish the serving bowl or individual bowls with the cilantro leaves and Crispy Garlic in Oil just before serving.

SERVES 4 TO 6.

NOTE • *You can use any cooked rice in this soup, including basmati, medium-grain rice, brown rice, or a combination of wild and white rice. ❖ The rice continues to absorb liquid, so when reheating the soup, thin with additional stock and season with salt.*

‿ LEMONGRASS SOUP WITH RICE AND BASIL CHEZ SOVAN ‿

Sovan Bounthuy is chef–owner of Chez Sovan, a wonderful Cambodian restaurant in San Jose, California. She kindly shared her recipe for this delicate soup, soothing with a heavenly lemongrass perfume and bracing with a sun-burst of citrus and lime. I have adapted it for vegetarian kitchens. In my Peace Corps days I lived in Surin province, which has strong Khmer cultural influ-ences due to its position on the border between Thailand and Cambodia. This soup, called *sgnor chhrok moin* in the Cambodian language, is a country–style *tome yum* that my student Onjan often made for our evening meal. It is as homey and satisfying as plain rice, dazzling in the way its flavors come together yet simple to prepare.

5 stalks lemongrass

3 cups Vegetable Stock (pages 204 and 205)

2 cups water

1 teaspoon sugar

¼ teaspoon salt

6 fresh button mushrooms, thinly sliced lengthwise (about ⅔ cup)

8 ounces firm tofu, cut into 1-inch chunks

2 cups cooked long-grain white rice

3 plum tomatoes, stemmed and cut into big bite-sized chunks, or 6 cherry tomatoes, halved lengthwise

3 to 4 tablespoons freshly squeezed lime juice

2 tablespoons coarsely chopped fresh cilantro

2 tablespoons coarsely chopped fresh basil

Trim the lemongrass, cutting away and discarding any withered outer leaves or roots. Cut the stalks into 3–inch lengths and then split each piece in half lengthwise, to expose its fragrant core.

In a large saucepan, combine the vegetable stock, water, lemongrass, sugar, and salt and bring to a rolling boil over high heat. Reduce the heat to main-tain a gentle boil and simmer for 5 minutes, stirring occasionally. Remove the lemongrass with tongs or strain the stock through a sieve and return it to the pan.

Add the mushrooms, the tofu, and the cooked rice and simmer only until the soup returns to a boil, about 2 minutes more. Remove from the heat and stir in the tomatoes, 3 tablespoons of the lime juice, and the salt. Taste and add a little more lime juice or salt if you need it for a pleasingly tart flavor.

Stir in the cilantro and basil, transfer to a serving bowl, and serve at once.

SERVES 4 TO 6.

NOTE • *If you would like some fireworks, dollop a little Roasted Chili Paste (page 222) onto each individual serving bowl. You can also add a few slices of fresh green jalapeño chili, or smash several tiny Thai bird chilies with the flat side of a knife and stir them into the soup just before serving. ❖ To prepare this soup in advance, pause after removing the rice-tofu soup from the heat. Let cool to room temperature, cover, and chill for a few hours. To serve, reheat gently; add the tomatoes, lime juice, and herbs and serve at once. If the rice has absorbed much of the soup, add additional stock and a little extra lime juice, or serve it as is, a rice stew. ❖ If your lemongrass is tired, brown, and pliable rather than fresh, green-tinged and stiff, use a few more stalks to intensify its flavor. I like to split open the lemongrass to expose its fragrant core, and then remove it after it has infused the soup with its flavor and perfume. This creates lots of tiny fibrous pieces that need to be strained out. Asian cooks usually smash the lemongrass with a cleaver, leaving it in large chunks, and then let it remain in the soup, since this saves a step and everyone knows not to try and eat it. ❖ If you do not have fresh lemongrass, you can still enjoy a version of this soup. Skip the first step of simmering the lemongrass in the stock and begin by adding the mushrooms, tofu, and rice to boiling stock. Add a little extra lime juice and a bit of lime zest and change the name to Rice Soup with Mushrooms and Fresh Herbs.*

∾ SWEET POTATO WONTON SOUP WITH CILANTRO AND CRISPY GARLIC ∾

What a heavenly, hearty soup you will have if you give this recipe a try! The wontons themselves take a bit of work, but it is a breeze when there is a part-ner to share the tasks and pass the time, and once they are filled and shaped, you can have the soup on the table in minutes. Soup wontons are traditionally cooked in quantity in boiling water until tender, then portioned into individual bowls, doused with hot, tasty broth, and crowned with herbs just before serv-ing. The uncooked dumplings freeze well, so you can make only half a batch of the soup and freeze half of the dumplings. That way you will have the foundation of a future feast on hand. To freeze, arrange the dumplings, not touching, on a baking sheet and place in the freezer until frozen solid. Then transfer them to lock–top bags or other airtight containers and freeze for up to 1 month. To cook, transfer them directly from the freezer to boiling water.

Wontons:

1 cup Mushroom Mince (page 206)

1 cup mashed cooked sweet potato

½ cup bread crumbs (page 40)

1 egg, lightly beaten

1 teaspoon soy sauce

¼ teaspoon sugar

¼ teaspoon salt

3 green onions, finely chopped

¼ cup finely chopped fresh cilantro leaves
    and stems

2 packages (12 ounces each) wonton
    wrappers

Soup:

3 quarts Vegetable Stock (pages 204
    and 205)

6 green onions, thinly sliced crosswise

⅔ cup chopped fresh cilantro leaves

About ¾ cup Crispy Garlic in Oil
    (page 221)

1 tablespoon salt

Vegetable oil, as needed

To make the wontons, combine the Mushroom Mince, sweet potato, bread crumbs, egg, soy sauce, sugar, salt, green onions, and cilantro. Mix until fully blended. Set up a work space with a clean, dry cutting board, a baking sheet, a small bowl of water, the wonton wrappers, and the sweet potato filling.

Place a wonton wrapper before you on the cutting board and place about 1 teaspoon filling in its center. Dip your finger in the water and moisten the edges of the wrapper. Fold it in half to form a small rectangle, enclosing the filling. Gently press out any air trapped inside and press the edges to seal it tight. With the flat, folded edge facing you, moisten the two sealed corners, pull them in toward each other, and press to seal them to each other well. This will make a plump dumpling; place it on the baking sheet. Continue shaping wontons until you have used up the filling, placing them without touching each other on the baking sheet. You should have about 96. (You can refrigerate these dumplings for 1 to 2 days if you take care to prevent them from touching each other, as they tend to stick and tear. Place them in a covered container with dry kitchen towels or plastic wrap between layers.)

To cook the wontons, fill a large pot with salted water (about 1 tablespoon salt), cover, and bring to a rolling boil over medium heat. Have a teakettle or a pitcher filled with cold water handy. When the water boils, uncover the pot and carefully add the wontons. Stir gently to discourage the dumplings from sticking together, and then let them cook, uncovered, until the pot returns to a boil. Add 1 cup or so of cold water, enough to stop the water from boiling, and then let it return to the boil a second time. Again add enough cold water to quiet the water, and when it comes to a boil again, quickly drain the dumplings into a colander, carefully transfer to a bowl, and gently toss with a little oil to discourage them from sticking together. (You can set the wontons aside to cool to room temperature, then cover and chill them for up to 1 day before reheating them gently in the hot soup.)

To make the soup, in a large saucepan over medium heat, bring the vegetable stock to a rolling boil. Meanwhile, place 8 wontons in each large, individual serving bowl. Pour about 1 cup of the hot stock into each bowl, and then garnish each with some green onions, cilantro, and a generous dollop of the Crispy Garlic in Oil. Serve at once. Or you can prepare a single large serving bowl of wontons, garnished as directed, and then ladle into individual bowls at the table.

SERVES 8.

NOTE • *Vegan readers can omit the egg and add an extra 2 tablespoons bread crumbs to the sweet potato mixture. The filling will be quite soft, so take extra care in transferring the cooked dumplings from the cooking water to the soup.* ❖ *You can also shape the wontons by folding them into triangles, pulling together the edges that are on the fold, and then sealing them securely to each other. Or you can fold them into rectangles or triangles, press out the air, seal tightly, and leave them as they are, with loose pasta "wings." If they burst, you can present them as open-face wontons, remembering that they will still taste great.* ❖ *I love this traditional method of cooking dumplings by adding cold water to the boiling water, because it solves questions of timing no matter how large or small your pot. Adding cold water paces the cooking process, so that the wrapper and its filling have time to cook evenly. That third return to the boil after you have added the wontons is the charm. Your wontons will be* sook laew!— *"ready, already!"*

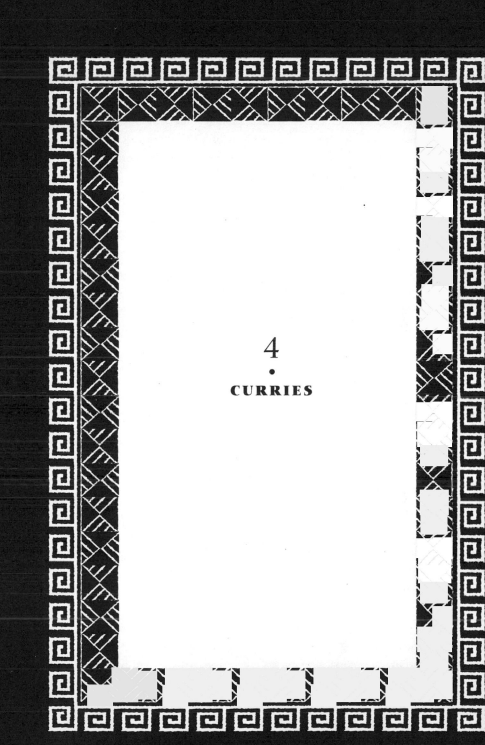

4

·

CURRIES

CURRIES

❧ The curry dishes of Thailand are Thai food in a nutshell. They contain Thai trademarks galore: lemongrass, galanga, wild lime leaves, and other aromatic Southeast Asian treasures; the juxtaposition of salty and sharp, tangy flavors against the luxurious sweetness of palm sugar and coconut milk; and the explosion of chili-pepper heat.

❧ The Thai word *gaeng* is both a verb and a noun. As a verb, it refers to the cooking of a meat, vegetable, or combination of the two with intense seasonings in abundant liquid, usually stock, water, or coconut milk, or a mixture. As a noun, it generally means a stew made with one of Thailand's signature curry pastes, but the same word can also mean a soup. *Gaeng jeute* is a mild, salty broth containing tofu, bean thread noodles, and greens, and *gaeng liang* is a clear, delicate soup made with Chinese okra, fresh straw mushrooms, baby corn, lemony *maengluk* basil leaves, and tender kabocha pumpkin vines, curly tendrils and all.

❧ The most common Thai curries make up a delicious quartet. *Gaeng peht* means "spicy-hot curry," and is made from red curry paste. *Gaeng kiow wahn* means "green sweet curry," although it is not particularly sweet. *Gaeng mussamun* is made with what Thais call Muslim-style curry paste, a red curry paste spiced with cinnamon, cloves, nutmeg, and cardamom and sharpened with a splash of tangy tamarind. *Gaeng kah-ree* means "curry curry," a red curry turned golden by turmeric and enlivened with curry powder, the latter known in Thailand as *pong kah-ree*. All curry pastes fall into one of two categories: green curry paste starts with fresh, ferociously hot green Thai chilies, and red curry paste starts with dried, ferociously hot red chilies. All other curry pastes are variations on red curry paste, with turmeric adding a golden hue and an assortment of ground, toasted spices adding a sweet, complex note. The curries do not display their namesake colors; the names refer to the original chili color or the particular spice combination, rather than the resulting curry's hue.

❧ The classic two- to three-quart saucepan of Thailand is known as *maw gaeng*, with *maw* meaning "cooking pot" and *gaeng* denoting the size and shape suitable for making a curry. The curry pastes used to work culinary magic are known as *kreuang gaeng*. You could translate this as "curry essence" or "curry base," but *kreuang* also means "engine" or "machine." This analogy delights me, that curry paste is the culinary equivalent of the key to the car, of the match that coaxes kindling into flames.

ᴄ∕ɔ *Kreuang gaeng* are part of Thailand's culinary legacy from India. Indian dishes defined in the West as curries include wet or dry *masalas*. *Masala* is a Hindi word denoting a concoction of herbs and spices ground together to breathe flavorful life into a dish. A dry *masala* would consist of whole dried spices such as cumin seeds, coriander seeds, and peppercorns, often toasted to jumpstart their aroma and taste and then ground to a powder known in Thai as *pong*. In India, a wet *masala* might include onion, cilantro, fresh ginger, and garlic ground with powdered spices to a glorious purée. Thai cooks adapted the wet *masala* to their own culinary repertoire, adding a profusion of herbs that thrive in the Southeast Asian countryside: lemongrass, galanga, and wild lime peel, along with fresh or dried chilies and the sturdy little roots of cilantro plants. Home cooks in Thailand pound their own curry pastes from scratch in the large, heavy mortars that are standard equipment in any Thai kitchen. But most Thai people will gladly purchase a meal's worth of ready-made curry paste from the curry vendors who set up shop in every market-place, enjoying a shortcut when they lack time to make their own.

ᴄ∕ɔ Traditional curries are easy to find in Thailand, although if you try to order a curry at just any upcountry restaurant you will probably be disappointed. Restaurants tend to specialize, doing one thing or a certain category of things repeatedly and consequently very well. At the café near the train station or bus depot you can feast on noodles, fried rice, and other one-dish specials. Here is where you take a load off after a hot, dusty journey, nursing a wonderfully tall Thai iced coffee as you cool your palms on the tiny pearls of cool water beading your glass in the heat of the day. If you are celebrating your birthday or otherwise feeling swell due to a burst of good fortune, you will host your friends at *rahn ahahn jeen*, the Chinese restaurant with that soupçon of uptown ambience, where the chef-owner cooks up seafood, Cantonese-style stir-frys, memorable soups, *yum*-style salads, and other fancy dishes. No curries here, but remember the national motto, *mai pen rai*, or "never you mind." Walk on, for even the smallest town upcountry supports at least one curry shop, whose proprietor cooks up a dozen or so curries first thing in the morning, and sets them out on display to entice you in. Here, customers can order a splash of curry over a mountain of rice for a quick one–plate lunch, or buy a family meal's worth for breakfast or supper, toting it home in a little plastic bag, which seems too full to survive the journey but invariably does.

ↂ If you are reading this worlds away from any upcountry curry shop, take heart, for Thai–style curries are among the easiest of Thai dishes to cook at home once you have the elements for creating them. These include curry paste and coconut milk, both of which are available in most Asian markets and many supermarkets, or are easily ordered through the mail (page 232). You can also make your own curry pastes from scratch, using recipes in the Basic Recipes chapter. You may find it essential to do so despite the work involved, since shrimp paste is a common ingredient in traditional Thai curry pastes, both those made commercially and in Thai homes.

ↂ Coconut milk is the most common base for Thai curries, but it is not the only one. If you use water or stock, you will have a traditional *gaeng bah*. This means "country–style curry," with the literal translation of *bah* meaning the "forest" or even the "jungle." In a remote village, coconut milk is a special-occasion ingredient, prepared for celebrations and honored guests. City folks can buy freshly ground coconut grated to a delicate floss by machine in the market, and squeeze out a batch of coconut milk in a few minutes' time. Country folks must usually go to the trouble to hack open a hairy brown coconut or two, grate it up laboriously by hand, soak the bright white confetti of coconut in rainwater, and then squeeze it through a wicker sieve into fresh coconut milk. Th.. is a lot of trouble on a weeknight when family members are tired and are hungry for rice. After a day working in the rice paddies, cooking up sweets and snacks to hawk at the bus stop, or making charcoal from wood gathered in the forest, *gaeng bah* will do just fine, as long as it is volcanically hot and ready by the time the rice is cooked.

ↂ A nontraditional alternative to coconut milk is to substitute soy milk or another nondairy milk, or a range of dairy milk products, including evaporated skim milk, for the coconut milk called for in these recipes. The choice depends on your culinary practices and the texture of sauce you prefer. You will notice that most curry recipes instruct you to begin by cooking the curry paste in a little coconut milk, to release its aroma. If you substitute another liquid for coconut milk, simply sauté the curry paste gently in a few tablespoons of oil first and then continue, adding the liquid of your choice along with the vegetables or tofu and seasonings.

❧ The most typical Thai curry has a texture closer to that of milk or soy milk, rather than that of thick gravy or cream soup. The reliance on thick coconut milk, frozen or from cans, has influenced the way curries are made in many Thai restaurants in the West, as has our affection for rich, thick, creamy sauces. You can adjust the texture of the curries you make to your liking, by thinning the coconut milk with vegetable stock and adjusting the seasonings to keep the flavors robust. I like Thai curries thick, thin, and in between. I like them ferociously hot, medium spicy, or mellow and sweet like *gaeng mussamun*. I like them with tofu and with wheat gluten, with sweet peppers, and with gnarly purple-skinned yams. I like them because they are easy to make, and I like them because their flavor improves with time. I like them because I can buy ready-made paste for a quick supper or create my own incredibly delicious paste by hand. I like them because despite their simplicity they remind me of all that is delightful and unique about Thailand and Thai food.

❧ RED CURRY WITH RED SWEET PEPPERS, SNOW PEAS, AND TOFU ❧

Think of this recipe as the basic game plan for a Thai curry, and vary it according to the produce you have on hand when you yearn for a Thai curry's appealing flavors. Use tempeh instead of tofu if you like, and change the vegetables, keeping in mind that firm vegetables like carrots, potatoes, and winter squash go in along with the tofu. Softer vegetables like zucchini need only a few minutes' cooking time, and delicate vegetables like snow peas and sugar snap peas go in when you are ready to remove the curry from direct heat.

1 can (14 ounces) unsweetened coconut milk (about 1¾ cups)

1 to 2 tablespoons Red Curry Paste (page 198)

8 ounces tofu, cut into ½-inch chunks

¼ cup Vegetable Stock (pages 204 and 205)

1 tablespoon palm sugar or brown sugar

½ teaspoon soy sauce

½ teaspoon salt

1 red sweet pepper, cut into long, thin strips

4 ounces snow peas, trimmed

Shake the coconut milk can well. Spoon out ⅓ cup into a medium saucepan and bring to a gentle boil over medium heat. Cook, stirring occasionally, until it thickens and releases its sweet fragrance, about 3 minutes.

Add the curry paste and cook for about 3 more minutes, mashing, scraping, and stirring often to soften the paste and combine it with the coconut milk. Add the tofu and stir gently to coat it with the curry paste. Add the remaining coconut milk, the vegetable stock, sugar, soy sauce, and salt and stir well. Bring to an active boil, reduce the heat to maintain a gentle boil, and simmer, stirring occasionally, for 15 minutes.

Add the red pepper and snow peas to the curry and stir gently. Remove from heat and let stand for 5 minutes. Serve hot or warm.

SERVES 4 TO 6.

NOTE • *Use a wooden spoon to stir the curry so that tofu chunks stay whole rather than break up or crumble.*

✑ RED CURRY WITH WINTER VEGETABLES AND CASHEWS ✑

Here is a pleasing pot full of harvest gold, perfect for a winter night's feast. You can use any combination of root vegetables—parsnips add a pleasing sweet note—or members of the pumpkin family. If you have time to prepare this curry in advance, do so, as its flavors will blossom as it stands. Keep the cashews and cilantro by the stove, and add them after you have gently reheated the curry, to get the most pleasure from their crunch and color.

1 can (14 ounces) unsweetened coconut milk (about 1¾ cups)

2 or 3 tablespoons Red Curry Paste (page 198)

1 yellow onion, thinly sliced lengthwise

1 cup wheat gluten, Wheatballs (page 207), or seitan, cut into bite-sized chunks

1 cup Vegetable Stock (pages 204 and 205)

1 pound assorted winter vegetables such as parsnips, carrots, sweet potatoes, and winter squash, in any combination, peeled and cut into 2-inch chunks

1 tablespoon palm sugar or brown sugar

1 teaspoon soy sauce

1 teaspoon salt

¾ cup salted, dry-roasted cashews

¼ cup chopped fresh cilantro

Shake the coconut milk can well. Spoon out ⅓ cup into a medium saucepan and bring to a gentle boil over medium heat. Cook, stirring occasionally, until it thickens and releases its sweet fragrance, about 3 minutes.

Add the curry paste and cook for about 3 more minutes, mashing, scraping, and stirring often to soften the paste and combine it with the coconut milk. Add the onion and the wheat gluten, Wheatballs, or seitan, and stir gently to coat them with the curry paste. Add the remaining coconut milk, the vegetable stock, winter vegetables, sugar, soy sauce, and salt and stir well. Bring to an active boil, reduce the heat to maintain a gentle boil, and simmer, stirring occasionally, until the vegetables are tender but not mushy, about 15 minutes.

Add the cashews to the curry and stir gently. Remove from the heat and let stand for 5 minutes. Transfer to a serving dish, sprinkle with the cilantro, and serve hot or warm.

SERVES 6 TO 8.

✑ RED CURRY WITH EGGPLANT AND SWEET PEPPERS ✑

This recipe makes a generous pot of curry, enough for a crowd of your favorite Thai food fans with a little left over for your next day's lunch. You can use any type of eggplant, including large globe, slender Japanese, or the golf ball–sized Thai variety called *makeuah poh*.

2 cans (14 ounces each) unsweetened
    coconut milk (about 3½ cups)
2 to 3 tablespoons Red Curry Paste (page
    198)
1 pound eggplant, cut into bite-sized
    chunks (about 3 cups)
12 wild lime leaves, torn in half length-
    wise
2 cups Vegetable Stock (pages 204 and 205)

1 tablespoon palm sugar or brown sugar
2 teaspoons soy sauce
1 ½ teaspoons salt
1 pound firm tofu, cut into ½-inch
    chunks
½ red sweet pepper, cut into 2-inch strips
½ green sweet pepper, cut into 2-inch
    strips
½ cup fresh cilantro leaves

Shake the coconut milk can well. Spoon out ⅓ cup into a medium saucepan and bring to a gentle boil over medium heat. Cook, stirring occasionally, until it thickens and releases its sweet fragrance, about 3 minutes.

Add the curry paste and cook for about 3 more minutes, mashing, scrap-ing, and stirring often to soften the paste and combine it with the coconut milk. Add the eggplant and stir gently to coat it with the curry paste. Add the remaining coconut milk, half of the lime leaves, the vegetable stock, sugar, soy sauce, and salt and stir well. Bring to an active boil, reduce the heat to main-tain a gentle boil, and simmer, stirring occasionally, just until the eggplant is tender, 10 to 15 minutes.

Add the tofu, the red and green sweet peppers, and the remaining lime leaves to the curry and stir gently. Let the curry return to a boil and then remove from the heat. Let stand for 5 minutes. Transfer to a serving dish, sprinkle with the cilantro leaves, and serve hot or warm.

SERVES 8 TO 10.

NOTE • *Use a wooden spoon to stir the curry so that the tofu chunks stay whole rather than break up or crumble.*

✍ RED CURRY WITH HARD-BOILED EGGS AND PEAS ✍

What a satisfying dinner this makes. Frozen green peas are added at the end of cooking since they only need to be heated until fully thawed. But if you have fresh green peas, add them after the curry has simmered for about 10 minutes. When they are tender, add the eggs, and remove from the heat.

1 can (14 ounces) unsweetened coconut
    milk (about 1¾ cups)
2 to 3 tablespoons Red Curry Paste
    (page 198)
1 yellow onion, thinly sliced lengthwise
¾ cup Vegetable Stock (pages 204
    and 205)

1 tablespoon palm sugar or brown sugar
1 teaspoon soy sauce
½ teaspoon salt
5 hard-boiled eggs, peeled and halved
    lengthwise
1 cup frozen green peas
¼ cup coarsely chopped fresh cilantro

Shake the coconut milk can well. Spoon out ⅓ cup into a medium saucepan and bring to a gentle boil over medium heat. Cook, stirring occasionally, until it thickens and releases its sweet fragrance, about 3 minutes.

Add the curry paste and cook for about 3 more minutes, mashing, scraping, and stirring often to soften the paste and combine it with the coconut milk. Add the onion and stir gently to coat it with the curry paste. Add the remaining coconut milk, the vegetable stock, sugar, soy sauce, and salt and stir well. Bring to an active boil, reduce the heat to maintain a gentle boil, and simmer, stirring occasionally, until the onion is tender and the curry thickens a bit, about 15 minutes.

Add the hard-boiled eggs and the peas to the curry and stir gently. Remove from the heat and let stand for 5 minutes. Transfer to a serving dish, sprinkle with the cilantro, and serve hot or warm.

SERVES 6 TO 8.

NOTE • *Vegan readers could substitute 8 ounces firm tofu, cut into 1-inch chunks, for the eggs, or add about 1 cup potato and carrot chunks when the curry begins its 15-minute simmer.*

ᴄ⦿ GREEN CURRY WITH ZUCCHINI AND BAMBOO SHOOTS ᴄ⦿

Green curry paste gets its fire from fresh green chili peppers, rather than dried red ones. If you can get fresh wild lime leaves, also called kaffir lime leaves, toss in a handful when you add the vegetable stock and seasonings, and add a few more just before serving. These add a lovely citrus note in fragrance and flavor. Think of them as equivalent to a bay leaf, added to impart their scent and taste but not to be eaten.

1 can (14 ounces) unsweetened coconut
    milk (about 1¾ cups)
1 to 2 tablespoons Green Curry Paste
    (page 199)
1 can (8 ounces) sliced bamboo shoots,
    rinsed and drained
1 yellow onion, coarsely chopped

½ cup Vegetable Stock (pages 204 and 205)
1 tablespoon palm sugar or brown sugar
½ teaspoon soy sauce
½ teaspoon salt
2 zucchini, sliced crosswise (about 1 cup)
½ bunch fresh cilantro, coarsely chopped

Shake the coconut milk can well. Spoon out ⅓ cup into a medium saucepan and bring to a gentle boil over medium heat. Cook, stirring occasionally, until it thickens and releases its sweet fragrance, about 3 minutes.

Add the curry paste and cook for about 3 more minutes, mashing, scraping, and stirring often to soften the paste and combine it with the coconut milk. Add the bamboo shoots and chopped onion and stir gently to coat it well with the curry paste. Add the remaining coconut milk, the vegetable stock, sugar, soy sauce, and salt and stir well. Bring to an active boil, reduce the heat to maintain a gentle boil, and simmer, stirring occasionally, until the onion is tender and the curry thickens a bit, about 15 minutes.

Stir in the zucchini, cook for 1 minute longer, and remove from the heat. Let stand for 5 minutes. Transfer to a serving bowl, sprinkle with the cilantro, and serve hot or warm.

SERVES 4 TO 6.

NOTE • *You can buy whole bamboo shoots and slice or tear them into thin, bite-sized pieces.*

✑ YELLOW CURRY WITH PINEAPPLE AND PEAS ✑

Here is a scrumptious curry with spicy notes and moderate chili heat. Green peas punctuate its sun-colored sauce, drawing everyone to the table. If you like, add a little of the Indian spice mixture called *garam masala,* or a mixture of freshly ground pepper and ground cinnamon and cloves, along with the curry paste. For more chili heat, cut a few fresh serrano chilies in half lengthwise and add them along with the pineapple and seasonings.

1 can (14 ounces) unsweetened coconut milk (about 1¾ cups)

1 to 2 tablespoons Yellow Curry Paste (page 200)

12 ounces potatoes, peeled and cut into bite-sized chunks

1 can (8 ounces) pineapple chunks, drained

½ cup Vegetable Stock (pages 204 and 205)

1 tablespoon palm sugar or brown sugar

½ teaspoon soy sauce

1 teaspoon salt

8 ounces firm tofu, cut into ½-inch cubes

1 red sweet pepper, cut into long, thin strips

¼ pound snow peas, trimmed

¾ cup frozen green peas

Shake the coconut milk can well. Spoon out ⅓ cup into a medium saucepan and bring to a gentle boil over medium heat. Cook, stirring occasionally, until it thickens and releases its sweet fragrance, about 3 minutes.

Add the curry paste and cook for about 3 more minutes, mashing, scraping, and stirring often to soften the paste and combine it with the coconut milk. Add the potatoes and pineapple chunks and stir gently to coat them with the curry paste. Add the remaining coconut milk, the vegetable stock, sugar, soy sauce, and salt and stir well. Bring to an active boil, reduce the heat to maintain a gentle boil, and simmer, stirring occasionally, until the potatoes are tender, about 15 minutes.

Add the tofu, red pepper, and peas to the curry and stir gently. Let the curry return to a boil and remove from the heat. Let stand for 5 minutes. Transfer to a serving bowl and serve hot or warm.

SERVES 4 TO 6.

NOTE • *Use a wooden spoon to stir the curry so that the tofu chunks stay whole rather than break or crumble.*

∽ MUSSAMUN CURRY WITH PEANUTS, POTATOES, AND CARDAMOM ∽

This delicious curry is a culinary legacy of Muslim traders from India, who traveled the sea coasts of Southeast Asia in centuries past. The use of peanuts, potatoes, and whole cardamom in a curry are unusual in most of Thailand, but not in the southern provinces where this curry originated and where Islam is a major religion. Mussamun curry paste is a red curry paste that includes not only the standard cumin, coriander, and peppercorns, but also an aromatic array of sweet spices, including cinnamon, cloves, nutmeg, and cardamom.

1 can (14 ounces) unsweetened coconut milk (about 1¾ cups)

1 to 2 tablespoons Mussamun Curry Paste (page 200)

1 can (8 ounces) wheat gluten, drained, or 2 cups Wheatballs (page 207)

1 small yellow onion, coarsely chopped

1 white potato, peeled and cut into 1-inch chunks

1 sweet potato, peeled and cut into 1-inch chunks

¾ cup Vegetable Stock (pages 204 and 205)

1 tablespoon palm sugar or brown sugar

½ teaspoon soy sauce

1 teaspoon salt

25 whole green or white cardamom pods

1 cup unsalted, dry-roasted peanuts

Shake the coconut milk can well. Spoon out ⅓ cup into a medium saucepan and bring to a gentle boil over medium heat. Cook, stirring occasionally, until it thickens and releases its sweet fragrance, about 3 minutes.

Add the curry paste and cook for about 3 more minutes, mashing, scrap-ing, and stirring often to soften the paste and combine it with the coconut milk. Add the wheat gluten or wheatballs and the onion and stir gently to coat them with the curry paste. Add the remaining coconut milk, the white potato, sweet potato, vegetable stock, sugar, soy sauce, salt, and cardamom pods and stir well. Bring to an active boil, reduce the heat to maintain a gentle boil, and simmer, stirring occasionally until the sweet potatoes are tender, about 15 minutes.

Add the peanuts to the curry and stir gently. Remove from heat and let stand for 5 minutes. Transfer to a serving bowl and serve hot or warm.

SERVES 4 TO 6.

∽ BURMESE-STYLE CURRY WITH YAMS, MUSHROOMS, AND GINGER ∽

Northern Thai cooks long ago adopted this deliciously earthy curry that originated in Burma. Its Thai name is *gaeng hahng ley*, and it provides a beautiful balance of spicy red–chili heat, sour tamarind punch, and sweet notes of brown sugar. Make it in advance and reheat it gently, as its flavors deepen in a pleasing way.

¼ cup peeled and slivered fresh ginger
2 tablespoons Red Curry Paste (page 198)
¼ cup brown sugar
2 teaspoons ground turmeric
2 ½ cups Vegetable Stock (pages 204 and 205)
1 teaspoon dark soy sauce or 2 teaspoons regular soy sauce
½ teaspoon salt

2 pounds yams or sweet potatoes, peeled and cut into 2-inch chunks
8 ounces small fresh button mushrooms, cut into ½-inch-thick slices
¼ cup thinly sliced shallots
2 tablespoons minced garlic
2 tablespoons Tamarind Liquid (page 212) or freshly squeezed lime juice
2 tablespoons chopped fresh cilantro

Place the slivered ginger in a small bowl, add warm water to cover, and set aside.

Combine the curry paste, brown sugar, and turmeric in a large, heavy (6-quart) saucepan or Dutch oven. Mash with a spoon to mix them together well. Add the vegetable stock, soy sauce, and salt and stir well. Bring to a rolling boil and add the yams. Reduce the heat to maintain a gentle boil, and cook, uncovered, until yams are tender and the sauce has cooked down and thickened a little, about 20 minutes.

Drain the ginger and add the soaking water to the curry. Place the ginger in a mortar and pound it lightly with a pestle to soften its fibers and release its flavor. Or place it on your cutting board and use the dull edge of your knife to bruise it.

Add the ginger, mushrooms, shallots, garlic, and tamarind or lime juice to the curry, stir well, and continue cooking for 10 minutes. Transfer to a serving bowl, sprinkle with the cilantro, and serve hot or warm.

SERVES 6.

ᥜ PANAENG CURRY WITH WHEATBALLS AND WILD LIME LEAVES ᥜ

Panaeng dishes are thick, rich, red–hot curries made with less coconut milk than most other Thai curries and enriched with coarsely ground peanuts. Traditionally, they are made with meat alone, rather than a combination of meat and vegetables. For a heady finish, whole fresh basil leaves and fine threads of wild lime leaves are stirred into the curry just before taking the pan off the heat, and the finished dish is garnished with thick coconut cream, lime leaves, and fire–engine–red *chee fah* chilies. This curry cooks fast, tastes great, and invites you to substitute what suits you. In place of the Wheatballs or wheat gluten, add firm tofu, fresh mushrooms (whole or sliced), chunks of cooked kabocha pumpkin or potato, or a mix of pineapple and zucchini.

1 can (14 ounces) unsweetened coconut milk (about 1¾ cups)

3 tablespoons Red Curry Paste (page 198)

2 cups Wheatballs (page 207), or 1 can (8 ounces) wheat gluten, drained

2 tablespoons Vegetable Stock (pages 204 and 205)

1 tablespoon brown sugar

1 teaspoon salt

½ teaspoon soy sauce

10 fresh horapah basil leaves or any other basil leaves

¼ cup coarsely ground or chopped salted dry-roasted peanuts

9 wild lime leaves, sliced crosswise into wire-thin threads

2 fresh red chee fah chilies, cut crosswise on the diagonal into ovals ¼ inch thick, or ¼ of a red sweet pepper, cut into long, thin strips

Scoop out about ¼ cup of the coconut milk from the top of the can and set aside to garnish the finished curry. In a skillet over medium heat, bring ½ cup of the coconut milk to a gentle boil. Cook, stirring occasionally, until it thickens a little and releases its sweet fragrance, about 3 minutes.

Add the curry paste and cook for about 3 more minutes, mashing, scraping, and stirring often to soften the paste and combine it with the coconut milk.

Add the Wheatballs or wheat gluten and toss to coat with the curry paste. Add the remaining coconut milk, vegetable stock, sugar, salt, and soy sauce and stir well. Bring to a gentle boil and cook, stirring occasionally, until the sauce is smooth and heated through, about 5 minutes more. Tear all but a few of the basil leaves in half crosswise and add to the curry along with the peanuts and most of the lime leaf threads.

Transfer to a serving platter. Pour the reserved coconut milk on top and sprinkle on the remaining lime leaf threads, the chilies or pepper strips, and the reserved whole basil leaves. Serve hot or warm.

SERVES 4.

NOTE • *To slice wild lime leaves, stack several leaves and cut them crosswise into extremely thin threads, using a sawing motion and a very sharp knife. If possible, without tearing the leaf in half, strip away and discard the center vein running lengthwise along each leaf. Wild lime leaves are too tough to eat whole, but cutting them into wire-thin strips allows them to impart their bright citrus flavor while making them fine enough to eat.*

❧ CHOO CHEE NEW POTATOES WITH FRESH BASIL ❧

Choo chee curries, which are traditionally made with seafood, are thick and rich. They call for less coconut milk than most Thai curries and use lots of pungent herbs. *Panaeng* curries (page 104) are similar, but they include ground peanuts. *Choo chee* curries are flavored with *krueng gaeng kua*, a red curry paste made without the toasted cumin, coriander seeds, and peppercorns used in most Thai curry pastes. You can make your own by using the Red Curry Paste recipe in the Basic Recipes chapter and omitting the spices. Or you can use any curry paste you like and be assured of a delicious result.

1 can (14 ounces) unsweetened coconut milk (about 1 ¾ cups)

2 tablespoons Red Curry Paste made without coriander, cumin, and peppercorns (page 198)

1 pound new potatoes, halved or quartered, cooked in boiling water for about 5 minutes, and drained

¼ cup Vegetable Stock (pages 204 and 205)

2 tablespoons palm sugar, light brown, or white sugar

1 teaspoon salt

½ teaspoon soy sauce

½ cup loosely packed fresh horapah basil leaves or any other basil leaves

12 wild lime leaves, sliced crosswise into wire-thin threads (see note, page 105)

Shake coconut milk can well. Spoon out about ½ cup into a medium saucepan and bring to a gentle boil over medium heat. Adjust heat to maintain a gentle boil, and cook, stirring occasionally, for 6 to 8 minutes. The coconut milk will become fragrant as it thickens. When you see tiny pools of oil glistening on the surface, add the curry paste and continue cooking for 1 to 2 minutes, stirring to dissolve the paste into the coconut milk.

Add the potatoes, the remaining coconut milk, the vegetable stock, sugar, salt, and soy sauce and stir well. Bring to an active boil, adjust the heat to maintain a gentle boil and cook, stirring occasionally, until the curry is thickened and the potatoes are cooked, about 10 minutes.

Cut all but a few of the basil leaves into thin strips and stir into the curry along with the lime leaves. Remove from the heat and transfer to a serving dish. Garnish with the reserved basil leaves and serve hot or warm.

Serves 4.

NOTE • *This dish traditionally calls for fresh horapah basil and wild lime leaves, but you can use any variety of fresh basil and a tablespoon of lime zest if you can't track down these particular fresh seasonings. Even if you omit them altogether, you'll still have a wonderful Thai dish. Dried basil and dried lime have too little fragrance and flavor, so I never use them, even if they are all I can find.*

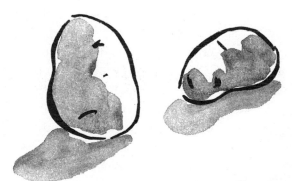

⌁ BUTTERNUT SQUASH IN FRESH GREEN CURRY ⌁

This simple fresh curry paste takes only minutes to prepare. It envelops sweet, golden chunks of butternut squash with a beautiful and savory green sauce in the time it takes the accompanying rice to cook. Try making it with any pre-pared curry paste for an even simpler dish (see note).

1 small butternut squash, about 1½ pounds

2 tablespoons coarsely chopped shallots or yellow onion

1 tablespoon coarsely chopped garlic

1 teaspoon peeled and coarsely chopped fresh ginger

2 fresh green jalapeño chilies or 1 fresh green serrano chili

3 tablespoons plus ½ cup water

¾ cup coarsely chopped cilantro leaves and stems

1 can (14 ounces) unsweetened coconut milk (about 1¾ cups)

1 teaspoon sugar

1 teaspoon salt

¼ cup fresh basil leaves

Trim off the stem and blossom end of the butternut squash. Halve lengthwise and scoop out and discard the seeds and fibers. Cut into large chunks and carefully peel each chunk. Cut the peeled chunks into 1–inch pieces. You will have about 4 cups. Set aside.

In a small food processor or the jar of a blender, combine the shallots or onion, garlic, ginger, chilies, the 3 tablespoons water, and ½ cup of the cilantro. Grind until you have a fairly smooth paste, pulsing the motor and stopping often to stir down the sides of the container and incorporate all the ingredi-ents. You will have about ¼ cup bright green paste. Set aside.

Shake the coconut milk can well. Spoon out ½ cup into a medium saucepan and bring to a gentle boil over medium heat. Cook, stirring occa-sionally, until it thickens and releases its sweet fragrance, about 3 minutes.

Add the curry paste and cook for 1 to 2 minutes, mashing, scraping, and stirring until the paste is dissolved into the coconut milk and is heated through. Add the remaining coconut milk, the remaining ½ cup water, the sugar, salt, and butternut squash. Raise the heat to high and bring the curry to a rolling boil. Stir well, reduce the heat to maintain a gentle boil, and continue cooking until the squash is tender and the sauce is smooth and evenly colored a soothing green, about 15 minutes.

Meanwhile, cut all but a few of the basil leaves crosswise into thin strips. When the curry is cooked, stir in the basil strips and the remaining ¼ cup cilantro. Remove from the heat and transfer to a serving bowl. Garnish with the reserved basil leaves and serve hot or warm.

SERVES 4 TO 6.

NOTE • *This recipe makes a moderately hot curry. If you like your curries very hot, increase the amount of fresh chilies to suit your palate.* ❖ *To substitute prepared curry paste (any type will do; see the Basic Recipes chapter), omit the shallots or onion, garlic, ginger, chili peppers, water, and cilantro, and begin by cooking 2 tablespoons prepared curry paste in the ½ cup coconut milk.* ❖ *Butternut squash and other hard winter squash are a challenge to peel. Use a chef's knife or a Chinese cleaver if you are handy with either one of these tools, or use a good paring knife, holding each chunk steady on your cutting board and cutting down along its side to remove the peel.*

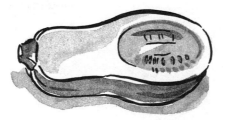

5
.
OTHER MAIN DISHES

OTHER MAIN DISHES

✿ This is the catch–all chapter for the Thai dishes that I have lassoed together because they share the distinction of not fitting in anywhere else in the book. If this cataloging decision suggests to you that the recipes to follow are ordinary, minor, or otherwise relegated to supporting roles, take another look. Along with the preceding chapters of Salads, Soups, and Curries, these recipes offer you plenty of options for Thai–style vegetarian feasts, anchored by an abundance of jasmine rice or sticky rice.

✿ The Mixed Grill included here is perfect for days when cooking outdoors is appealing and possible. If you were using an upcountry kitchen in Thailand, this would be an everyday dish, since a traditional kitchen like the one I had during my Peace Corps days becomes almost a patio when the wooden shutters and door are thrown open to greet the dawn. My Thai kitchen included a pair of bucket–sized charcoal stoves that we used for the grilling technique known charmingly as *ping*.

✿ Most of the following recipes are for traditional stir–frys, the Chinese cooking method Thais call *paht* and use at almost every meal. Whenever you stir–fry, set the scene to make your work easier when it's time to cook. Prepare the main ingredients, such as vegetables and tofu, washing and chopping as necessary and setting them near the stove. In a small bowl, combine any liquid ingredients, such as water, stock, and soy sauce. In another small bowl, combine any dry ingredients such as sugar, salt, and spices. Set these bowls near the stove, along with any herbs or garnishes. Then you are ready for the demands of a stir–fry, cooking through from start to finish without a pause.

✿ There is a quartet of hearty classics, all fortified with tofu but each with its own special spark. Oyster Mushrooms with Red Sweet Peppers and Ginger is *paht king*, lit up with a shower of shredded ginger and studded with fresh mushrooms. You can throw in softened, shredded cloud ear mushrooms if you want to give it a traditional spin. Following is Baby Corn and Tofu with Cashews. Its Thai name is *paht meht mamuang Himapahn*, with the three enchanting but unwieldy modifying words adding up to the concise English word *cashew*. *Meht* is "seed" or "nut," *mamuang* is "mango," and *Himapahn* is an enchanted forest locale in the jataka tales of Theravada Buddhist tradition. In Thai, cashews are "mangoes of the forest of Himapahn," a poetic reference probably springing from the fact that the nuts are shaped like the incomparable mangoes of Southeast Asia.

❧ Completing this classic quartet are *paht briow-wahn*, the pleasing Thai version of Chinese sweet–and–sour dishes, and *paht bai graprao*. The latter is a stir-fry with holy basil, a delicious and delicate herb for which you can substitute any variety of its first cousins, fresh basil and fresh mint. Each of these classic stir-fry recipes calls for tofu, but you could substitute other protein–rich ingredients such as wheat gluten, seitan, or tempeh, with tasty results.

❧ Next come recipes in which successive vegetables deliciously take a bow in the spotlight, including Bean Sprout Toss–up, Chinese Cabbage with Black Pepper and Garlic, and Triple Mushroom Feast. Following are *paht* dishes jazzed up with some of the voluptuous sauces you will find in the Basic Recipes chapter. If you lay in a supply of these concoctions, you will have the short, high road to incredible flavor in remarkably little time. Start with my favorite, Butternut Squash and Spinach in Roasted Chili Paste, and progress and work your way through tasty dishes spiked with curry paste to the deceptively simple Firecracker Broccoli, a gorgeous sparkler fueled by Sweet and Hot Garlic Sauce.

❧ All the previous dishes are vegan, but this *gahp kao*–"with rice"–parade concludes with four traditional Thai egg dishes, beginning with two unique Asian ways with hard–boiled eggs and ending with a savory custard and a simple omelet served with fiery Sri Racha chili sauce. Vegans can adapt the first two dishes by substituting crisp–fried tofu or wheat gluten for the hard-boiled eggs. The recipes in this chapter will feed four people, when served along with rice and several other dishes, such as a curry, a salad, and a soup.

✑ MIXED GRILL ✑

This spectacular rainbow of vegetables, seasoned with the traditional Thai combination of cilantro, garlic, and peppercorns, makes a fine companion to a pot of curry, a simple green salad, and a mountain of jasmine rice. If you can grill outdoors on a summer afternoon, add a pitcher of lemonade and make Sticky Rice (page 150) rather than jasmine; the former is finger food and perfect for picnics. Cook up a double batch of grilled vegetables, as you can turn the leftovers into instant feasts galore. Pile the garlicky morsels onto a veggie burger, stack them on crusty peasant bread for a sensational sandwich, or toss with noodles.

1½ cups coarsely chopped fresh cilantro leaves and stems

2 tablespoons coarsely chopped garlic (8 to 12 cloves)

1 teaspoon freshly ground pepper

2 tablespoons soy sauce

2 tablespoons Vegetable Stock (pages 204 and 205)

½ cup vegetable oil

About 3 pounds vegetables in any combination, such as portobello mushrooms; zucchini; yellow summer squash; eggplants; yellow onions; large green onions; whole heads of garlic; firm small to medium tomatoes; asparagus spears; red, yellow, or green sweet peppers; New Mexico, Anaheim, or Hungarian wax peppers.

In a food processor fitted with the metal blade, combine the cilantro, garlic, pepper, and soy sauce and pulse to mince and combine well. With the machine running, pour in the oil and process to a fairly smooth marinade. If using a blender, combine cilantro, garlic, pepper, soy sauce, stock, and oil and blend to a fairly smooth marinade, pulsing, and scraping down the sides as needed. Transfer the marinade to a large, shallow baking dish and set aside.

Next, prepare the vegetables for the grill: Rinse the mushrooms and pat them dry. Remove the stems and make 3 shallow diagonal slashes on the dark side of each cap. Or slice whole mushrooms through the stem about ¾ inch thick. Trim the ends of the zucchini or yellow squash and halve them lengthwise. Trim the ends of a large globe eggplant and slice crosswise into rounds 1 inch thick. For long, slender Asian eggplant, trim the ends and halve lengthwise.

Cut the onions crosswise into 1-inch-thick slices, or cut in half lengthwise.

Trim the green onions, slicing off the roots and any fading tips or greens. Leave garlic heads whole, or cut crosswise just below the pointed tip, exposing the cloves.

Cut the tomatoes in half crosswise. Snap off and discard the woody base of each asparagus stem. Cut the peppers in half lengthwise and remove stems, seeds, and ribs. Leave in halves, or cut pepper halves lengthwise into wide strips.

Place the prepared vegetables in the baking dish with the marinade and toss to coat well. Let stand at room temperature for 30 minutes to 1 hour, tossing occasionally.

Prepare the grill or preheat the broiler. Grill or broil the vegetables until tender, shiny, and nicely browned, using tongs to turn them often and removing them to a plate as they are ready. Serve hot, warm, or at room temperature.

SERVES 4.

NOTE • *If you like, mask the grill rack with aluminum foil to minimize flare-ups and discourage vegetables from slipping through the grate onto the coals.*

ᏚᏅ OYSTER MUSHROOMS WITH RED SWEET PEPPERS AND GINGER ᏚᏅ

This flavorful stir-fry marries velvety mushrooms with flame-colored peppers and a shower of piquant ginger shreds. This dish goes beautifully with a creamy curry and steamed broccoli or a simple green salad, all to be savored over a plate or two of jasmine or basmati rice. Dove-gray oyster mushrooms can be found in Asian grocery stores and some supermarkets. You can leave them whole, or cut them lengthwise into thick strips. The cloud ear mushrooms add a handsome note of color and crunch, but omit them if they are difficult to find.

4 large pieces dried cloud ears or black
    tree fungus

4 cups plus 1 tablespoon water

8 ounces firm tofu, cut into ¼-inch cubes

2 tablespoons vegetable oil

1 tablespoon coarsely chopped garlic (4 to
    6 cloves)

½ cup long, thin peeled strips fresh ginger
    (see note)

1 yellow onion, cut lengthwise into thick
    wedges

2 cups fresh oyster mushrooms or any
    other sliced mushrooms

2 tablespoons soy sauce

1 tablespoon sugar

1 teaspoon salt

½ red sweet pepper, cut into 2-inch-long
    strips

Place the cloud ears in a bowl, add warm water to cover, and soak until softened, about 30 minutes.

Meanwhile, bring the 4 cups water to a rolling boil in a saucepan. Gently add the tofu to the water and cook for 1 minute. Drain and place near the stove along with the oil. When the cloud ears have softened, drain them and cut away any tough stem ends. Slice into thin strips and set near the stove.

Heat a wok or a large, deep skillet over medium-high heat for 30 seconds. Add the oil and swirl to coat the surface. Add the garlic and toss for 10 seconds. Add the ginger and toss for 1 minute. Add the onion and toss 1 minute more.

Add the mushrooms and cloud ears and toss until the mushrooms are shiny and softened, about 2 minutes. Add the tofu, 1 tablespoon water, and soy sauce and toss gently to coat everything well while keeping the tofu pieces whole. Add the sugar, salt, and red pepper strips, toss gently to combine, and cook until everything is heated through, 1 to 2 minutes. Transfer to a serving platter and serve hot or warm.

SERVES 4.

NOTE • *To prepare fresh ginger, select plump, shiny chunks that are heavy and firm for their size. Peel away the skin using a paring knife. Alternatively, use the tip of a spoon to peel it: Holding the ginger chunk in one hand and an ordinary spoon, bowl up, in the other, place the bowl of the spoon face down over the ginger and press the tip into the ginger, pulling down toward you and scraping away the peeling. Cut peeled ginger into very thin slices and then stack and cut these slices into delicate strips.*

❧ BABY CORN AND TOFU WITH CASHEWS ❧

You will love this tumble of petite, crunchy corn cobs and luscious cashews. Look for large, dark red New Mexico and California chilies wherever ingredients for Mexican cooking are sold. They add a subtle, smoky heat. You can, however, use a handful of small, fiery chilies if you prefer a volcanic note. In the summer, make this dish with fresh corn, shaving the kernels off the cob.

4 large, mild dried red chilies such as New Mexico or California chilies
4 cups plus 2 tablespoons water
8 ounces firm tofu, cut into 1-inch cubes
3 tablespoons vegetable oil
1 yellow onion, sliced lengthwise into thick wedges
1 tablespoon soy sauce
1 can (14 ounces) baby corn, rinsed and drained
1 teaspoon sugar
½ teaspoon salt
½ cup salted, dry-roasted cashews
3 green onions, cut into 2-inch lengths

To prepare the chilies, cut off their stems and shake out most of the seeds. Cut the chilies into quarters lengthwise and set aside.

Bring the 4 cups water to a rolling boil in a saucepan. Gently add the tofu to the water and cook for 1 minute. Drain and place near the stove along with the oil and a serving platter for the finished dish.

Heat a wok or a large, deep skillet over medium-high heat for 30 seconds. Add the oil and swirl to coat the surface. Add the chilies, toss for 1 minute, and transfer to the serving platter, leaving the oil in the wok. Add the onion, and toss until shiny and softened, 1 to 2 minutes.

Add the tofu, the 2 tablespoons water, and soy sauce and cook for 1 minute, tossing gently. Add the corn, sugar, and salt and toss gently. Return the chilies to the pan and add the cashews and green onions. Toss gently and cook until heated through, about 1 minute. Transfer to the serving platter and serve hot or warm.

SERVES 4.

∾ MUSHROOMS AND TOFU WITH FRESH MINT ∾

I learned this delicious stir-fry recipe from Mrs. Wongkiow, a great home cook in northern Thailand's Chiang Rai province. She used fresh straw mushrooms and lots of pepper, and cooked up an array of other dishes to go with mountains of sticky rice. This vegetarian version of her recipe works beautifully with almost any fresh mushroom. If you can find small button mushrooms, trim their stems and leave them whole. Halve regular button mushrooms lengthwise or cut them into thick slices. Leave oyster mushrooms whole, and cut portobellos or other large mushrooms into bite-sized pieces.

4 cups plus 1 tablespoon water

8 ounces firm tofu, cut into ¼-inch cubes

1 tablespoon vegetable oil

1 tablespoon coarsely chopped garlic
(4 to 6 cloves)

1 or 2 fresh green serrano chilies, stemmed
and minced

8 ounces fresh mushrooms (see introduction)

1 teaspoon regular soy sauce

1 teaspoon dark soy sauce

1 tablespoon sugar

1 teaspoon salt

½ red sweet pepper, cut into 2-inch-long
strips

1 cup lightly packed fresh mint leaves

Bring the 4 cups water to a rolling boil in a medium saucepan. Gently add the tofu to the water and cook for 1 minute. Drain and place near the stove along with the oil.

Heat a wok or a large, deep skillet over medium-high heat for 30 seconds. Add the oil and swirl to coat the surface. Add the garlic and chilies and toss for 10 seconds. Add the mushrooms and cook until shiny and softened, about 2 minutes. Add the tofu, the 1 tablespoon water, and both soy sauces and toss for 1 minute. Add the sugar and salt, toss well, and add the sweet pepper and mint. Toss until heated through, about 1 minute. Transfer to a serving platter. Serve hot or warm.

SERVES 4.

NOTE • *If you do not have dark soy sauce, you can leave it out; its main culinary role here is to add a handsome caramel color to the dish.*

↭ SWEET-AND-SOUR TEMPEH WITH CUCUMBER AND CAULIFLOWER ↭

The Thai take on sweet–and–sour dishes is light and crunchy. Here, a chorus of tomatoes, cauliflower, and cucumber is bathed in a tangy sauce. Cucumber, a sturdy member of the melon family, is much appreciated in the Thai pantry, where it is cooked in soups and stir–frys as well as used raw in salads. Chinese stir–fry dishes are often thickened with cornstarch, tapioca starch, arrowroot powder, or other flours, but Thai cooks prefer to leave the sauce in its natural state and use it as a flavorful juice perfect for seasoning a plate of rice. You can substitute broccoli florets or chunks of fresh or canned pineapple for the cauliflower.

2 tablespoons vegetable oil

1 tablespoon coarsely chopped garlic (4 to 6 cloves)

8 ounces tempeh, cut into bite-sized pieces

1½ cups small cauliflower florets

½ cup Vegetable Stock (pages 204 and 205)

1 yellow onion, cut lengthwise into thick wedges

1 tablespoon soy sauce

2 tablespoons distilled white vinegar

3 tablespoons sugar

1 teaspoon salt

½ hothouse cucumber, peeled, halved lengthwise, and cut crosswise into thick slices

8 cherry tomatoes, halved lengthwise

Heat a wok or large, deep skillet over medium–high heat for 30 seconds. Add the oil and swirl to coat the pan. Add the garlic and toss for about 10 seconds. Add the tempeh, toss well, and spread it out in a single layer. Cook, turning once, until lightly browned, about 1 minute on each side.

Add the cauliflower and toss well to coat with the other ingredients. Add the stock and cook, tossing occasionally, until the cauliflower is tender, 2 to 3 minutes. Add the onion, soy sauce, vinegar, sugar, and salt and toss well. Cook for 2 minutes.

Add the cucumber and cook for 1 minute, tossing once. Add the cherry tomatoes, toss well, and cook until heated through, about 1 minute. Transfer to a serving platter and serve hot or warm.

SERVES 4.

∽ TRIPLE MUSHROOM FEAST ∽

For this simple stir-fry, you can splurge on exotic mushrooms such as shiitake, oyster, or crimini, or make it with familiar button mushrooms. Either way you will have a tasty dish with lots of flavorful broth for seasoning a steaming plate of jasmine rice. The dish can be served hot, warm, or at room temperature, and it reheats nicely. Its flavor note is salty, so accompany it with a fiery curry and a soup or salad with the sharp edge of freshly squeezed lime juice. A wok is best here for ease in tossing the mushrooms as they cook, but you can use a large skillet and turn them carefully.

3 ounces fresh shiitake mushrooms	2 small shallots, thinly sliced lengthwise
3 ounces fresh oyster mushrooms	½ teaspoon salt
8 ounces fresh button mushrooms	1 teaspoon sugar
2 tablespoons vegetable oil	¼ cup water
6 large cloves garlic, thinly sliced cross-	½ teaspoon freshly ground pepper
wise	3 green onions, thinly sliced crosswise

Remove and discard the stems from the shiitakes, and separate any clusters of oyster mushrooms into individual mushrooms. Score the dark cap of each shiitake with an X. Combine the shiitake and oyster mushrooms in a large bowl. Slice the button mushrooms and add them to the bowl as well; set aside.

Heat a wok or a large, deep skillet with a tight-fitting lid over medium-high heat for 30 seconds. Add the oil and swirl to coat the pan. Add the garlic and shallots and cook, tossing occasionally, until fragrant and coated with oil, about 1 minute. Add the mushrooms and toss until shiny and beginning to soften, about 1 minute. Add the salt, sugar, and water and toss well. Reduce the heat to medium, cover, and cook for 2 minutes.

Uncover and toss well. Stir in the ground pepper and green onions, toss to mix, and transfer the contents of the pan, including the liquid, to a serving dish. Serve hot, warm, or at room temperature.

SERVES 4.

NOTE • *You can use a total of about 1 pound button mushrooms in place of the combination suggested with good results. You can also make this dish with whole oyster mushrooms, which are often available in Asian markets at reasonable prices.*

◌ BEAN SPROUT TOSS-UP ◌

Thais adore fresh mung bean sprouts and use them in abundance, both raw and cooked. In a classic *paht Thai* (page 162), the cook tosses a handful of sprouts in with the noodles to wilt them in the sauce. The finished dish is then garnished with another handful of raw bean sprouts as a cool, crunchy foil to the tasty, tangy noodles. Here is a simple symphony in homage to beans: tofu from soybeans, green beans from the garden, and a confetti of crisp sprouts from the tiny green mung bean.

2 tablespoons vegetable oil

2 tablespoons coarsely chopped garlic (8 to 12 cloves)

10 green beans, trimmed and thinly sliced crosswise

8 ounces firm tofu, cut into 1-inch cubes

¼ cup Vegetable Stock (pages 204 and 205)

1 tablespoon sugar

1 teaspoon salt

1 teaspoon regular soy sauce

½ teaspoon dark soy sauce

8 ounces fresh mung bean sprouts (about 4 cups)

2 or 3 plum tomatoes, cut into bite-sized chunks

Heat a wok or a large, deep skillet over medium–high heat for 30 seconds. Add the oil and swirl to coat the pan. Add the garlic and toss until it is fragrant and coated with oil, about 1 minute. Add the green beans and toss until tender and bright green, about 2 minutes. Add the tofu, vegetable stock, sugar, salt, and both soy sauces and toss gently. Spread out the tofu in a single layer and cook, tossing it gently every now and again to coat with the sauce, until heated through, about 2 minutes.

Raise the heat to high and add the bean sprouts and tomatoes. Cook, tossing often, until hot, shiny, and beginning to wilt, about 1 minute. Transfer to a deep serving platter and serve hot or warm.

SERVES 4.

NOTE • *If you do not have dark soy sauce, you can leave it out; its main culinary role here is to add a handsome caramel color to the dish.*

✌ GARLICKY BRUSSELS SPROUTS ✌

Vegetarian stir-fry sauce is a commercially made substitute for oyster sauce, sold in Asian markets and some supermarkets with extensive Asian food selections. Dried shiitake mushrooms give it its deep, rich flavor, and its thick, rich texture gives a boost to the simplest stir-fry. Thais use traditional oyster sauce often, particularly with broccoli, bok choy, and other members of the cabbage family. Brussels sprouts are not common in Thailand, but they take beautifully to this Thai way of cooking sturdy greens. Look for small, tightly furled sprouts that are bright green. Yellow or brown leaves indicate aging, so avoid them. Substitute 2½ cups shredded cabbage or florets of broccoli and cauliflower for the Brussels sprouts if they are not in season. This is a salty stir-fry, made to go with a spicy or sweet-and-sour dish and a plateful of grains.

1 pound Brussels sprouts, trimmed and
  halved lengthwise (about 3 cups)
½ teaspoon salt
¾ cup water
1 tablespoon vegetarian stir-fry sauce

2 teaspoons soy sauce
1 teaspoon sugar
½ teaspoon freshly ground pepper
2 tablespoons vegetable oil
1 tablespoon chopped garlic

In a saucepan, combine the Brussels sprouts, salt, and ½ cup of the water and bring to a rolling boil over medium heat. Reduce the heat to maintain a simmer, cover, and cook until tender and bright green, 7 to 9 minutes. Meanwhile, in a small bowl, combine the vegetarian stir-fry sauce, soy sauce, sugar, pepper, and the remaining ¼ cup water. Stir well and set aside.

When the sprouts are tender, remove from the heat and set aside. Heat a wok or large, deep skillet with a tight-fitting lid over medium-high heat. Add the oil and swirl to coat the pan. Add the garlic and cook, tossing often, for 30 seconds. Add the braised Brussels sprouts and cook, tossing often, until the sprouts are shiny, about 1 minute longer.

Quickly stir the sauce mixture to combine and add to the pan. Cook, tossing to coat well with the sauce, until heated through, about 1 minute. Transfer to a serving dish and serve hot, warm, or at room temperature.

SERVES 4.

✂ SPINACH IN SWEET-SOUR TAMARIND SAUCE ✂

Thais gladly eat their greens, which is no surprise given their brilliant touch in cooking them to create lots of flavor with little time and effort. A wok is ideal here because of the sheer volume of this much spinach in the raw. A wokful of unwieldy leaves swiftly sizzles down into a tidy tender platter for four, but if a big, deep skillet is all you have to work with, that's fine, too. Simply ease the spinach into the pan in batches, adding fresh leaves as soon as the previous batch wilts down to make room for more. Serve this dish Thai style, with plenty of rice, and remember to spoon on lots of the thin, vitamin-packed pan sauce, known in my home of North Carolina as pot liquor, where it is treasured along with the greens from which it came.

1½ tablespoons palm sugar or brown sugar
1½ tablespoons Tamarind Liquid (page 212)
2 teaspoons soy sauce
½ teaspoon salt

¼ teaspoon freshly ground pepper
2 tablespoons vegetable oil
1 tablespoon coarsely chopped garlic (4 to 6 cloves)
1¼ pounds spinach leaves (18 to 20 loosely packed cups)

In a small bowl, combine the sugar, tamarind, soy sauce, salt, and pepper. Stir well and place near the stove.

Heat a wok or a large, deep skillet with a tight-fitting lid over medium-high heat for 30 seconds. Add the oil and swirl to coat the pan. Add the garlic and toss until it is fragrant and shiny, about 1 minute. Add the spinach and toss to begin coating it with the oil. You may need to add the spinach in batches, tossing and turning until it all fits into the pan.

When all of the spinach has been touched by the oil, reduce the heat to medium. Quickly stir the sauce mixture to combine and add to the pan. Toss well and cover immediately. Cook until the spinach is wilted but still bright green, 1 to 2 minutes. Transfer the spinach, including its cooking liquid, to a deep serving platter and serve hot, warm, or at room temperature.

SERVES 4.

NOTE • *This is a salty dish, so you may want to serve it with a sweet dish such as Mee Grop (page 158), a crispy, tangy noodle dish, and a hot, spicy curry.* ❖ *If you have some left over, sautéed spinach is quite tasty the next day, although it will lose much of its sparkle in the presentation department. Reheat gently, as more actual cooking will tire it out rather than wake it up.*

✌ CHINESE CABBAGE WITH BLACK PEPPER AND GARLIC ✌

This quick-and-easy stir-fry of healthful greens spiked with garlic and pepper is destined to become a standard whenever your menu centers on rice. This is my version of *pahk boong fai daeng*, or "water spinach on fire." *Pahk boong*, a broccoli-green member of the Asian vegetable family, has delicate, arrowhead-shaped leaves attached to long, slender, hollow stalks. In Thailand's restaurants, cooks tilt the pan so that a tower of flame briefly engulfs the greens, giving them a fabulous charred flavor difficult to obtain on a home stove. *Pahk boong* is available seasonally in Asian markets, but you can enjoy this dish made with other greens as well. My favorite alternative is half napa cabbage and half bok choy for a gorgeous display of shades of green. The dish is wonderfully salty, so serve it with mountains of rice and something sweet, perhaps Son-in-Law Eggs (page 136), and something hot and spicy, such as Tome Yum Soup with Mushrooms and Tofu (page 76).

*1 ¼ pounds napa cabbage, bok choy, or
    other leafy Asian cabbage
1 tablespoon Vegetable Stock (pages 204
    and 205) or water
2 teaspoons sugar
½ teaspoon soy sauce*

*½ teaspoon salt
¼ teaspoon freshly ground pepper
2 tablespoons vegetable oil
2 tablespoons coarsely chopped garlic
    (8 to 12 cloves)*

Trim the napa cabbage or bok choy, cutting away and discarding the core end and cutting the remaining leaves crosswise into 1-inch-wide pieces. Place in a large bowl, add cold water, swish around with your fingers, and then drain well, allowing some water to cling to the leaves. Set aside.

In a small bowl, combine the vegetable stock, sugar, soy sauce, salt, and pepper and stir well. Set aside near the stove.

Heat a wok or a large, deep skillet with a tight-fitting lid over high heat for 30 seconds. Add the oil and swirl to coat the pan. Add the garlic and toss until fragrant and beginning to brown, about 30 seconds. Add the greens and toss (2 slotted spoons work well) until they are coated with oil and begin to wilt, about 1 minute. Quickly stir the sauce mixture to combine and add to the pan. Toss well and cover immediately. Cook until the greens are somewhat wilted and tender but still bright green, 1 to 2 minutes. Transfer the greens, including their cooking liquid, to a deep serving platter and serve hot or warm.

SERVES 4 TO 6.

NOTE · *You can use this same recipe with sturdy winter greens such as collards, mustard greens, or chard. For best results, separate the leaves and stems; cut the stems on the diagonal into bite-sized spears and cut the leaves into generous 2- to 3-inch pieces. Blanch them for 1 to 3 minutes in wildly boiling water to make them tender, then drain well and proceed as directed, adding them to the oil and garlic. You can also use spinach, which needs no blanching.*

ఴ BUTTERNUT SQUASH AND SPINACH IN ROASTED CHILI PASTE ఴ

Roasted chili paste, a sensational combination of sweetness and heat, complements the pairing of butternut squash and spinach. You can make your own paste or buy it prepared in Asian groceries. If you bake the butternut squash in advance and have chili paste on hand, this dish goes together in a flash.

1 small butternut squash, about 1 pound

2 tablespoons vegetable oil

1 tablespoon coarsely chopped garlic (4 to 6 cloves)

1 yellow onion, cut lengthwise into thin strips

6 ounces spinach leaves (7 to 8 loosely packed cups)

2 tablespoons Roasted Chili Paste (page 222)

1 tablespoon water

1 teaspoon soy sauce

½ teaspoon salt

Preheat the oven to 400 degrees F. Cut the butternut squash in half lengthwise, scoop out and discard the seeds, and place cut side down on a baking sheet. Bake until tender, about 30 minutes. Remove from the oven and set aside until the squash is cool enough to handle. Peel the squash and cut it into 1-inch chunks.

Heat a wok or large, deep skillet over medium-high heat. Add the oil and swirl to coat the pan. Add the garlic and onion and cook, tossing often, until the onion is shiny and softened, 1 to 2 minutes. Add the butternut squash and spinach and cook for 1 minute, turning so that the spinach leaves begin to wilt. Add the chili paste, water, soy sauce, and salt and toss well. Cook until the spinach is tender, shiny, and brilliant green and the squash is heated through, 1 to 2 minutes. Transfer to a serving dish and serve hot or warm.

SERVES 4.

NOTE • *Avoid baking the butternut squash too long, as you want it sturdy enough to cut into chunks that will hold their shape when cooked on the stove top. You can bake it several hours in advance, let it cool to room temperature, and then cover and chill until cooking time.*

ᔂ EGGPLANT AND RED SWEET PEPPERS IN ROASTED CHILI PASTE ᔂ

In this dish, eggplant's slightly bitter note is softened by the pepper's sweetness and the tangy explosion of the extraordinary chili sauce. The slender, deep purple Japanese eggplants are ideal here, but chunks cut from a large globe eggplant, or golf ball–sized Thai eggplants halved lengthwise would work as well.

1¼ pounds eggplants (see introduction)

3 tablespoons vegetable oil

1 tablespoon coarsely chopped garlic (4 to 6 cloves)

1 purple onion, cut lengthwise into thin strips

2 tablespoons Roasted Chili Paste (page 222)

1 tablespoon palm sugar or brown sugar

1 tablespoon water

1 teaspoon soy sauce

½ teaspoon salt

1 red sweet pepper, cut into long, thin strips

Trim off the stems from the eggplants. If using Japanese eggplants, cut each one in half lengthwise and then cut each half crosswise into 1–inch pieces. If using Thai eggplants, quarter lengthwise. If using one or more globe eggplants, cut into 1–inch chunks.

Heat a wok or a large, deep skillet over medium–high heat. Add the oil and swirl to coat the pan. Add the garlic and onion and cook, tossing often, until the onion is shiny and softened, 1 to 2 minutes. Add the eggplant pieces and cook, tossing often, until they are tender but still hold their shape, 5 to 7 minutes. Add the chili paste, sugar, water, soy sauce, and salt and toss well. Add the red pepper and cook, tossing often, until it is shiny and beginning to wilt, about 2 minutes longer. Transfer to a serving dish and serve hot or warm.

SERVES 4 TO 6.

∽ ZUCCHINI AND TOFU IN ROASTED CHILI PASTE ∽

Make a double batch of Roasted Chili Paste so that you can use it often in this satisfying dish. You can switch the vegetables to suit your whim or your garden's bounty, or merely to make supper out of what you have on hand. Use yellow squash or pattypan squash instead of the zucchini, and add a handful of halved cherry tomatoes at the end for a burst of color.

4 cups water

8 ounces firm tofu, cut into 1-inch cubes

2 tablespoons vegetable oil

1 tablespoon coarsely chopped garlic (4 to 6 cloves)

1 onion, cut lengthwise into thick strips

3 zucchini, cut into ¼-inch-thick rounds

3 tablespoons Roasted Chili Paste (page 222)

¼ cup Vegetable Stock (pages 204 and 205)

1 teaspoon soy sauce

½ teaspoon salt

Bring the water to a rolling boil in a saucepan. Gently add the tofu to the water and cook for 1 minute. Drain and place near the stove.

Heat a wok or a large, deep skillet over medium-high heat. Add the oil and swirl to coat the pan. Add the garlic and onion and cook until shiny, fragrant, and softened, about 1 minute. Add the zucchini and cook, tossing occasionally, until shiny, tender, and a brilliant green, about 2 minutes.

Reduce the heat to medium and add the chili paste, vegetable stock, soy sauce, and salt. Toss well. Add the tofu and cook, giving it an occasional gentle toss, until it is heated through and evenly coated with the sauce, about 1 minute. Transfer to a serving dish and serve hot or warm.

SERVES 4.

ᥬ EGGPLANT PAHT PEHT ᥬ

If you adore the fiery flavors of Thai curries but want a quicker, lighter dish, try this one. *Paht* means "to stir-fry in a wok" and *peht* means chili-pepper hot. Here, curry paste is softened in oil and then tossed with vegetables and kissed with a bouquet of Asian herbs. The resulting dish is served up with plain rice, untempered by the velvety sweetness of coconut milk that would extinguish a bit of a curry paste's fire. This is Thai home cooking at its delicious best.

Eggplant is part of the classic *paht peht*, and the standard choice is the golf ball–sized Thai eggplant known as *makeuah poh*. It is hard and seedy, and you will find it with green, purple, or white skin in Asian markets. This dish is also delicious made with everyday globe eggplants or long, slender Japanese egg-plants. Traditionally, the dish includes fresh green peppercorns, but I have never seen them outside of Southeast Asia, so I have omitted them. But if you would like to get an idea of the pleasing jolt they deliver, look for canned green peppercorns in Asian markets, and toss in about ¼ cup of them, rinsed and drained, just before you remove the pan from the heat.

3 tablespoons vegetable oil

3 tablespoons Red Curry Paste (page 222)

1 yellow onion, cut lengthwise into thick strips

1 pound eggplant (see introduction), cut into large bite-sized chunks (about 4 cups)

¾ cup Vegetable Stock (pages 204 and 205)

1 tablespoon palm sugar or brown sugar

1 teaspoon salt

½ teaspoon soy sauce

2 tablespoons peeled and finely shredded fresh ginger

¼ cup fresh basil leaves

12 wild lime leaves

Pour the oil into a wok or large, deep skillet and place over medium heat for about 1 minute. Add the curry paste and mash and scrape the paste against the pan to soften it and combine it with the oil. Adjust the heat so that the paste and oil sizzle pleasantly without a lot of popping, sticking, or burning. Cook, stirring occasionally, until fragrant and well mixed with the oil, about 2 minutes. Add the onion strips and toss to coat them with the paste. Add the eggplants, toss well, and cook, tossing occasionally, for 2 minutes. Add the vegetable stock, sugar, salt, soy sauce, and ginger, toss well and cook until the eggplant is tender and everything is well combined, 5 to 7 minutes.

Add the basil and wild lime leaves, toss well, and turn out onto a serving plat–ter. Serve hot or warm.

SERVES 4.

NOTE • *If you do not have wild lime leaves or fresh basil, leave them out. You can even omit the ginger, if it calls for a trip to the store. These traditional ingredients inarguably enhance the dish, but it is delicious even without them. In the small upcountry Thai town where I lived, wild lime leaves were a luxury. When we had them, we tossed them into soups, curries, and stir-frys, but when we had none, we simply did without. ❖ The final cooking time will depend on the type of eggplant you use, with Japanese eggplant cooking the quick–est, small, round Thai eggplant taking the longest, and friendly globe eggplant in between.*

✺ RED CURRY VEGETABLE STIR-FRY ✺

Put your homemade Thai curry paste to work when your hunger for curry heat and flavor insists on instant satisfaction. Use green, yellow, or mussamun curry paste (pages 199–203) instead of red, and vary the vegetables to suit your fancy, adding longer–cooking vegetables early on and delicate ones toward the end of cooking time. When you request this *paht peht*, or "red–hot stir–fry dish" from a Thai cook, you will generally be asked, "*Peht towrai kah?*" or, in other words, "Just how much fire are we looking for here?" This is hot stuff to my palate, but you can increase the amount of curry paste if you crave food at what my friend Jim O'Connor calls "the core temperature of the sun."

8 ounces firm tofu, cut into ½-inch chunks

4 ounces green beans, trimmed and cut
    into 2-inch lengths

3 tablespoons vegetable oil

3 tablespoons Red Curry Paste (page 198)

2 Japanese eggplants, cut crosswise on the
    diagonal into thick slices

⅓ cup Vegetable Stock (pages 204 and 205)

1 teaspoon soy sauce

2 teaspoons sugar

1 teaspoon salt

½ cup loosely packed fresh basil leaves

¼ red sweet pepper, cut into 2-inch-long
    strips

Fill a 2–quart saucepan with water and bring to a rolling boil over high heat. Gently add the tofu and cook for 1 minute. Using a slotted spoon, remove to a plate. Add the green beans to the same water and cook for 2 minutes. Drain and transfer them to the plate.

In a wok or skillet over medium–low heat, warm the oil until it is very warm but not hot. Add the curry paste and cook, mashing and scraping to mix it with the oil, until it is well–blended and fragrant, about 2 minutes.

Add the green beans, eggplant, vegetable stock, soy sauce, sugar, and salt and toss well. Cook for 5 minutes, tossing occasionally. Add the tofu and con–tinue cooking, tossing gently, until the vegetables are tender and the tofu is heated through, about 2 minutes.

While the vegetables are cooking, set a few of the basil leaves aside. Stack the remaining leaves and cut them crosswise into thin ribbons. When the veg–etables are ready, toss in the basil ribbons and sweet pepper, and transfer to a serving platter. Garnish with the reserved basil leaves and serve hot or warm.

SERVES 4.

✑ YELLOW CURRY CABBAGE WITH MUSHROOMS AND PEAS ✑

Cabbages are popular year–round in Thailand, where cooks stir-fry them quickly in a hot wok to preserve their flavor and crunch. Make this satisfying winter vegetable braise on a blustery day while dreaming of a rainbow of produce in your garden next summer.

1 small head cabbage, about 1 pound
2 tablespoons vegetable oil
2 tablespoons coarsely chopped garlic
1 yellow onion, cut lengthwise into thin
  strips
1 cup sliced fresh mushrooms (about 6
  ounces)

2 to 3 teaspoons Yellow Curry Paste
  (page 200)
¼ cup water
1 teaspoon soy sauce
1 teaspoon salt
1 teaspoon sugar
1 cup green peas

Trim the cabbage, removing and discarding its hard core and outer leaves. Quarter it lengthwise and cut into thin shreds. You will have 5 to 6 cups. Set aside.

Heat a wok or a large, deep skillet with a tight–fitting lid over medium–high heat. Add the oil and swirl to coat the pan. Add the garlic and onion and toss until shiny and fragrant, about 1 minute. Add the mushrooms and cook, tossing often, until shiny, darkened, and tender, about 5 minutes.

Add the cabbage and toss until shiny and beginning to wilt, about 1 minute. Add the curry paste, water, soy sauce, salt, and sugar and toss well. Cover and cook, tossing occasionally, until cabbage is shiny and tender but still crisp, about 5 minutes. Add the peas, toss well, and remove from the heat. Transfer to a deep serving platter and serve hot or warm.

SERVES 4 TO 6.

✺ FIRECRACKER BROCCOLI ✺

Charlisa Cato of Arkansas became famous last Christmas by making my dia-
bolically delicious Sweet and Hot Garlic Sauce (page 224) by the gallon to share
with her friends. She was kind enough to pass along her recipe for broccoli.
This makes broccoli taste so good so fast that you will put on your cha–cha
heels and dance around the kitchen.

1 tablespoon vegetable oil
8 ounces broccoli florets (about 4 cups)
¼ cup Vegetable Stock (pages 204 and 205)

Dash of salt
1 tablespoon Sweet and Hot Garlic Sauce
(page 224)

In a skillet with a tight–fitting lid over medium–high heat, warm the oil for
about 1 minute, or until a bit of broccoli tip sizzles at once. Add the broccoli
florets and toss until they are bright green and beginning to shine, about 1
minute. Add the vegetable stock, cover, reduce the heat to medium, and cook
until tender but still crisp, 1 to 2 minutes.

Uncover, add the Sweet and Hot Garlic Sauce, toss well, and remove from
the heat. Transfer to a serving dish and serve hot, warm, at room temperature,
or cold.

Serves 4.

NOTE • *With adjustments to the timing and amount of liquid, you can enjoy this quick
fix with other gifts from the garden, including asparagus, carrots, cauliflower, snow peas, and
sugar snap peas. It can be covered and stored in the refrigerator for up to 2 days.*

ೞ **SON-IN-LAW EGGS** ೞ

This unique dish is hearty and delicious, with its combination of golden hard–
boiled eggs napped with a pungent tamarind sauce and enlivened with crispy
garlic and shallots. It is one of my favorites, perhaps because I often enjoyed
it as part of a banquet menu in Thailand when friends were celebrating a
wedding, a birth, the ordination of a family member as a Buddhist monk, or
some other auspicious occasion. These eggs have a chewy–crisp texture, which
is unusual by Western standards but prized in Asian cuisines. Try them with
lots of jasmine rice, or serve the halved or quartered eggs in lettuce cups with
a dollop of sauce and toppings as an exotic starter to offer as guests arrive.
Vegans can enjoy this fabulous sauce and its accompaniments on large chunks
of tempeh sautéed with garlic, soy sauce, and a little sugar and salt, or with
chunks of pressed tofu (purchased or homemade, page 218), fried to golden
crispiness in hot oil.

Sauce:
½ cup *Vegetable Stock (pages 204 and 205)*
1 tablespoon *Asian bean sauce*
⅓ cup *Tamarind Liquid (page 212)*
¼ cup *palm sugar or brown sugar*
1 teaspoon *soy sauce*
½ teaspoon *salt*

Eggs:
Vegetable oil for deep-frying
10 shallots, sliced crosswise into thin
  rings (about ½ cup)
20 garlic cloves, thinly sliced lengthwise
  (about ½ cup)
8 hard-boiled eggs, peeled
1 to 2 teaspoons red chili pepper flakes

A handful of fresh cilantro leaves,
  coarsely chopped

To make the sauce, in a mini processor or blender, combine ¼ cup of the vegetable stock and the bean sauce and blend until smooth. Pour into a saucepan
and add the tamarind, sugar, soy sauce, and salt. Place over medium heat and
bring to a rolling boil. Stir well and reduce the heat to maintain a gentle but
active boil. Simmer until the sugar is dissolved and the sauce is smooth and
slightly thickened, about 10 minutes. Remove from the heat and set aside to
cool to room temperature.

To make the eggs, line a baking sheet with a double thickness of paper towels and place it next to the stove along with a slotted spoon, the sliced shallots and garlic, and the eggs. Fill a wok or large, deep skillet with vegetable oil to a depth of 3 inches. Heat the oil over medium heat until a bit of garlic dropped into the pan sizzles at once. The oil should register 350 to 375 degrees F on a cooking thermometer.

Sprinkle the shallots into the oil and cook until golden brown but not burned, 1 to 2 minutes. Using the slotted spoon, transfer to the lined baking sheet to drain. Sprinkle in the sliced garlic and cook until golden brown but not burned, about 1 minute. Remove with a slotted spoon to the baking sheet.

Pat the eggs dry with paper towels and gently add 3 eggs to the oil, sliding them gently down the side of the wok or lowering them into the oil with the slotted spoon. Cook, using the spoon to turn them occasionally and to keep them from settling on the bottom of the pan, until evenly colored, golden brown, and crisp, 5 to 7 minutes. Using the spoon, transfer the eggs to the baking sheet and repeat with the remaining eggs.

To serve, cut the eggs in half lengthwise; coat a deep serving platter with the sauce. Place the eggs on the sauce and sprinkle them with the shallots and garlic, some chili flakes, and the cilantro. Serve hot, warm, or at room temperature.

SERVES 6 TO 8.

NOTE • *For a traditional presentation, leave the eggs whole. Coat a deep serving platter with about half the sauce and place the eggs on the sauce. Pour the remaining sauce over the eggs and sprinkle them with the shallots, garlic, chili flakes, and cilantro.* ❖ *You can serve these as an appetizer to be eaten out of hand. Cut the eggs in half lengthwise, place each half on a lettuce leaf, and sprinkle with the shallots, garlic, chili flakes, and cilantro. Serve the sauce on the side to be added at serving time by each guest.* ❖ *To peel the garlic easily, soak the whole cloves in water for about 30 minutes. Or bruise each clove lightly with the flat side of your cleaver or a full can and then shake the papery peeling until the garlic is released.* ❖ *It is frustratingly easy to burn the garlic and shallots, so have handy two slotted spoons, if possible, to help you corral them and get them out in a flash. Start removing them before they are all done to your liking, as you may have to make several passes to remove them all, and they continue to cook briefly out of the oil. If they burn, strain the oil through a fine-mesh sieve and start again. To get them all out fast, position a large fine-mesh strainer over a large, deep saucepan placed near the stove. When the garlic and shallots are nearly ready, simply* empty the oil into the saucepan through the sieve. Then turn the contents of the sieve onto the towel-lined baking sheet. ❖ You can prepare the sauce an hour or so in advance and let it stand, covered, at room temperature. Reheat gently over low heat just before serving. You can also fry the shallots and garlic several hours in advance and set them aside at room temperature until serving time. ❖ If you long to try this but have neither tamarind nor Asian bean sauce on hand, improvise a tangy sauce using hoisin sauce, sugar, salt, vegetable stock, and freshly squeezed lime. ❖ Ready to test this recipe and eat it for dinner one evening, I found myself with a paltry amount of vegetable oil in the pantry. I decided to make do and ended up with only an inch of oil in my cast-iron skillet. I was amazed at how beautifully the garlic, shallots, and eggs came out, browning handsomely without sticking and minus the effort of dealing with a major quantity of hot oil in a hot wok. I recommend this West-meets-East method highly.

✥ FIVE-SPICE HARD-BOILED EGGS IN SWEET SOY STEW ✥

This is *kai pa-loh*, a direct Chinese import, combining the sweetness of cinnamon, cloves, and star anise with the richness of *si-yu wahn*, the dark sweet soy sauce found in every Thai pantry. Like curry powder, five-spice powder is widely available in Thai kitchens, although its use is limited to stews similar to this one. You can substitute cinnamon, cloves, and star anise, whole or ground, for the five-spice powder; check the note at the end of this recipe for the amounts to use. This dish comes together quickly once the eggs are cooked and peeled, and it keeps beautifully, blossoming to a deeper, richer flavor in the refrigerator overnight. Offer lots of rice to savor with this luxurious mahogany sauce.

2 tablespoons coarsely chopped garlic
    (8 to 12 cloves)
2 tablespoons coarsely chopped cilantro
    roots or cilantro leaves and stems
½ teaspoon freshly ground pepper
2 tablespoons water
2 tablespoons vegetable oil
1 yellow onion, sliced lengthwise into
    thick wedges
2 teaspoons five-spice powder

3 cups Vegetable Stock (pages 204 and 205)
⅓ cup dark sweet soy sauce, or 3 tablespoons dark soy sauce and 2 tablespoons molasses or honey
3 tablespoons brown sugar
1 tablespoon soy sauce
1 teaspoon salt
7 hard-boiled eggs, peeled
8 ounces firm tofu, cut into 1-inch chunks
⅓ cup coarsely chopped fresh cilantro

In a mini processor or blender, combine the garlic, cilantro root (or leaves and stems), pepper, and water and grind to a fairly smooth paste. Heat the vegetable oil in a saucepan over medium heat for about 30 seconds. Add the garlic-cilantro paste and cook for 1 minute, stirring and scraping. Add the onion wedges and cook, tossing often, until they are shiny and fragrant, about 2 minutes.

Add the five-spice powder and toss to mix with the onions. Add the vegetable stock, dark sweet soy sauce (or dark soy and molasses or honey), sugar, soy sauce, and salt and stir well. Add the eggs and tofu and bring to a boil. Adjust the heat to maintain an active simmer and cook, stirring now and then, until the eggs and tofu are a rich, deep brown and the sauce is a smooth, pleasing blend of soy sauce, sugar, salt, and spice, about 25 minutes.

Transfer the eggs, tofu, and a generous pool of sauce to a serving bowl. Sprinkle with the cilantro and serve hot or warm. Or let cool to room temperature, cover, and refrigerate for up to 2 days.

SERVES 6 TO 8.

NOTE • *Vegans can omit the eggs and add 2 cups Wheatballs (page 207) or wheat gluten, or a combination of potatoes and sweet potatoes, totaling about 2 cups peeled, bite-sized chunks. ❖ I like to remove the eggs, halve them lengthwise, and return them to the sauce just before serving to add color, but you can also serve them whole, the traditional way. ❖ You can substitute whole or ground spices for the five-spice powder if you like. If using whole spices, add 3 cinnamon sticks, 12 whole cloves, ¼ teaspoon whole fennel seeds, and 3 whole star anise. If using ground spices, add ½ teaspoon cinnamon, ¼ teaspoon cloves, ¼ teaspoon fennel, and ½ teaspoon star anise.*

✎ STEAMED EGGS WITH CILANTRO AND CRISPY GARLIC ✎

This classic dish, called *kai toon*, fortified me many a night during the two years I lived in the small northeastern Thai town of Thatoom. My students used duck eggs for everyday and chicken eggs if we had guests, and we never found out about the keeping properties of this old favorite, since we always ate up every bite. As with rice soup, it is often on the menu for a family member who is ailing, and it is a traditional favorite of children. Once you have a means of steaming food, it is very simple to make. Thais eat this egg dish plain, but if you like a bit of fire, enjoy it with a little Sri Racha chili sauce.

3 eggs
½ cup Vegetable Stock (pages 204 and 205)
½ teaspoon soy sauce
¼ teaspoon salt
¼ teaspoon freshly ground pepper

1 small shallot, minced (about 1 tablespoon)
1 green onion, minced
1 tablespoon coarsely chopped fresh cilantro
2 tablespoons Crispy Garlic in Oil (page 221)

Place a wok or the base of a large steamer on the stove and add 3 to 4 inches of water. Place a steaming rack over the water, cover, and bring to a rolling boil over high heat.

Meanwhile, in a bowl, beat the eggs with a fork until frothy. Add the vegetable stock, soy sauce, salt, pepper, shallot, and green onion and beat to combine well. Pour into a shallow, heatproof bowl and set aside.

When you have a strong, steady flow of steam, uncover and carefully place the bowl of eggs on the steaming rack. Place a paper towel on top of the bowl to prevent condensing steam from dripping onto the eggs. Cover the wok or steamer and reduce the heat a bit to maintain a steady flow of steam without the water boiling away. Check often to be sure that the water level remains high and the steam is flowing, adding very hot or boiling water as needed if the level drops.

Steam the eggs until they are firm, pale yellow, and a little puffed up, 25 to 45 minutes. They are ready when a fork inserted near the center comes out clean. Uncover, turn off the heat, and let stand for 5 minutes while the steam subsides. Carefully remove the bowl from the steamer. Sprinkle with the cilantro and then pour the Crispy Garlic in Oil over the top. Serve hot, warm, or at room temperature.

SERVES 4 TO 6.

NOTE • *If you do not have a steaming rack, you can use the standard Asian shortcut: two long, sturdy chopsticks laid in an X in the bottom of the wok. Place the bowl of eggs on the spot where the chopsticks intersect and steam away. Be sure to use blunt-tipped Chinese-style chopsticks, rather than pointed-tipped Japanese-style ones for this job, as their extra length is needed.* ❖ *You will probably need to add water at least once during the steaming process, so have a kettle simmering. If you add boiling or very hot water to the pan, you will avoid losing cooking time while the steaming water pokes its way back to a boil. Do your best to prevent the water inside the lid from dripping into the custard. And take great care to avoid burning your hands as you check on the progress of your eggs.*

☙ THAI OMELET WITH SRI RACHA SAUCE ☙

Plates of this homey dish appeared as a last course when the principal of the secondary school where I taught English took his staff out for a dinner banquet. We gathered at Thatoom's finest eatery, officially called Thatoom Pochanah, but known affectionately around town as *rahn ahahn jeen,* the "Chinese restaurant." After a parade of delicious dishes, including volcanic *tome yum* soup, stir–fried water spinach with brown bean sauce, and an array of Cantonese–style stir–frys, we knew the omelets were a gentle and satisfying signal that it was time to finish up the feast and stroll home surrounded by a chorus of crickets, bullfrogs, radio music, and children's laughter decorating the dark. The green onions and cilantro are my addition to the Thai classic. Use any hot–chili sauce if you do not have Sri Racha sauce, or mix up a bowl of ripe tomato salsa spiked with onion, cilantro, serrano chilies, and freshly squeezed lime juice.

4 eggs

2 tablespoons Vegetable Stock (pages 204 and 205) or water

½ teaspoon soy sauce

½ teaspoon salt

2 green onions, thinly sliced crosswise

2 tablespoons finely chopped fresh cilantro

2 tablespoons vegetable oil

Sri Racha sauce or other hot-chili sauce

In a bowl, combine the eggs, vegetable stock, soy sauce, salt, green onions, and cilantro and beat to mix well. Heat the vegetable oil in a skillet over medium heat until it is very hot. When a drop of the egg mixture sizzles and blooms at once, the oil is ready.

Add the eggs and tilt the pan to spread them out evenly. Using a spatula, pull the puffy edges in toward the center, working around the edges to coax any liquid pooling in the center to seep out and extend the borders of the omelet. Cook until the edges are golden and the top is opaque and nearly set, about 2 minutes. Gently flip the omelet over and brown the top for about 1 minute.

Turn the omelet out onto a plate and serve hot or warm with a small saucer of chili sauce.

SERVES 4 TO 6.

NOTE • *For a truly Thai version, omit the green onions and cilantro and increase the oil to 3 or 4 tablespoons. Be sure that it is very hot before you add the eggs. The extra oil makes the omelet puff up beautifully and brown in a pleasing, tasty manner.* ❖ *I serve this omelet almost every time I cook Thai food for a crowd because it is easy to prepare at the last minute and is a hit with children and other guests who may be new to Thai food and are looking for something familiar.*

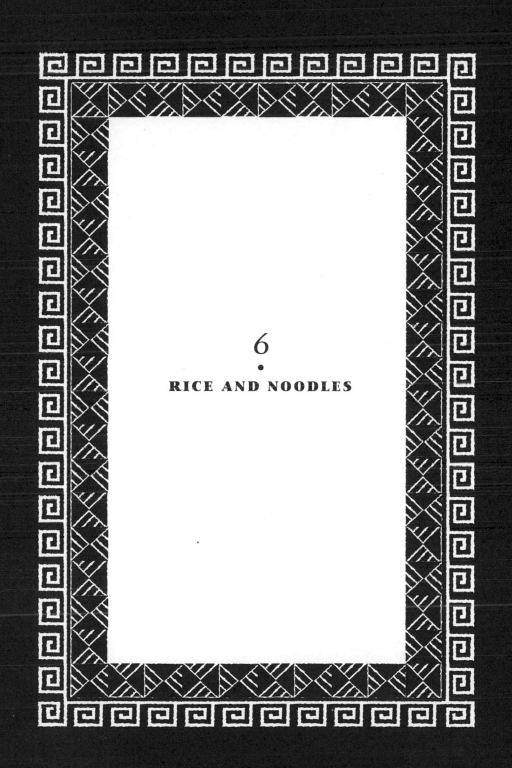

6
·
RICE AND NOODLES

RICE AND NOODLE DISHES

ᴄᴓ No matter how much you cherish chilies, savor satay, or plow through platters of *paht Thai*, you will be missing the essential nature of Thai food unless you learn to love rice. Plain white rice, cooked in water without seasoning—not even salt—is the heart of Thai cooking, the field on which all the intense flavors and dishes of Thai cuisine come together to play. To Thai people, rice is what fills them up, what comforts them, what makes them feel they are living an abundant life. This holds true even when the dishes that come with the rice are simple and few, and the surroundings in which they are eaten are equally plain.

ᴄᴓ Thais eat long-grain white rice morning, noon and night, plates and plates of it, spooned up in the presence of family and friends to make it taste even better. When I lived in Thatoom, in a teacher's house with four students from the middle school where I taught English, supper began with a yell from the kitchen, *"Cheun mah kin kao!"* ("Y'all come and get it, the rice is ready!") One or two of the students had cooked dinner, using whatever I had brought home from the morning market to make a soup, a curry, an egg dish, and *nahm prik*, a chili-hot, tangy dipping sauce with raw vegetables. Five or six such dishes were placed in the center of a handwoven straw mat spread out over the concrete floor of our kitchen, ringed by five plates mounded with steaming jasmine rice and stainless steel spoons shaped like porcelain soup spoons used at Chinese banquets. In the course of our meal, each of us had at least a second plateful of rice, and it was not uncommon to request a third helping if we were especially hungry or the dishes were particularly good.

ᴄᴓ Unlike the Western practice of loading a full portion of each dish onto a plate of rice before eating, we ate Thai style, spooning a bite or two of one dish at a time onto the rice and savoring it before moving on to the next. This kept the meal at a graceful pace, and we dawdled along, indulging our culinary whims as we visited and unwound from the cares of the day. The meal ended with a big bowl of rainwater placed in the center, into which we dipped our cups to cleanse our palates and satisfy the thirst created by the roller coaster of flavors that decorated the evening's rice.

ᴄᴓ The category of dishes that are served with rice has a Thai name that perfectly expresses the elevated status of rice in Asian cusines. All the dishes are lumped together as *gahp kao*, literally "with rice." This phrase acts as a noun, rounding up what Westerners would separate into main courses, side dishes, salads, sauces, dips, omelets, and even soups in a bundle defined as accompaniments to rice. "What's for dinner?" in Thai becomes *"Dai arai gahp kao?"* ("What have you got with the rice tonight?"). This in no way implies that Thai people are indifferent to the quality and variety of the dishes that go with rice. They are in fact quite passionate about them in every detail, from shopping for the ingredients through cooking them, devouring them, and reminiscing about them at a later date. What they do not do is see rice as a starch that stands by to round out the meal or soak up the extra sauce. Rice sustains life, and tasty *gahp kao* make the human task of taking in the nourishment given by the rice a delight rather than a chore.

✿ I learned to love rice effortlessly by eating Thai home cooking with my students at breakfast, lunch, and dinner for two years. It was not my intention to open a new door, but this happened because I had the good fortune to eat Thai food in its traditional context over time. I urge you to put rice at the center of your Thai menus, not to convert you to a particular way of eating, but because rice explains and enhances the intense seasonings and textures present in Thai dishes.

✿ In this chapter you will find basic rice recipes, as well as seasoned rice dishes. The first recipe is for jasmine rice, the aromatic long-grain rice Thais grow in the green checkerboard of paddy fields that quilt the Central Plain and the Korat Plateau of the northeastern region. If you have a rice cooker, you can make great rice on your countertop. I like to add a little less water than the cooker directions call for, since the ones imported from Asia tend to be designed for making Japanese- or Chinese-style rice, which is shorter grained and needs to be moist enough to eat with chopsticks from a rice bowl. Thai people eat rice from plates using a spoon, and often using a fork to help mix the flavors and push food onto the spoon. They cook it in the South Asian manner, so that it comes out fluffy and separate, rather than moist and clinging together as is preferred in East Asian countries.

✿ The second recipe is for sticky rice, a long-grained white rice that the people of Laos eat at every meal instead of jasmine rice or a more ordinary long-grain rice. Sticky rice contains prodigious amounts of a starch that causes it to cling together in a most pleasing, chewy manner. Because northern and northeastern Thailand have strong historical and cultural ties to Laos, the Thais of those regions eat sticky rice as their daily grain. It steams quickly once it has soaked in water for several hours, and is delightful to eat with finger-food dishes. Serve yourself a fist-sized hunk and then pinch off bites of rice, roll them into little balls, and pop them into your mouth along with your *gahp kao*.

✑ There are also several recipes for special-occasion rice dishes, special in that they are particularly handsome and delicious, but not so special that you could not enjoy them on short notice for a quick weeknight supper. These include two recipes for rice in coconut milk and three versions of the beloved Thai dish, fried rice.

✑ The chapter ends with a few noodle favorites, including the spectacular crispy-sweet confection called *mee grop*, an appealing broccoli-soy sauce stir-fry, and my version of *paht Thai*.

✑ JASMINE RICE ✑

Jasmine rice is a treasure of Thailand's fertile fields, naturally endowed with a delicate nutty flavor and toasty aroma that gently draws everyone within olfactory range right to your table. The rice thrives in Thailand's seemingly infinite paddy fields, which stretch from the lush central plain to the vast northeastern plateau. In Asian markets, jasmine rice is sold for a song in 25- and 50-pound sacks, but it is also increasingly available in supermarkets and specialty stores in smaller packages. If you have storage space for a large quantity, buy yourself a great sack, as it is a lovely everyday rice and keeps well for many months.

2 cups jasmine rice or other long-grain white rice
3 cups cold water

Place the rice in a medium saucepan that has a tight-fitting lid, and rinse it several times with cold water. Drain well and add the 3 cups water to the saucepan. Bring to a rolling boil over medium heat and stir well. Reduce the heat to low, cover, and cook for 20 minutes. The rice kernels will be tender and the liquid will be absorbed.

Remove the saucepan from the heat without lifting the lid and let stand, covered, for 10 minutes. Uncover, fluff gently with a fork, and serve hot or warm.

MAKES ABOUT 5 CUPS; SERVES 3 OR 4.

NOTE • *The label "new crop" on your rice sack tells you that the contents are from a recent harvest and therefore retain more moisture than rice from a few crops back. This alerts you to use less water for cooking, to avoid mushy rice. Try 2¾ cups water to start with, and adjust as needed to cook up firm, fluffy, distinctively separate grains.*

✌ STICKY RICE ✌

Allow plenty of time to prepare sticky rice, as it needs at least 3 hours to soak before you steam it. Sticky rice is finger food, so each diner should pull off a fist-sized hunk and place it on his or her plate. Then eat it by pinching off a walnut-sized lump, rounding it off quickly with fingers, and either dipping it into a sauce, using it as a means to pick up chunks of vegetables, or simply enjoying it neat.

This flat-white, long-grain rice, often called glutinous rice or sweet rice, is the daily bread of the people of Laos. It is also the staple grain of northern and northeastern Thailand, the two regions that border Laos and consequently share with it an abundance of cultural and culinary traditions. In the West, long-grain sticky rice is found predominantly in markets that serve customers who have migrated from Laos and Thailand. It is seldom labeled in English or any Asian language, since most customers who seek it will recognize it on sight. Many Asian markets break up large sacks into smaller lots and seal it in plastic bags, so look for long-grain rice with a startlingly flat, whitewashed color. You could also check the mail-order section (page 232) and send away for a supply. What you will find more easily is short-grain sticky rice, popular in Japan, Korea, and China, and often labeled "sweet rice." It is widely used by Asian cooks in an array of sweets and desserts, but it is seldom eaten with savory dishes. It is considerably less sticky than its long-grained cousin and cooks up differently, so if you hanker to try sticky rice Thai and Lao style, take the time to find the long-grain variety.

2 cups long-grain sticky rice

Soak the rice in cold water to cover by 2 inches for at least 3 hours or for as long as overnight.

Drain the rice and transfer it to a bamboo steaming basket specifically designed for steaming sticky rice, or to another steaming vessel such as a colander or a sieve that can be suspended above boiling water.

Fill a wok or the bottom of a steamer pan with several inches of water. Place the steaming basket or other container inside the wok or steamer pan so that it holds the soaked rice at least 1 inch above the water level. Bring the water to a rolling boil over high heat. When steam is rising steadily through the rice, place a damp kitchen towel over the rice, folded to cover the rice fully and to slow the escape of steam from the pan. Reduce the heat to maintain a steady flow of steam and cook until the rice swells, glistens, and becomes sticky enough to be easily shaped into little balls, 30 to 45 minutes. Keep a teakettle filled with simmering water handy, to add to the wok or pan as needed to maintain the original water level.

As soon as the rice is ready, turn it out onto a large tray or a baking sheet. Dampen a wooden spoon with water and quickly and gently spread the rice out into a shallow layer to release some of the steam and moisture. As soon as it is cool enough to touch, gently gather the rice into a large lump and place it in a sticky–rice basket or on a serving platter. Serve hot, warm. or at room temperature.

MAKES ABOUT 5 CUPS; SERVES 3 OR 4.

NOTE • *The cooking time for sticky rice will vary according to its soaking time. The longer the rice soaks, the shorter its steaming time will be.* ❖ *If you like sticky rice, treat yourself to a Laotian-style bamboo steaming basket and steamer base, both widely available in Southeast Asian markets. The base is a large, tall, shiny aluminum or tin pot without handles and with a 3-inch-high slanted rim around the opening. The steaming basket is shaped like an enormous straw ice cream cone, and its pointed base fits snugly into the opening of the metal pot, holding a quantity of water well away from the soaked rice. To clean the basket, remove as much of the rice as possible, and then let the rest dry for a day or so until the remaining grains harden and become easy to brush away. Occasionally you will find rounded, flat-bottomed steaming baskets as well. These are the style used in northern Thailand, and they work fine in the same metal steaming base.* ❖ *Look for sticky-rice serving baskets in Asian markets. You will find handsomely simple ones about the size and shape of a Dutch oven or a domed layer-cake cover, and fancy ones with an X-shaped base and an apple-shaped body, which I think of as small wicker spaceships. Either shape may be found in individual-serving sizes with a string handle to make it easy to tote one's lunch off to the rice fields. You will also find them in large family-sized versions.* ❖ *Traditional cooks avoid using a metal lid to hold in the steam, as it traps too much steam and drips it back onto the cooking rice. Using a damp cloth (or a folded banana leaf) traps enough of the steam for cooking and then releases it into the air.* ❖ *Sticky rice does not reheat well, so once hardened past a pleasingly chewy stage, you can shape it into small balls and simmer it in soup.*

☙ STICKY RICE WITH COCONUT SAUCE ☙

This rich, salty–sweet rice is a velvety foil to both sweet and savory dishes, notably ripe sweet mangoes as a dessert (page 176), and the hot and garlicky green papaya slaw known as *som tum* (page 60). Allow lots of time to fix this luxurious grain dish, as you will need about 4 hours to soak and steam the rice, season it with coconut cream, and let it cool to room temperature. You can use black sticky rice in this recipe, cooking it as directed or simply soaking it for an hour and cooking it on the stove as you would cook jasmine rice (see page 149). It is less sticky than white long–grain sticky rice, and when cooked, it develops a magnificent purple hue.

1½ cups long-grain sticky rice   *1 cup sugar*
2 cups unsweetened coconut milk   *2 teaspoons salt*

Cook the sticky rice as directed on page 150. While it steams, combine the coconut milk, sugar, and salt in a saucepan. Stir to combine well and then bring to a gentle boil over medium heat. Stir well, remove from the heat, and set aside.

When the rice is soft, swollen, and shiny and can be easily shaped into a small ball, transfer 3 cups of it to a large bowl. Pour the coconut milk mixture over the rice and stir well. Cover and set aside for 30 minutes to 1 hour to allow the rice to absorb most of the sauce. Serve at room temperature with ripe fruit or with savory dishes.

MAKES ABOUT 3 CUPS; SERVES 4.

NOTE • *The rice will keep at room temperature for 6 to 8 hours. While it is best freshly made, you can keep it for 1 to 2 days and reheat it gently in a steamer or microwave. Aim to warm and soften it rather than to make it hot.*

ఴ FRIED RICE ఴ

In upcountry households and small cafés, this dish is the simplest one-dish meal offered. You can serve it instead of plain rice with curries and other main dishes, but if you need a quick hot supper, this is a winner. The ingredients are always on hand, and fried rice satisfies hunger with little fuss. You can add firm tofu, tempeh, or wheat gluten for protein, and you can omit the eggs. Thais toss in a squeeze or two of lime juice just before eating. Some Thais spike it with chopped fresh or dried chilies as well.

4 cups cooked long-grain rice (page 149), preferably jasmine rice and preferably chilled

3 tablespoons vegetable oil

1 tablespoon coarsely chopped garlic (4 to 6 cloves)

1 yellow onion, coarsely chopped

1 cup sliced fresh button mushrooms (about 6 ounces)

2 eggs, beaten

1 teaspoon salt

½ teaspoon sugar

2 plum tomatoes, coarsely chopped, or 9 cherry tomatoes, halved lengthwise

½ cup coarsely chopped fresh cilantro

1 hothouse cucumber, peeled and sliced into ¼-inch-thick rounds

1 lime, quartered lengthwise

A few fresh cilantro sprigs

Using your hands, crumble the cold rice gently between your fingers to separate it into individual grains. Set aside.

In a wok or a large, deep skillet, heat 2 tablespoons of the oil over medium-high heat, swirling to coat the pan, until a bit of garlic added to the pan sizzles at once, about 1 minute. Add the garlic and onion and toss until shiny, fragrant, and softened, 1 to 2 minutes. Add the mushrooms and cook, tossing often, until darkened, shiny, and tender, 3 to 4 minutes.

Push the onion and mushrooms to the edges of the pan and add the egg to the center of the pan. Cook until set and then scramble, breaking the set egg into small pieces.

Add the remaining 1 tablespoon oil, heat for about 1 minute, and then add the rice. Toss for about 1 minute, breaking up any lumps and mixing it with the onion, mushrooms, and eggs. Add the salt, sugar, and tomatoes and toss until the ingredients are well combined and the rice is softened and heated through, 2 to 3 minutes.

Remove from the heat, add the cilantro, and toss well. Transfer to a serving platter and garnish with the cucumber slices, lime wedges, and cilantro sprigs. Limes can be squeezed over individual portions before eating. Serve hot or warm.

SERVES 4.

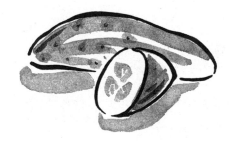

❧ PINEAPPLE FRIED RICE ❧

This dish is yummy, pretty, and quick. Serve as is as a foil for a stir-fry, a curry, or a platter of grilled vegetables, or add small cubes of firm tofu at the end and serve as a hearty main dish.

4 cups cooked long-grain rice (page 149), preferably jasmine rice and preferably chilled

3 tablespoons oil

1 tablespoon coarsely chopped garlic (4 to 6 cloves)

1 yellow onion, coarsely chopped

1 cup shredded carrots

1 can (8 ounces) crushed pineapple, with juice, or 1 cup finely chopped fresh pineapple

1 teaspoon salt

½ teaspoon sugar

3 green onions, thinly sliced crosswise

Using your hands, crumble the cold rice gently between your fingers to separate it into individual grains. Set aside.

In a wok or a large, deep skillet, heat 2 tablespoons of the oil over medium-high heat, swirling to coat the pan, until a bit of garlic added to the pan sizzles at once, about 1 minute. Add the garlic and onion and toss until shiny, fragrant, and softened, 1 to 2 minutes.

Add the remaining 1 tablespoon oil, heat for about 1 minute, and then add the rice. Toss for about 1 minute, breaking up any lumps and mixing it with the garlic and onion. Add the carrots, pineapple, salt, and sugar and toss until the ingredients are well combined and the rice is softened and heated through, 2 to 3 minutes. Add the green onions, toss well, and remove from heat. Transfer to a serving platter and serve hot or warm.

SERVES 4.

NOTE • *If a smashing presentation is in order, use a fresh pineapple for serving: Halve a ripe pineapple lengthwise, cutting through its leafy top as well as the fruit. Hollow out each half, reserving 1 cup of the fruit for the rice and some extra for a garnish; set aside the remainder for other uses. Make a small slice on the outside of each half, to create a flat base to hold the hollow pineapple steady on its side. Fill each half with the warm rice, mounding it high and garnishing the top with a flourish of cilantro leaves and chunks of pineapple.*

∽ YELLOW CURRY FRIED RICE WITH CRISPY POTATOES AND PEAS ∽

Fried rice works best with leftover rice that has been chilled until its grains are firm and dry. Make extra the next time you cook rice and then turn it into a quick meal the following day. For this recipe you will also need leftover baked or boiled potatoes. If you do not have any on hand, boil 2 cups diced peeled potato until tender, drain well, and then proceed as directed in the recipe.

4 cups cooked long-grain rice (see page 149), preferably jasmine rice and preferably chilled

3 tablespoons vegetable oil

1 tablespoon chopped garlic (4 to 6 cloves)

2 cups peeled, cooked, and diced potatoes

1 cup chopped yellow onions

2 tablespoons Yellow Curry Paste (page 200)

1½ cups frozen green peas

1 teaspoon salt

¼ cup chopped fresh cilantro leaves and stems

Using your hands, crumble cold rice gently between your fingers to separate it into individual grains. Set aside.

Line a plate with paper towels and place near the stove. In a wok or a large, deep skillet, heat 2 tablespoons of the oil over medium–high heat, swirling to coat the pan, until a bit of garlic added to the pan sizzles at once, about 1 minute. Add the potatoes and cook, tossing occasionally, until golden brown and crisp, 4 to 5 minutes. Using a slotted spoon, transfer the potatoes to the towel–lined plate.

Add the remaining 1 tablespoon oil to the wok along with the garlic and onions. Reduce the heat to medium and toss until shiny and slightly softened, about 1 minute. Add the curry paste and cook, mashing and scraping often to soften the paste and mix it with the onions, until the paste is fragrant and mixture is well combined, about 1½ minutes.

Add the rice and toss well. Return the potatoes to the wok along with the peas and salt and cook, tossing occasionally, until rice is softened, mixed with the curry paste, and heated through, 2 to 3 minutes. Transfer to serving platter, garnish with the cilantro and serve hot or warm.

SERVES 4.

NOTE • *You can substitute any Thai-style curry paste for the Yellow Curry Paste.*

∽ COCONUT RICE WITH CILANTRO AND FRESH GINGER ∽

Pair this luscious alternative to plain jasmine rice with grilled vegetables or your favorite Thai curry. Thais serve it with *som tum*, sharp and spicy green papaya salad (page 60). You can use basmati rice or any long-grain white rice if you are out of jasmine rice.

1 can (14 ounces) coconut milk

1¾ cups water

6 quarter-sized slices peeled fresh ginger

1 teaspoon salt

2 cups jasmine rice

½ cup coarsely chopped fresh cilantro

In a saucepan with a tight-fitting lid, combine the coconut milk, water, ginger, and salt and bring to a rolling boil over medium heat. Add the rice and stir well. When the liquid boils again, cover, reduce the heat to low, and cook for 25 minutes. The rice kernels will be tender and the liquid will be absorbed.

Remove the saucepan from the heat and let stand, covered, for 10 minutes. Uncover and remove and discard the ginger. Add the cilantro and, using a fork, toss gently to distribute the cilantro evenly. Fluff the rice kernels and serve hot or warm.

SERVES 4 TO 6.

∽ MEE GROP ∽

Here is a spectacular dish. Wiry rice noodles are deep–fried to a light, crisp
tangle, tossed in a piquant chili sauce, and then garnished with pickled garlic,
bean sprouts, green onion brushes, and strips of red chili. The result is an
extraordinary dish, unlike any other in its juxtaposition of textures and in its
classic Thai explosions of flavor. A traditional version would also include lacy
nets of egg fried to a puffy golden brown and draped over the mound of noodles, which is studded with dried shrimp and sharpened by the juice of *som-
sah*, a particularly sour orange unavailable in the West.

Since *mee grop* is served at room temperature, it makes a grand centerpiece
for a celebration meal. Thais prepare it in large quantitites for the feasts that
accompany a wedding, Buddhist ordination, moving into a new home, or wel-
coming a baby to the world. Sweet and delicate and traditionally containing a
little seafood and no meat, it is especially appropriate for serving to the
monks who are invited to bless these occasions.

Although I have given you a simplified recipe, you are nonetheless in for a
considerable amount of work, from deep–frying the noodles to making their
tangy sauce and tossing them in it. You can turn its preparation into a pleasure by calling in culinary reinforcements as Thais do. Have a friend or two
come over to provide good company along with extra hands under your
instruction, and the time will sail by, leaving you all with a small, glorious
mountain of scrumptious Thai noodles to enjoy.

8 ounces wire-thin dried rice noodles
Vegetable oil for deep-frying and sautéing
4 ounces firm tofu, cut into slender,
    1-inch-long rods
¼ cup finely chopped garlic
8 ounces fresh button mushrooms, thinly
    sliced
1¼ teaspoons salt
2 tablespoons coarsely chopped shallots
½ cup Vegetable Stock (pages 204 and
    205)

2 tablespoons distilled white vinegar
1 tablespoon Asian bean sauce
½ teaspoon soy sauce
1 teaspoon red chili pepper flakes
½ cup palm sugar or brown sugar
¼ cup granulated sugar
¼ cup Tamarind Liquid (page 212)
2 tablespoons freshly squeezed lime juice
1 bunch fresh garlic chives or 9 green
    onions, cut into 1-inch lengths
1 cup coarsely chopped fresh cilantro

Garnishes:

3 cups bean sprouts

5 heads Thai pickled garlic, cut crosswise
  into rounds ¼ inch thick, or 24 cloves
  pickled garlic

1 red sweet pepper, cut into long, thin
  strips

A handful of cilantro leaves

To prepare for frying the noodles, gently pull the bundle of dried rice noodles apart, breaking them into small handfuls about 3 inches long. Set them aside in a heap. Tiny shards will fly around the room as you complete this task, so you could do it outside, weather permitting, or break them up inside a paper grocery bag, or simply plan to sweep up after you are finished. Select a utensil suitable for removing batches of fried noodles from the hot oil with speed and dexterity. A large, long-handled Asian wire strainer is ideal, and 2 long-handled metal slotted spoons will work well. Line a large tray or 2 baking sheets with paper towels and place near the stove to hold the fried noodles. Have handy a large serving platter, a dinner plate, a large, deep bowl, and 2 long-handled spoons or pasta forks for tossing the puffed noodles with the sauce.

To fry the noodles, pour oil into a wok or a large, deep skillet to a depth of about 3 inches. Place over medium heat and heat to 325 to 350 degrees F. Drop a piece of rice noodle into the pan. If it sinks and then floats and puffs immediately, the oil is ready.

Drop a small handful of the noodles into the oil. Turn them once and remove them as soon as they swell and change color from ivory to white to a very faint golden brown. This takes only seconds, so slip the telephone off the hook until you are done. Using the wire strainer, scoop out the puffed noodles, holding them over the pan briefly to drain, and then transfer them to the towel-lined tray. Repeat this process until all the noodles are cooked.

In the same hot oil, cook the little rods of tofu, adding them in small batches to discourage them from sticking together. Fry, turning to cook evenly, until crispy and golden, 1 to 2 minutes. Remove them as quickly as you did the noodles, draining them briefly, and then transfer them to the towel-lined tray to cool. Turn off the heat and let the oil return to room temperature.

In a medium skillet, heat 2 tablespoons vegetable oil over medium heat until a bit of garlic added to the pan sizzles at once. Add half of the garlic and toss until fragrant and shiny, about 1 minute. Add the mushrooms and cook, tossing occasionally, for 1 minute. Add ¼ teaspoon of the salt, toss well, and then cook, tossing often, until the mushrooms are softened, shiny, and handsomely browned, about 5 minutes. Transfer to the plate and set aside.

Add 2 more tablespoons vegetable oil to the skillet and heat over medium–high heat until a bit of garlic added to the pan sizzles at once. Add the remaining garlic and the shallots and cook, tossing often, until shiny, fragrant, and tender, about 2 minutes. Add the remaining 1 teaspoon salt, vegetable stock, vinegar, bean sauce, soy sauce, chili pepper flakes, both sugars, and tamarind and bring to a gentle boil. Stir to dissolve the sugars, mixing well. Reduce heat to medium and cook gently until the sauce is a thin, shiny syrup, 5 to 7 minutes.

Add the lime juice and then taste and adjust the seasoning for a pleasing balance of sweet, salty, and sour flavors.

Transfer the sauce to a large bowl, add the noodles and mushrooms, and toss gently, thoroughly, and patiently to coax apart the clumps, distributing the sauce and coating the noodles evenly. Add the garlic chives or green onion and the cilantro and toss again to mix well.

Mound the noodles on the serving platter. Arrange the bean sprouts attractively on one side or surrounding them. Garnish with the rounds or cloves of pickled garlic, red pepper strips, and cilantro leaves. Serve at room temperature.

SERVES 6 TO 8.

NOTE • *If you enjoy making green onion brushes and chili flowers, this is the time to pull out your garnishing tools and go to town. For simple green onion brushes, cut a trimmed green onion to a length of about 5 inches, including its base. Using a clean sewing needle, poke the needle into the onion where the green part begins and pull up gently until the needle comes out at the tip of a stalk. Repeat repeatedly, shredding the greens as much as you can, remembering that more cuts mean more curlicues. Drop these shredded green onions into a bowl of ice water to chill for an hour or more. You can also use a sharp paring knife to shred the greens while holding the onion on a cutting board. You can make "firecrackers" by shredding both ends of plump 2- or 3-inch lengths of green onion. You can make chili flowers by cutting through long, slender chilies from points ¼ inch or more below where the stem is attached through to the tip, and continuing around the chili until the tip is divided into* *sixths or eighths. Chill in ice water for an hour or so, to encourage the strips to curl, then drain and use to decorate the platter.* ❖ *You can purchase Thai pickled garlic in an Asian market. What you buy will be petite whole heads, with papery sheaths still in place, packed in their brine. These should be drained and then sliced crosswise into ¼-inch-thick rounds that display a pleasing mosaic of round cloves clustered into a large circle. These delicate slices are placed decoratively on the mountain of noodles just before serving.*

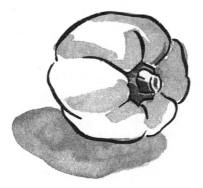

↣ PAHT THAI ↢

In Thailand, most noodle dishes have clear Chinese origins, and have been adapted very little, since they please Thais just the way they are. This is the exception, a Thai invention, with the basic technique of stir–frying applied to seasonings that marry sweet with sour and salty with hot in a way Thais adore. The full name for this dish is *kwaytiow paht Thai*. The first word means rice noo–dles, and *paht* means to stir–fry in a wok or shallow skillet. The word *Thai* says that the use of tamarind, sugar, peanuts, bean sprouts, and lime in this dish is a signature of Thai ingenuity in the kitchen. The classic version of *paht Thai* includes crispy little tofu rods, minced pickled turnip (known as *tay-po*), and a handful of little salty dried shrimp. Raw bean sprouts and a wedge of purple–and–yellow banana flower (if it can be found) always garnish the plate, as these two add a cool, raw crunch. The addition of fresh seafood and meat is a mod–ern one, as is the inclusion of tomato paste or ketchup. The latter is common in Thai restaurants in the West, probably added more for color than for flavor. Noodle chefs in Thailand freely include their own touches to create a signature version, so use your ingenuity once you get the hang of cooking the noodles.

4 ounces dried rice noodles, the width of linguine or fettuccine

Vegetable oil for deep-frying and stir-frying

8 ounces firm tofu, cut into slender 1-inch-long rods

1 tablespoon coarsely chopped garlic (4 to 6 cloves)

1 egg, lightly beaten

¼ cup Vegetable Stock (pages 204 and 205)

2 tablespoons Tamarind Liquid (page 212) or freshly squeezed lime juice

1 tablespoon Asian bean sauce

1 tablespoon sugar

2 teaspoons soy sauce

1 teaspoon salt

½ teaspoon ground red chili pepper flakes

½ cup finely chopped salted, dry-roasted peanuts

2 cups bean sprouts

3 green onions, whites thinly sliced cross-wise and tender green tops cut into 1-inch lengths

1 lime, quartered lengthwise

Place the dried rice noodles in warm water to soak for 15 to 20 minutes. Meanwhile, pour vegetable oil into a medium skillet to a depth of about 2 inches. Place over medium heat until a bit of tofu added to the pan sizzles at once. Line a plate with paper towels and place near the stove. When the oil is ready, add the tofu in small batches to discourage them from sticking together. Fry, turning to cook evenly, until crispy and golden, about 2 minutes. Using a long-handled wire strainer or a slotted spoon, remove from the oil, draining over the pan briefly, and transfer to the paper-lined plate.

When the noodles are very limp and white, drain and measure out about 2½ cups. Set these near the stove.

Heat a wok or a large, deep skillet over medium-high heat. Add 1 tablespoon oil and swirl to coat the pan. Add the garlic and toss until golden, about 1 minute. Add the egg and tilt the pan so it coats the surface in a thin sheet. As soon as it is opaque and beginning to set, scramble it well and transfer it to a serving platter.

Add 2 more tablespoons oil to the pan and heat for 30 seconds. Add the softened noodles and, using a spatula, spread and pull the noodles into a thin layer covering the surface of the pan. Then scrape them down into a clump again and gently turn them over.

Add the vegetable stock, tamarind or lime juice, bean sauce, sugar, soy sauce, and salt and toss well. Hook loops of noodles with the edge of your spatula and pull them up the sides, spreading them out into a layer again. Repeat this process several times as the stiff, white noodles soften and curl into ivory ringlets. Add the chili flakes and about half of the peanuts and turn the noodles a few more times.

Set aside a little less than half of the bean sprouts for garnish. Add the remainder to the pan along with all the green onions and the cooked egg. Toss well and cook until the bean sprouts and green onion tops are shiny and beginning to wilt, 1 to 2 minutes more. Transfer to the serving platter and squeeze the lime wedges over the top. Garnish with the remaining peanuts and bean sprouts on one side and serve at once.

SERVES 1 AS A MAIN COURSE OR 2 AS AN APPETIZER.

NOTE • *Vegans can omit the egg.* ❖ *This makes only one or two portions, which is the best I can do with a wok on a Western stove. In Thailand, expert cooks do only a batch or two at a time, too, even when a tableful of diners orders* paht Thai. *A wok can only do justice to so many noodles at one time.* ❖ *My recipe instructs you to squeeze the lime juice over the noodles just before serving. This is because I have found that if I present the dish Thai style, with a lime wedge on the side, it is left behind like a parsley garnish on a dinner plate at a* *banquet. Thais always squeeze on lime juice, so I like to include some and then offer extra lime wedges to those who like an extra sour hit.* ❖ *You can omit the step of frying the tofu rods and simply add them to the pan along with the bean sprouts. For a simple, home-style* paht Thai, *you can leave out the tamarind and bean sauce as well.*

↳ RICE NOODLES WITH EGGS, BROCCOLI, AND DARK SWEET SOY SAUCE ↲

In Thailand, this classic dish is almost as popular as *paht Thai*, plus it is a boon for home cooks because it is easier to prepare. The dark sweet soy sauce, known as *si-yu*, bestows a gorgeous mahogany color to the noodles, while the broccoli turns a brilliant green. Instead of fresh, soft rice noodles, you can use dried rice noodles, which must be first soaked until softened, or even cooked fettuccine or linguine with tasty results. Check the menu at your favorite Thai restaurant for this one, which may be listed under its Thai name, *paht si-yu*. Widely available in the West, it is easily adapted for vegetarian diners since it is always cooked to order. If you want an authentic dish, be sure to doctor up your portion with a little extra sugar, salt, and chilies, and then dollop on a little Chili–Vinegar Sauce before you dig in.

2 tablespoons dark sweet soy sauce, or 2 tablespoons dark soy sauce and 1 tablespoon molasses or brown sugar

2 tablespoons Vegetable Stock (pages 204 and 205)

1 tablespoon soy sauce

1 teaspoon salt

½ teaspoon freshly ground pepper

3 tablespoons vegetable oil

1 tablespoon coarsely chopped garlic (4 to 6 cloves)

8 ounces fresh mushrooms, sliced

3 cups bite-sized broccoli florets

1 pound soft, fresh flat rice noodles, or 8 ounces dried rice noodles, soaked in warm water for about 20 minutes until pliable

2 eggs, lightly beaten

Condiments:

Chili-Vinegar Sauce (page 226)

Sugar

Red chili pepper flakes

In a small bowl, combine the dark sweet soy sauce or dark soy sauce mixture, vegetable stock, regular soy sauce, salt, and pepper. Stir well and place near the stove along with a serving platter.

Heat a wok or a large, deep skillet over medium-high heat. Add 1 tablespoon of the oil and swirl to coat the pan. Add the garlic and toss until fragrant and just beginning to brown, about 1 minute. Add the mushrooms and cook, tossing often, until they are dark, softened and shiny, about 3 minutes. Add the broccoli and cook, tossing often, until shiny and bright green, about 2 minutes. Scoop out the mushrooms and broccoli and place on the serving platter; set aside.

Add the remaining 2 tablespoons oil to the pan and heat for about 30 seconds. Add the noodles and toss until they are separated and heated through. Push the noodles to one side of the wok and add the eggs. Swirl to spread out the eggs and let cook for about 30 seconds. Then scoop and toss everything together gently, scrambling the eggs and mixing well.

Quickly stir the soy sauce mixture to combine and then pour it over the noodles. Add the reserved broccoli and mushrooms and their juices and toss until the noodles are handsomely colored and evenly coated with the sauce, about 1 minute. Transfer to the serving platter and serve at once, offering the condiments– Chili-Vinegar Sauce, sugar, red chili pepper flakes– in small bowls on the side.

SERVES 4.

NOTE • *Vegans can omit the eggs and add about a cupful of crumbled firm tofu in their place.* ❖ *Thai cooks make this noodle dish with the sturdy dark green cabbage cousin called pahk ka–nah, rather than broccoli. You could use any member of the healthful family known as cruciferous vegetables, all of which have a cross-shaped formation of leafy stem at the base. Cabbages, winter greens, broccoli, and cauliflower are part of this group, and any of them would work nicely in this recipe. Be sure to cut them on the diagonal into thin, bite-sized pieces so they will cook quickly. Try winter greens such as kale, collards, or Swiss chard. You can also use bok choy, napa cabbage, or any of the Asian greens Cantonese speakers refer to as choy. These include ong–choy, yu–choy and choy–sum, all of which are often sold in bloom with tiny white or yellow flowers. You could also use spinach if you stir it in just before the dish is ready, and cook it only long enough for it to wilt.*

✣ MEE GA-TI RICE NOODLES WITH COCONUT-BEAN SAUCE ✣

Try this terrific noodle dish when you crave noodles but find stir–frying them too much work. The noodles are tossed with the sauce and then enjoyed warm or at room temperature, so it makes a good choice for serving on a buffet. Asian bean sauce is the flavor note here, a sharp, salty concoction of salted fermented soybeans that is a terrific foil for the richness of *ga-ti* (coconut milk). Like *paht Thai* (page 162), this delicious sweet–and–tangy rice noodle classic is traditionally garnished with raw bean sprouts and chunks of fresh banana flower. These flourishes provide what Thais call *rote faht-faht*, a cool, raw taste and texture that are welcome counterpoints to the lush, sweet, salty, and sour flavors of many Thai dishes. Should you be fortunate enough to be cooking this in a tropical clime, find a teardrop–shaped banana flower, quarter it lengthwise, and offer it to diners to nibble along with the noodles. Or pull off some delicate and colorful portions, slice them, and use to garnish the platter

8 ounces dried rice noodles, either wire-thin or about the width of linguine or fettuccine

1 tablespoon vegetable oil

2 eggs, beaten

3 cups unsweetened coconut milk

½ cup minced shallots

⅓ cup Asian bean sauce

8 ounces firm tofu, cut into slender 1-inch-long rods

2 zucchini, halved lengthwise and cut crosswise into thin half-moons, or cut into slender 2-inch-long rods

2 tablespoons Tamarind Liquid (page 212) or freshly squeezed lime juice

2 tablespoons Vegetable Stock (pages 204 and 205)

2 tablespoons sugar

1 teaspoon salt

1 teaspoon freshly ground pepper

1 teaspoon red chili pepper flakes

A handful of fresh garlic chives, cut into 2-inch lengths, or 3 green onions, white part thinly sliced crosswise and green part cut into 2-inch lengths

2 cups bean sprouts

½ cup coarsely chopped fresh cilantro

1 lime, cut lengthwise into 6 wedges

Put the dried rice noodles in a bowl, add warm water to cover, and let stand until limp and pliable, 15 to 20 minutes. Put a large pot of water on to boil.

Meanwhile, heat the vegetable oil in a medium skillet over medium–high heat until a drop of egg added to the pan sizzles at once, about 1 minute. Add only enough of the eggs to coat the pan, swirling to make a thin sheet. Cook until the egg sets, about 30 seconds. Flip it to warm the other side, and then turn it out onto a cutting board to cool. Repeat with the remaining egg. When the egg sheets are cool, shred them into fine strips and set aside.

Drain the noodles and add them to the boiling water. Cook until tender but still firm, 1 to 2 minutes. Drain well and set aside.

Pour the coconut milk into a medium skillet, place over medium heat, and bring to a gentle boil. Adjust the heat to maintain an active simmer and cook, stirring occasionally, until it gives off a sweet aroma and thickens a little, 3 to 5 minutes. Add the shallots, bean sauce, tofu, and zucchini and cook, stirring occasionally, for 3 minutes. Add the tamarind or lime juice, vegetable stock, sugar, salt, pepper, and chili flakes. Stir well and cook for 2 minutes more.

Add the noodles, the garlic chives or green onions, and most of the bean sprouts, reserving a handful for garnish. Toss well to coat everything with the sauce. Transfer to a serving platter and sprinkle with the cilantro. Garnish with the reserved bean sprouts and the lime wedges and serve warm or at room temperature.

SERVES 4.

NOTE • *Vegans can omit the eggs and vegetable oil. Add a handful of shredded carrots to the coconut milk along with the shallots, if you like.* ❖ *If you have a heavy Thai-style mortar and pestle, do not mince the shallots. Instead, chop the shallots coarsely and then pound them to a coarse mush, to release their flavor and juice.* ❖ *This dish is also served with the cooked noodles served up in small heaps and the sauce on the side, to be added by each diner along with the garnishes. You could do this on individual plates, or offer the noodles on a platter with the bowl of sauce alongside.*

7

·

SWEETS AND DRINKS

SWEETS AND DRINKS

෨ Thai people have an undeniable sweet tooth, but sweetness plays a different role in Thailand than it does in Western food. Thais consider sweetness
one of the four essential flavors that make eating a pleasure, along with saltiness, sourness, and chili-pepper heat. It is not reserved for cake, candy, and
cookies, but rather included at all levels of eating. A little palm sugar slips into
curries, sauces, and stews to balance the equation of flavors. Sweetness even
stars in some dishes such as *Mee Grop* (page 158) and Son-in-Law Eggs (page
136). By Western standards, these dishes are savory main-course foods, but
your palate will tell you that you are in Asia, where no clear line is drawn
between savory and sweet.

෨ Sweet dishes designed for eating apart from rice abound in Thai cuisine.
They are enjoyed not as dessert following a main course, but as snacks to satisfy hunger or whims between meals, as food for children, or as breakfast-time
treats. These treats come under the general category of *kanome*, which can be
translated as both "snack" and "sweet treat," although it also covers bread,
certain kinds of noodles, and other dishes made mostly from flour.

෨ The majority of traditional Thai sweets involve coconut milk, palm sugar,
and an array of substantial ingredients, including tapioca pearls, sticky rice,
squiggly little rice-flour noodles, cooked mung beans or black beans, shreds of
freshly grated coconut, and gelatins made with the seaweed extract agar-agar.
Both fruits and vegetables play a role in Thai sweets. Kabocha pumpkins are
hollowed out and filled with custard for steaming, and taro root, potatoes, cassava, fresh ginger, and several varieties of bananas are candied and preserved
in sugar syrup in a process called *chu-am*.

෨ Eggs appear in a number of Thai sweets, including *sangkayah*, simple
steamed custards of coconut milk, palm sugar, and duck or chicken eggs, and
the baked custard crowned with crisp fried shallots and garlic known as
kanome maw gaeng, a dish of foreign origin that is baked in a land where an
oven is as exotic as a Thai granite mortar and pestle is in the West. This dish is
the signature sweet treat of Petchaburi, the *kanome* capital of the Thai kingdom,
where Thais on vacation at the nearby seaside towns of Hua Hin and Cha-Am
stop off to stock up on edible souvenirs for themselves and their loved ones
who were not lucky enough to come along.

෨ Eggs also star in a group of sunburst-orange treats that are trompe l'oeil re-creations of pure gold. *Tong* means "gold," and it appears in an array of goodies made with a dough of egg yolks and sugar cooked in syrup. *Tong yip* are plump golden teardrops, *tong yode* are like flowers, and *tong aek* are shaped in leaf and flower molds and garnished with real gold leaf. *Foi tong* are diminutive hanks of golden threads. These are ringers for the skeins of raw silk women spin at home during the winter break from rice farming in rural northeastern Thailand. *Meht kanoon* are a chunky golden rendering of jackfruit seeds.

Like *kanome maw gaeng* and *foi tong*, the gorgeous tiny sweets called *look choop* suggest a culinary connection to the West dating back several centuries to early contact between European nations and Thailand via seagoing trade. *Look choop* are an Asian version of marzipan, the almond paste treats formed into tiny fruits and vegetables so as to delight the eye as well as the palate. Made from a paste of coconut, palm sugar, and steamed *tua tong*, the yellow centers of hulled mung beans, *look choop* are shaped into miniature tropical fruits, painted with food color to complete the illusion, and then dipped in gelatin to make them shine.

While the traditional sweets of Thailand appear throughout the day as snacks rather than following a meal, Thais do love a simple dessert of the season's freshest, ripest fruits, carefully prepared and presented so that guests are relieved of the hassle of peeling it or dealing with seeds. I remember my first experience of this brilliant, healthful custom in the northernmost Thai town of Chiang Rai, where I joined a group of diners for a late lunch at a restaurant where we feasted away the heat of the day. As we lingered, enjoying the company and the lacy shade of a tamarind tree protecting our alfresco table, the dishes were cleared away and replaced with an enormous platter. It held juicy chunks of sweet watermelon and triangles of ripe, perfect pineapple of the short, squat variety that thrives in the north. This red-and-yellow mountain was showered with crushed ice to keep it cold while we enjoyed it in the withering heat. While I am a dedicated fan of Western desserts, I cannot imagine a better ending to that meal.

This chapter is an intriguing collection of sweets, some of them from the repertoire of traditional Thai *kanome* and some my Thai-inspired creations. Each and every one would work beautifully as a dessert course to your Thai or Western feast. Cool, Crisp Rubies in Coconut Milk and *Maengluck* Basil Seeds in Coconut Milk are two old-time Thai sweet things that I adore for a summertime breakfast, as well as for a snack or dessert. Coconut Ice Cream is spectacular, providing the owners of an ice cream maker with an unbelievably good, completely authentic Thai sweet treat in exchange for a very small amount of time and work.

✎ Additional desserts are my East-West inventions. If you do not have an ice cream maker, please buy or borrow one so that you can churn out my two ice creams flavored respectively with Thai iced coffee and Thai iced tea. You will also find a lovely sorbet infused with the heavenly flavor of lemongrass, and another with the delicate, delectable notes of galanga and wild lime leaves. These two Asian herb confections can also be made into granitas, which are a bit grainier than sorbets but every bit as good.

✎ Winding up this sweet parade is a rice pudding made with coconut milk and toasted coconut that can be eaten hot or cold. To ease your thirst, I have included Thai iced coffee and iced tea, with instructions on making them in a drip coffee maker or straining them more traditionally. Finally, for those of you with a lemongrass patch in a pot or yard, there is Fresh Lemongrass Lemonade.

✎ For vegans, there is much to enjoy here. The two sorbets are made without dairy products, as are the Coconut Ice Cream, Thai Ice Cream Sandwich, and the first two Thai sweets, Cool, Crisp Rubies in Coconut Milk and Maengluck Basil Seeds in Coconut Milk. You can adapt the Coconut Rice Pudding by using soy milk instead of dairy milk, and enjoy Thai iced tea and iced coffee without the milk that is traditionally included.

☙ COOL, CRISP RUBIES IN COCONUT MILK ☙

This beloved traditional sweet is called *tuptim grop*, and it has delighted Thais for centuries. Made from the most ordinary of Asian ingredients, its name embodies a double pun for both eye and ear. *Tuptim* can be translated both as "ruby" and as "pomegranate seed," and the dessert looks very much like the jewels or seeds, shimmering in a bowl of snowy, sweet coconut milk. In Thailand, it is purchased from a sweets vendor, either in individual serving bowls for eating at a market stall or in separate plastic bags for transporting home. Thais add crushed ice to each bowl at serving time, but if you prefer, simply chill the coconut milk and syrup well and serve it cold.

Red food coloring
1 can (8 ounces) whole water chestnuts,
  drained and cut into pea-sized chunks
About 1 cup tapioca flour

⅔ cup water
⅔ cup sugar
1¼ cups unsweetened coconut milk
Crushed ice

Fill a medium bowl with water, add a few drops of red food coloring, and stir well. Add the water chestnuts and let stand until they absorb the red color fully, 15 to 20 minutes. Drain well.

Place the tapioca flour in a medium bowl and add the water chestnut pieces a handful at a time, tossing them gently with your fingers to coat them evenly and well with the tapioca flour. Scoop them out with a slotted spoon, shake gently to remove any excess flour, and set aside on a plate in a single layer.

Place a saucepan filled with water over medium heat and bring to a rolling boil. Add the water chestnut pieces in handfuls, stirring well to discourage them from clumping together. Boil until the flour coating is clear and red, 3 to 4 minutes. Drain well, add cool water to cover, let stand for 1 minute, and then drain well again. Set aside in a bowl.

Combine the water and sugar in a saucepan, place over medium heat, and bring to a rolling boil. Cook, stirring once, until the sugar dissolves completely and you have a light syrup, about 3 minutes. Remove from the heat and set aside to cool.

To serve this sweet, divide the "rubies" evenly among 5 small shallow serving bowls, preferably made of glass to show off the colors of the finished dish. Stir the coconut milk well and divide it among the bowls, putting about ¼ cup in each bowl; the "rubies" should still be quite visible and appear to be floating in the coconut milk. Add 3 tablespoons of the syrup to each bowl and then sprinkle with a tablespoon or two of crushed ice. Serve at once.

SERVES 5.

NOTE • *Dishes like this are typically served as an afternoon snack or in the night market, where you perch on a stool at the vendor's rickety table and enjoy a cool, sweet treat before strolling home. This dish acts as a refreshing dessert after nearly any Thai meal, particularly since sweet coconut milk can quell the fires of chili-pepper heat. I use canned coconut milk in lieu of freshly made. If you make coconut milk from scratch, here is a great place to use it, however. It is uncooked for this dish, so its fresh flavor can shine. For the traditional version, use fairly thick coconut cream from the first pressing (see page 236), as this dish calls for that level of richness. ❖ These "pomegranate seeds" are best made within a few hours of serving. They cling together into a gelatinous mass as time passes and as they chill. If you make them ahead, cover and chill for up to 2 days, and then turn the cool red blob out onto a cutting board and gently separate it into individual "seeds" with your fingers. ❖ Tapioca flour is found in Asian markets and through some of the mail-order sources listed in this book (page 232). It has the gelatinous property needed to give the water-chestnut pieces a colorful and plump jellylike coating. Store extra tapioca flour in an airtight container, where it will keep indefinitely. ❖ You can make "crisp emeralds" by using green food coloring instead of red, and your* tuptim grop *would become* kaew grop, kaew *being the word for "emerald." You can also combine the two colors for a red, white, and green treat. ❖ If you want to use fresh water chestnuts in this recipe, purchase 30 to 40 firm chestnuts. Using a very sharp knife, peel them to remove all of their thick, tough brown exterior. Boil the peeled ivory-colored chestnuts in water to cover, until tender enough to bite but still nicely crunchy and firm, about 30 minutes. Drain and immerse in cold water until cooled to room temperature, then use as directed.*

✂ MAENGLUK BASIL SEEDS IN COCONUT MILK ✂

Bai maengluk, a member of the Thai basil trio, has a delicate lemony aroma and tang. In Thailand, *maengluk* basil leaves are tossed into soups and curries just before serving. Its tiny black seeds are sold in Thai markets year–round, often labeled "dried sweet basil" in English and "hot e" in Vietnamese. They are purchased not only for planting in herb gardens, but also for their unique capacity to swell into gelatinlike pearls for serving in Thai soups and sweets. Once you have the seeds in hand, you are minutes away from a down–home Thai–Chinese treat beloved by children and grown–ups alike. The delicately sweet, translucent meat of young green coconuts is the classic companion to this dessert of swollen basil seeds in coconut cream; it is sometimes available canned or frozen in Asian markets, packed in juice, which is drained before use. You can also use any other sweet, ripe fruit or a combination of several if young, green coconut is difficult to find.

1 tablespoon maengluk *basil seeds*

1½ cups water

½ cup young coconut meat or 1 bite-sized chunks sweet, ripe fruit such as banana, cantaloupe, honeydew melon, mango, papaya, or pineapple or whole strawberries, raspberries, or blueberries

1 cup unsweetened coconut milk, stirred to combine well before measuring

⅓ cup palm sugar or brown sugar

Place the *maengluk* basil seeds in a medium bowl and add ¾ cup of the water. Let stand, stirring occasionally, until the seeds absorb the water and transform themselves into about 1 cup tiny gray–blue "eggs" with a clear gelatin encasing each one. This should take about 15 minutes. Set aside along with the prepared fruit.

In a medium bowl, combine the coconut milk with the remaining ¾ cup of water and stir well. Add the sugar and mix well, stirring, scraping, and mashing to dissolve the sugar completely in the coconut milk. If some chunks refuse to dissolve, strain them out, place them in a small saucepan with a little water, heat, and stir just until they dissolve. Then stir this liquid into the bowl of sweetened coconut milk. Cover and place in the refrigerator until well chilled, 1 to 2 hours or more.

To serve, set out small, individual bowls and pour about ⅓ cup of the chilled sweet coconut milk into each bowl. Place 2 tablespoons or so of the basil seeds in each bowl and then divide the fruit among the bowls. Serve at once.

SERVES 6.

NOTE • *Try this with frozen coconut milk as well as canned, since the coconut milk is served without any cooking and frozen coconut milk has a pleasing note. If you have time and energy, make coconut milk from scratch (page 210), using some for a curry and some for this sweet. It will not be as thick and creamy as canned or frozen coconut milk, but its clear, fresh flavor makes up for what is lost in texture. ❖ To chill the sweet coconut milk quickly, nestle the bowl into a bigger bowl about three-fourths full of ice. Or try the traditional Thai method of chilling sweets: Add a handful of crushed ice to each bowl just before serving. ❖ In addition to its pleasing, caviarlike texture, basil seeds have another strong appeal to Thai people. No scientific research studies have hit the journals, but Thai market ladies always assured me that eating soaked* maengluk *basil seeds causes one to* lote nahm nahk, *or "release unwanted pounds." ❖ Soaked* maengluk *basil seeds are an unusual sight, and their odd appearance has been compared to everything from tapioca pearls and caviar to tiny fish eyes and tadpoles. Use tiny tapioca pearls cooked until clear and tender if you cannot find the seeds.*

❧ STICKY RICE WITH MANGOES ❧

This is heavenly. It is also simple to make once you are in possession of some sweet, ripe mangoes, which are worth their weight in gold on a sweltering day in Thailand. During mango season, Thai people often skip supper and instead stroll to the night market to indulge in this local treat. If you do not have wonderful mangoes handy to pair with the sticky rice, use summer's sweetest peaches, nectarines, or plums, or a red, white, and blue rainbow of strawberries, bananas, and blueberries. Plan ahead, as the sticky rice needs 3 hours to soak and then an hour or so to cool to room temperature after steaming. Thais sometimes use black sticky rice, which actually has a gorgeous purple hue after cooking.

Sticky Rice in Coconut Sauce (page 152)
3/4 cup unsweetened coconut milk
1/2 teaspoon salt

6 ripe, sweet mangoes or about 1 1/2 cups
per person of any ripe, sweet fruit (see
introduction)

Prepare the sticky rice as directed and set it aside to cool to room temperature. In a saucepan over medium heat, heat the coconut milk gently over medium heat until it comes to a gentle boil. Add the salt, stir well, and cook until the coconut milk thickens a bit and releases its sweet fragrance, about 3 minutes. Transfer to a small bowl and set aside to cool.

Shortly before serving, peel and slice the mangoes, removing as much meat as you can in large, tender pieces. Avoid cutting very close to the seed where the meat is quite fibrous. For each serving, arrange a fist-sized serving of coconut rice on a dessert or salad plate along with several chunks of mango or other fruit. Spoon about 2 tablespoons of the coconut milk over the rice and serve at once.

SERVES 6.

You can keep the coconut rice for 6 to 8 hours at room temperature. Do not refrigerate, as it will harden.

NOTE • *For a traditional presentation, sprinkle each serving of sticky rice with toasted tua tong, or "golden beans," which are the tiny, bright yellow oval centers that are at the heart of mung beans. They are widely available in Asian markets in small cellophane bags. To toast them, put a handful in a small skillet, place over medium heat, and toast, shaking the pan often, until lightly browned, 5 to 10 minutes. Then divide them among the servings of rice. ❖ Mangoes are about one-third seed, making a great deal of scrumptious fruit too fibrous to cut off and enjoy delicately in polite company. For this reason, I strongly suggest you retire to the kitchen sink (or the backyard) along with the 6 mango seeds and your closest family and friends. Then take turns leaning over the sink and gnawing on the meaty seeds with messy, joyous abandon.*

ꙮ COCONUT ICE CREAM ꙮ

Here is the classic Thai ice cream that sweetens the hottest evening in
Thailand's upcountry small towns. It could not be simpler and it could not be
better. You can jazz it up with flavors and additions in the modern manner,
but in my opinion it is perfect as is. Thais love it sprinkled with chopped
peanuts and served in tiny bowls, or in Thai Ice Cream Sandwiches (page 179).

2 cans (14 ounces each) unsweetened   *1 cup sugar*
  coconut milk (about 3½ cups)   *½ teaspoon salt*

In a heavy saucepan, combine the coconut milk, sugar, and salt. Place over
medium–high heat and bring to a boil, stirring often to dissolve the sugar and
salt. Remove from the heat and pour into a bowl.

Cover the bowl and refrigerate until very cold, about 2 hours. Freeze in an
ice cream maker according to the manufacturer's directions. Serve at once, or
transfer to an airtight container and place in the freezer for up to 3 weeks.

MAKES ABOUT 1 PINT; SERVES 4.

NOTE • *You can make the ice cream base in advance, cover, and chill it for up to 1 day
before you churn it into ice cream.* ❖ *If the ice cream loses its pleasing texture and becomes
grainy, break it into chunks and briefly process it in a food processor fitted with the metal
blade to restore its creaminess.*

❧ THAI ICE CREAM SANDWICHES ❧

This East–West snack exhibits Thai ingenuity in translating two Western imports, ice cream and sliced white bread, into a sweet and portable treat. Thailand's urban centers now have ice cream parlors with many flavors and a choice of plain or chocolate sprinkle cones, but in the countryside you may still find night markets where the flavor is coconut and your serving dish and spoon is washable rather than disposable. As a greenhorn Peace Corps volunteer, I remember my surprise on being handed my first coconut ice cream sandwich, since it broke one of my Western culinary rules (bread equals savory; ice cream equals sweet). But as I devoured this revelation while meandering home through the steamy summer night, I decided many a culinary concept gains something in the translation. Use miniscule scoops of firm ice cream and soft white bread rather than the proverbial crusty peasant loaf for best results.

Very firm ice cream, preferably Coconut Ice Cream (page 178), about 12 small scoops
4 slices soft white bread

About ½ recipe Sticky Rice (page 150), warm or at room temperature
2 cups coarsely chopped salted, dry-roasted peanuts

For each sandwich, scoop out 3 small, golf ball–sized lumps ice cream and line them up in the center of a slice of soft white bread. Shape a handful of sticky rice into a plump, finger-length log and place it on the bread alongside the ice cream. Sprinkle with ½ cup of the peanuts, fold up into a rectangle, and serve at once. Repeat with the remaining ingredients to make 4 sandwiches in all, also served at once.

SERVES 4.

NOTE • *Use any flavor ice cream you like. I am partial to coconut ice cream purely for sentimental reasons, and it is the traditional Thai choice in a land where dairy products are a recent addition to the market and remain relatively rare. Vegans can use coconut milk–based ice creams or fruit-based sorbets for their sandwiches.*

↢ THAI COFFEE ICE CREAM ↢

I adore the flavor of Thai iced coffee, with its deep, dark coffee kick fortified with ground dried corn and sesame seeds that have been roasted to a robust turn. In the spring of 1989, I returned to Thailand to research my first cookbook, *Real Thai*. My dear friend and fellow former Peace Corps volunteer Sandi Younkin joined me on this mission, and together we survived the fierce heat of Thailand's April afternoons by collapsing into chairs in Chiang Mai's hyper-air-conditioned Black Mountain Cafe and swilling Thai iced coffee from enormous frosty mugs. Had they served this ice cream, we might be there still.

1½ cups milk	1 cup sugar
1½ cups heavy cream	3 egg yolks
¼ cup Thai coffee powder	

In a heavy saucepan, combine the milk and cream. Place over medium-high heat and bring to a boil. Quickly remove from the heat and stir in the coffee powder. Set aside to steep for 20 minutes.

Strain the cream through a fine-mesh sieve into a bowl to remove the coffee powder. Rinse out the saucepan to remove any grounds, return the strained coffee cream to the pan, whisk in half the sugar, and set aside.

Place the egg yolks in a medium bowl and, using a whisk or an electric mixer at medium speed, whisk in the remaining sugar, beating until the mixture is smooth, lightened in color, and as thick as softly whipped cream. Keep whisking the egg–sugar mixture as you pour about one-third of the warm coffee cream into the bowl, to heat the egg-sugar mixture gently and combine everything well.

Return the saucepan containing the remaining coffee cream to the stove over medium heat. Using a wooden spoon, stir constantly as you pour the egg–sugar mixture into the warm coffee cream. Stirring constantly in a figure-eight motion, cook the coffee cream until it is satiny and thickened and coats the back of a spoon, 2 to 3 minutes. The mixture should register 190 degrees F on a cooking thermometer; do not allow it to come to a boil. Pour into a bowl and set aside to cool to room temperature. (To cool it quickly, nestle the bowl into a bigger bowl about three-fourths full of ice.)

When the ice cream base has cooled to room temperature, cover and chill for several hours until very cold. Then freeze in an ice cream maker according to the manufacturer's directions.

MAKES ABOUT 1 PINT; SERVES 4.

NOTE • *Allow plenty of time to prepare the ice cream, since it needs to be heated and then chilled until very cold so that it will freeze well. If possible, make the base a day in advance, as it keeps well and will then be ready when you are. It is also ideal to return the frozen ice cream to the freezer to "ripen" and set for an hour or two before you serve it. Leftover ice cream may freeze solid after a day or more in the freezer. In this case, cut it into large chunks and process in a food processor fitted with the metal blade until smooth.*

༣ THAI TEA ICE CREAM ༣

If you love Thai iced tea as I do, you will love this ice cream, too. Soft and creamy, it has the intriguing flavor of Thai black tea laced with cinnamon and vanilla, as well as the trademark pumpkin color Thai tea fans adore.

1½ cups milk

1½ cups heavy cream

¼ cup Thai tea

1 cup sugar

3 egg yolks

In a heavy saucepan, combine the milk and cream. Place over medium–high heat and and bring to a boil. Quickly remove from the heat and stir in the Thai tea. Set aside to steep for 20 minutes.

Strain the cream through a sieve lined with a triple thickness of cheese-cloth or a clean kitchen towel into a bowl. (Whatever you use will take on a terra–cotta hue.) Rinse out the saucepan to remove any tea leaves, return the strained mixture to the pan, whisk in half the sugar, and set aside.

Place the egg yolks in a medium bowl and, using a whisk or an electric mixer at medium speed, whisk in the remaining sugar, beating until the mixture is smooth, lightened in color, and as thick as softly whipped cream. Keep whisking the egg–sugar mixture as you pour about one–third of the warm tea cream into the bowl, to heat the egg–sugar mixture gently and combine everything well.

Return the saucepan containing the remaining tea cream to the stove and over medium heat. Using a wooden spoon, stir constantly as you pour the egg–sugar mixture into the saucepan of warm tea cream. Stirring constantly in a figure–8 motion, cook the tea cream until it is satiny and thickened and coats the back of a spoon, 3 to 4 minutes. The mixture should register 190 degrees F on an instant–read thermometer; do not allow it to come to a boil. Pour into a bowl and set aside to cool to room temperature. (To cool it quickly, nestle the bowl into a bigger bowl about three–fourths full of ice.)

When the ice cream base has cooled to room temperature, cover and chill for several hours until very cold. Then freeze in an ice cream maker according to the manufacturer's directions.

MAKES ABOUT 1 PINT; SERVES 4.

✑ LEMONGRASS-GINGER SORBET ✑

Track down fresh lemongrass and make this even if you never use lemongrass in soups and curry pastes. It is fabulous, taking the incomparable essence of lemongrass from the savory side to the sweet. You can make this tangy celebration of Southeast Asian herbs even if you do not have an ice cream freezer. This sorbet needs only a food processor to transform it from syrup to icy perfection. Or you can make it into a wonderfully grainy confection called a granita, using that low-tech kitchen gadget, the fork.

4 stalks lemongrass
¼ cup thin strips peeled fresh ginger
(from about a 3-inch chunk)
1½ cups water

1 cup sugar
1 cup freshly squeezed lemon juice (about
5 lemons)

Cut away and discard any tough root portions from the lemongrass stalks, leaving a smooth, flat base just below the bulb. Trim away the tops, including any dried brown leaf portions; you should have handsome stalks about 6 inches long, including the bulbous base. Slice each stalk crosswise into thin rounds and place in a heavy saucepan along with the ginger, water, and sugar. Stir well and bring to a boil over medium heat. Adjust the heat to maintain a gentle boil and cook, stirring occasionally to help the sugar dissolve, for about 5 minutes. Remove from the heat and let steep for 10 minutes. Strain through a fine-mesh sieve into a bowl. Stir in the lemon juice.

Pour the sorbet base into 2 ice-cube trays and freeze until almost completely set but not rock hard, 2 to 4 hours. Remove from the freezer and turn into a food processor fitted with the metal blade. Process until creamy and uniformly combined. Transfer to an airtight container and return to the freezer to harden for at least 1 hour or overnight. Serve ice cold.

MAKES ABOUT 1 PINT; SERVES 4.

NOTE • *If the sorbet has become too hard when you are ready to serve it, simply break it into big chunks and reprocess it in the food processor.* ❖ *If you do not have a food processor, you can make a granita, which is a delicious icy version of ice cream made by a wonderfully low-tech, old-fashioned method. Pour the warm lemongrass-ginger base into a pie plate and* *place in the freezer until slushy but not frozen solid, about 30 minutes. Using a fork, reach into the freezer and quickly "rake" the granita to break it up and encourage it to form small ice crystals. Repeat this step every 30 minutes until the granita is uniformly frozen yet somewhat creamy, about 2 hours. Then freeze for at least 1 hour or overnight and serve ice cold.*

∾ WILD LIME LEAF SORBET ∾

Wild lime leaves are a treasure of the Southeast Asian kitchen. These shiny, emerald green ovals poke up from the branches of their thorny mother tree in chic pairs attached seamlessly end to end. Tear one and smell it to understand the pleasure Thai cooks take in having some on hand. Seldom eaten outright due to their toughness, they are tossed into soups, curries, and stir-frys for the incomparable explosion of delicate citrusy aroma and flavor they impart to a dish. If you have some, enjoy them in this wildly delicious sorbet, and if you have none, simply leave them out. If you omit the wild lime leaves and lemongrass, you will still have a lovely lime sorbet with fresh ginger. See note on page 183 on how to make a granita.

20 wild lime leaves
2 stalks lemongrass
1 piece fresh galanga or ginger, about 3
*   inches long, thinly sliced*

2 cups water
1 cup sugar
½ cup freshly squeezed lime juice

Using kitchen scissors or a sharp knife, cut the lime leaves crosswise into very thin strips. Cut away and discard any tough root portions from the lemongrass stalks, leaving a smooth, flat base just below the bulb. Trim away the tops, including any dried brown leaf portions; you should have handsome stalks about 6 inches long, including the bulbous base. Slice each stalk crosswise into thin rounds and place in a heavy saucepan along with the galanga or ginger, water, and sugar. Stir well and bring to a boil over medium heat. Adjust the heat to maintain a gentle boil and cook, stirring occasionally to help the sugar dissolve, for 5 minutes. Remove from the heat and let steep for 10 minutes. Strain through a fine-mesh sieve into a bowl. Stir in the lime juice.

Pour the sorbet base into 2 ice–cube trays and freeze until almost com–pletely set but not rock hard, 2 to 4 hours. Remove from the freezer and turn into a food processor fitted with the metal blade. Process until creamy and uniformly combined. Transfer to an airtight container and return to the freezer to harden for at least 1 hour or overnight. Serve ice cold.

MAKES ABOUT 1 PINT; SERVES 4.

NOTE · *You can substitute 5 pieces dried galanga in place of the fresh galanga or ginger.*
❖ *When I was a child, lime sherbet was my favorite ice cream, and I still love its cool, green color, even though I now know the truth. Limes create lots of flavor but no color, so the folks at the ice cream factory used green food coloring to do the job. If you are nostalgic for that look, add 1 or 2 drops green food coloring to the sorbet base along with the lime juice.*

✑ SPEEDY FROZEN FRUIT SORBET ✑

Frozen fruit is the secret of this quick treat, which is made in a food processor. Frozen mangoes are particularly good, but you can also use frozen peaches, cherries, or strawberries with great results, so check the freezer case at your supermarket to see what your options are. If you have an abundance of ripe mangoes, strawberries, or peaches, simply peel, stem, and chop 1 pound's worth into big chunks and freeze them first. Then use this frozen fruit as directed in the recipe. Taste the sorbet before you freeze it, adding a little extra sugar and lemon juice as needed to get the flavor just right.

1 bag (1 pound) frozen mangoes, peaches,
  strawberries, or cherries
¼ cup sugar, or as needed

1 tablespoons freshly squeezed lemon
  juice, or as needed
1 can (12 ounces) lemon-lime soda

Place the still-frozen fruit in a food processor fitted with the metal blade. Process until finely chopped. If the fruit is very hard, let it thaw slightly before processing, about 5 minutes.

Stop the machine and add the ¼ cup sugar and the lemon juice. Process again, adding the soda through the feed tube. Continue processing until creamy and well combined. Do not overprocess or the sorbet will melt. Taste and adjust with the lemon juice and sugar. Quickly transfer to an airtight container and freeze for 1 to 2 hours. If it freezes longer, you may need to break the sorbet into chunks and process again until soft enough to eat.

MAKES ABOUT 1 PINT; SERVES 4.

NOTE • *Peaches and strawberries will need more sugar and lemon juice than mangoes. Add a tablespoon or two of each until you have a balance you like, up to a total of ½ cup sugar and 3 tablespoons lemon juice.*

ᆬ COCONUT RICE PUDDING ᆬ

Thais cook and eat rice in almost every form, but the traditional rice pudding I adore is a Western creation. Deliciously creamy and rich, my Thai–inspired version of this tempting comfort–food classic has a tropical twist, with coconut milk in the custard and a confetti of toasted coconut on top. Almost any type of rice can be used, including sticky rice and jasmine rice. You can enjoy the pudding as is, serve it with chunks of fresh ripe pineapple or mango, or pair it with Orange Salad in Ginger Syrup (page 70). Vegans can omit the egg yolks and substitute soy milk for the dairy milk.

1 cup long-grain sticky rice or jasmine rice

3 cups unsweetened coconut milk

5 cups milk

¾ cup sugar

¾ teaspoon salt

2 egg yolks

1 teaspoon vanilla extract

1 cup sweetened shredded dried coconut

¼ cup Toasted Coconut (page 217)

In a large, heavy saucepan, combine the rice, coconut milk, milk, sugar, and salt and stir well. Place over medium–high heat and bring to a boil, stirring often and well. Reduce the heat to medium, adjusting it to maintain a gentle boil without burning, and cook, stirring often, until the rice is tender and the pudding thickens, about 25 minutes.

Remove from the heat. Combine the egg yolks and vanilla in a small bowl and stir well. Slowly stir the yolk mixture into the pudding to combine well, then add the 1 cup coconut. Return the pan to the stove and cook over medium heat until the pudding is smooth and well combined, 3 to 4 minutes.

Remove from the heat and pour into a medium bowl or gratin dish or an oval baking pan. Sprinkle with the Toasted Coconut. Serve warm or at room temperature, or cover and chill until shortly before serving time and serve cold.

SERVES 6 TO 8.

NOTE • *If you want to prepare the pudding in advance and serve it warm, reheat it gently in a warm oven or a microwave.*

✑ THAI ICED COFFEE ✑

Dark, rich, and sweet, with an earthy note created by the addition of roasted corn and roasted sesame seeds to the coffee, Thai coffee powder is a Chinese legacy. Imported from China and packed in 1-pound cellophane packages, it is widely available in Asian grocery stores. The label may read "Thai coffee powder" or "*oliang,*" the latter a Chinese dialect name for the flavored coffee powder as well as the beverage when it is served cold and sweetened but without milk. The Thai version, with a luxurious crown of evaporated milk cascading into the dark iced brew, is extraordinary. The electric coffee maker does a great job on Thai iced coffee, so I have given you two methods.

Electric Drip Coffee Maker Method:

¼ cup Thai coffee powder
¾ cup sugar
Ice, preferably crushed

1 to 1½ cups evaporated milk or
    half-and-half

Place a paper filter in the basket of an electric drip coffee maker, add the Thai coffee, and fit the basket into place on the coffee maker. Fill the coffee pot with water up to the 8-cup mark and pour it into the coffee maker as directed. This will be about 6 cups of water. Turn the coffee maker on and let the Thai coffee brew.

When the brewing cycle is completed, add the sugar to the coffee and stir well to dissolve it completely. Transfer to a serving pitcher and set aside to cool to room temperature. Refrigerate until serving time, or for up to 1 week.

To serve, fill tall glasses with ice, add coffee almost to the top of each glass, and carefully float about ¼ cup evaporated milk or half-and-half on top of each glass. Serve at once.

Regular Method:

4 cups water
¼ cup Thai coffee powder
¾ cup sugar, or as needed

Ice, preferably crushed
1 to 1½ cups evaporated milk or
    half-and-half

In a medium saucepan over high heat, bring the water to a rolling boil. Add the coffee powder and stir gently to moisten the grounds fully. Reduce the heat and simmer gently for 3 minutes. Remove from the heat, add ¾ cup sugar, and stir well to dissolve. Taste and add more sugar if needed. Set aside and let cool to room temperature.

Strain the coffee through a coffee filter basket or a fine-mesh sieve into a pitcher and refrigerate until serving time, or for up to 1 week.

To serve, fill tall glasses with ice, add coffee almost to the top of each glass, and carefully float about ¼ cup evaporated milk or half-and-half on top of each glass. Serve at once.

EACH METHOD SERVES 6 TO 8.

NOTE • *Thais always serve this iced coffee very sweet, but you can adjust the amount of sugar to suit your taste. ❖ Crushed ice is ideal for Thai iced coffee because it enhances the pleasing visual effect of a glass when the milk is added. Crushed ice captures the dollop of milk and holds most of it aloft as tendrils of it drift down into the dark coffee in mesmerizing swirls. Ice cubes do a good job, too. ❖ Evaporated milk is the traditional choice, since fresh dairy products are a luxury in Thailand, but half-and-half also works well.*

✄ THAI ICED TEA ✄

There is nothing in the world quite like Thai iced tea. Thai tea is simply finely chopped black tea that is spiced with cinnamon, vanilla, star anise, and a bit of food coloring to give it that trademark cinnamon–rose hue. While it is not to everyone's liking, I adore it and feel lucky that it is remarkably simple to make. The only challenge is securing the tea itself, which can be ordered by mail (page 232) if you do not live near an Asian market. The powdery leaves keep for months; buy a good supply so that you can keep a pitcher of tea on hand in your refrigerator at all times. While it is traditionally sweetened in advance with sugar and served with a dollop of evaporated milk, you can enjoy it hot or iced with honey and lemon. The electric coffee maker does a great job on Thai iced tea, so I have given you two methods for making it. See the note accompanying Thai Iced Coffee (page 189); it applies to tea as well.

Electric Drip Coffee Maker Method:

½ cup Thai tea

¾ cup sugar

Ice, preferably crushed

1½ cups evaporated milk or half-and-half

Place a paper filter in the basket of an electric drip coffee maker, add the tea, and fit the basket into place on the coffee maker. Fill the coffee pot with water up to the 8–cup mark and pour it into the coffee maker as directed. This will be about 6 cups of water. Turn the coffee maker on and let the tea brew.

When the brewing cycle is completed, add the sugar to the tea and stir well to dissolve it completely. Transfer to a serving pitcher and set aside to cool to room temperature. The tea will be a brilliant orange. Refrigerate until serving time, or for up to 1 week.

To serve, fill tall glasses with ice, add tea almost to the top of each glass, and carefully float about ¼ cup evaporated milk or half-and-half on top of each glass. Serve at once.

Regular Method:

4 cups water

1 cup Thai tea

¾ cup sugar, or as needed

Ice, preferably crushed

1½ cups evaporated milk or half-and-half

In a medium saucepan over high heat, bring the water to a rolling boil. Add the tea and stir gently to moisten the leaves fully. Reduce the heat and simmer gently for 1 minute. Remove from the heat, add ¾ cup sugar, and stir well to dissolve. Taste and add more sugar if needed. Set aside and let cool to room temperature. The tea will be a brilliant orange.

Strain the tea through a coffee filter basket or a fine-mesh strainer into a pitcher and refrigerate until serving time, or for up to 1 week.

To serve, fill tall glasses with ice, add tea almost to the top of each glass, and carefully float about ¼ cup evaporated milk or half-and-half on top of each glass. Serve at once.

EACH METHOD SERVES 6 TO 8.

ℰᔕ MAENGLUK BASIL SEED DRINK WITH FRESH FRUIT AND HONEY ℰᔕ

Cooling beverages similar to this one are popular throughout Southeast Asia, having spread from southern China down through Vietnam, Thailand, and beyond. You will find tiny black *maengluk* basil seeds sold in small cellophane bags at Asian markets, possibly labeled "sweet basil" or with the Vietnamese name, *hot e*. Soaking the *maengluk* basil seeds creates an amazing transformation you must see to believe. Provide a spoon when you serve this in tall glasses. I like to pour it over ice cubes, but if you chill it well, you can serve it without them, which is the traditional way.

3 cups water
3 tablespoons honey
3 tablespoons palm sugar or brown sugar
1 tablespoon maengluk *basil seeds*

2 cups ripe bananas, strawberries, and
pineapple, cut into chunks
Ice cubes

In a saucepan, combine the water, honey, and sugar. Place over medium heat and stir well only until the honey and sugar dissolve completely. Remove from the heat and set aside to cool to room temperature.

Stir in the basil seeds, and watch in astonishment as they swell from tiny black sesame seedlike bits into countless little blue–gray balloons, with a gelatinlike coating enclosing each seed. Chill until very cold.

When you are ready to serve, fill 4 to 6 tall glasses halfway with ice cubes. Add a few chunks of banana, strawberries, and pineapple to each glass. Fill to the top with the sweet basil seed drink and serve at once with spoons.

SERVES 4 TO 6.

✌ FRESH LEMONGRASS LEMONADE ✌

I first enjoyed this pleasing Thai herbal version in the lovely northern city of Chiang Mai, seated on the patio of a restaurant called *Takrai*. *Takrai* means "lemongrass" in the central Thai dialect, and the restaurant was graced with numerous large pots of its namesake herb, placed among the outdoor tables as a portable and accessible herb garden. To find the long, slender leaves for this recipe, you will need to grow your own supply (page 214), as lemongrass is invariably sold with its willowy leaves trimmed away. If that is not possible, use about 2 cups finely chopped lemongrass stalks for a tasty version with a milder flavor and color.

3 ¼ cups cold water
¼ cup sugar

2 cups coarsely chopped fresh lemongrass, preferably the soft, grassy tops from 4 or 5 stalks
Ice cubes

In a small, heavy saucepan, combine ¼ cup of the water with the sugar and bring to a gentle boil over medium heat. Stir to dissolve the sugar and remove from the heat.

Combine the remaining 3 cups water with the chopped lemongrass leaves in the jar of a blender and add the warm sugar syrup. Blend at high speed until the water is intensely green and the lemongrass leaves are reduced to a fine, aromatic mush, 1 to 2 minutes. Stop once or twice to scrape down the sides of the container and grind the lemongrass evenly. Strain through a fine-mesh sieve into a pitcher, discarding the residue in the sieve.

Cool and then chill for up to 1 day. To serve, fill tall glasses with ice cubes and fill with the lemongrass drink. Serve at once.

SERVES 4.

8

·

BASIC RECIPES

BASIC RECIPES

✐ In this chapter are recipes for preparations you will need to cook the dishes in this book. Look here for instruction on making curry pastes and coconut milk from scratch, as well as for Roasted Rice Powder, Toasted Coconut, and other ingredients called for throughout the book. You will also find a fantastic array of sauces, including Roasted Chili Paste, Tangy Tamarind Sauce, and Sweet and Hot Garlic Sauce. In some cases you can purchase a shortcut, such as canned or frozen unsweetened coconut milk and chili garlic sauce. In other cases you will need to rely on these basic recipes, or improvise a substitute on your own.

✐ Vegetarian cooks have an extra incentive for taking the time to make their curry pastes from scratch, since shrimp paste, known in Thailand as *gapi*, is a basic ingredient in traditional Southeast Asian curry pastes and is included in almost all the commercial pastes imported from Thailand or made in the Thai manner. Homemade curry paste offers a great return on the time and energy you spend transforming my recipes into jars of flavor-filled curry paste standing by in your kitchen. You will need such uncommon ingredients as lemongrass, galanga, wild lime peel, and cilantro roots, although you can make a good adapted version by substituting widely available items for these Asian treasures. You must chop it all and pound or grind it into a paste, which takes time and elbow grease, whether you use a blender, food processor, or Thai-style mortar and pestle. Although most of the commercial curry pastes are of good quality, the fruit of your labors in grinding your own from scratch will be worlds better than anything you can buy.

✐ Thai curry pastes call for lemongrass, galanga, wild lime peel, and wild lime leaves, which have a sturdy, often fibrous texture that is difficult to chew. For this reason, Thai cooks add them to soups and stews in large pieces to infuse their flavor and aroma into the food. These pieces may be fished out or left in a dish, where they are clearly not to be eaten. Sometimes these herbs are minced or very thinly sliced before they are added to a dish. For curry paste, they are ground beyond recognition. A large food processor chops curry paste ingredients into bits that are small but still unpleasant to eat. If you prefer to use a large food processor, check the texture of the finished paste, and if it is still too coarse, consider finishing off the batch of curry paste with a whirl in the blender. If you add water to help with grinding, your paste will be softer and moister, and tend to separate a little as it stands. Give it a stir before you use it.

✌ If you make your own curry pastes, you will benefit from the fact that they keep well in the refrigerator or freezer, and have many uses beyond the basic Thai curry made with coconut milk. Consider making several pastes at once, since the basic ingredients are the same, with variations only in the type of chili and inclusion of certain spices. Even more important, take the authentic Thai step of recruiting help in the form of extra hands and good company to lighten the burden of cooking alone. In exchange for a portion of the curry paste or a curry feast, you will probably have a flock of volunteers.

✑ RED CURRY PASTE ✑

Red curry paste takes its name from the dried red chilies peppers that set it on fire. Thais use hot chilies known collectively as *prik haeng*, which simply means "dried chilies." You can find dried red chilies in cellophane bags and sometimes loose in Asian markets. I often use the chilies sold in many supermarkets along-side ingredients for cooking Mexican food. *Chiles de árbol* or *chiles japones* will work nicely in this recipe. You can also experiment with a combination of large and small dried red chilies, keeping in mind that the smaller chilies are the hottest. For tips on making the paste, see the chapter introduction on page 196.

20 dried red finger-length chilies such as chiles de árbol or chiles japones
1 tablespoon whole coriander seeds
1 teaspoon whole cumin seeds
10 white or black peppercorns or 1 teaspoon freshly ground pepper
3 stalks lemongrass
¼ cup coarsely chopped fresh cilantro roots, or leaves and stems

¼ cup coarsely chopped shallots
2 tablespoons coarsely chopped garlic (8 to 12 cloves)
1 tablespoon coarsely chopped peeled fresh galanga or fresh ginger
1 teaspoon finely minced fresh wild lime peel or domestic lime peel
1 teaspoon salt

Stem the chilies and shake out and discard a lot of the seeds. Break into large pieces. Place the chilies in a small bowl, add warm water to cover, and set aside to soften for about 20 minutes.

In a small skillet over medium heat, dry-fry the coriander seeds until they darken a shade or two, shaking the pan or stirring often, 2 to 3 minutes. Tip out onto a saucer. Toast the cumin seeds in the same way, until they darken and release their rich aroma, 1 to 2 minutes. Add to the saucer along with the peppercorns and then grind the three spices to a fine powder in a mini processor or a Thai-style mortar. Set aside. You can substitute the same amount of ground spices, dry-frying the ground coriander and cumin together for a minute or two, stirring often to prevent burning, and then combining them with the ground pepper.

To prepare the lemongrass, trim away and discard any root section below the bulb base, and cut away the top portion, leaving a stalk about 6 inches long, including the base. Remove any dried, wilted, and yellowed leaves. Finely chop the stalk.

Drain the chilies and combine them with the lemongrass, the ground toasted spices, and the remaining ingredients in a blender or mini processor. Grind everything to a fairly smooth purée, stopping often to scrape down the sides and adding a few tablespoons of water as needed to move the blades. Transfer to a jar, seal airtight, and store at room temperature for up to 1 day, or refrigerate for up to 1 month.

MAKES ABOUT 1 CUP.

ꙮ GREEN CURRY PASTE ꙮ

Green curry paste takes its name from the vibrant color of the fresh hot chili peppers from which it is made, rather than from the color of the finished paste and curry, which are an earthy brown with a greenish tinge. I like the idea of green curry actually being green, so I sometimes grind in a half cup or so of fresh cilantro leaves or even Italian parsley, to give it a burst of emerald color. Thais make this with the petite, pointy chili peppers called *prik kii-noo*, or Thai bird chilies. Available in Asian markets, they are among the world's hottest peppers. I like to use chopped fresh serranos or jalapeños, since they are easy to come by and plenty hot for a fiery curry paste. For tips on making the paste, see the chapter introduction on page 196.

5 fresh green serrano chilies, 4 fresh green jalapeño chilies, or 10 fresh green Thai bird chilies
1 tablespoon whole coriander seeds
1 teaspoon whole cumin seeds
5 white or black peppercorns or ½ teaspoon freshly ground pepper
3 stalks lemongrass
¼ cup coarsely chopped fresh cilantro roots, or leaves and stems

¼ cup coarsely chopped shallots
2 tablespoons coarsely chopped garlic (8 to 12 cloves)
1 tablespoon coarsely chopped peeled fresh galanga or ginger
1 teaspoon finely minced fresh wild lime peel or domestic lime peel
1 teaspoon salt

Stem the chilies, chop them coarsely, and set aside. In a small skillet over medium heat, dry-fry the coriander seeds until they darken a shade or two, shaking the pan or stirring often, 2 to 3 minutes. Tip out onto a saucer. Toast the cumin seeds in the same way, until they darken and release their rich aroma, 1 to 2 minutes. Add to the saucer along with the peppercorns and then grind the three spices to a fine powder in a mini processor or a Thai-style mortar. Set aside. You can substitute the same amount of ground spices, dry-frying the ground coriander and cumin together for a minute or two, stirring often to prevent burning, and then combining them with the ground pepper.

To prepare the lemongrass, trim away and discard any root section below the bulb base, and cut away the top portion, leaving a stalk about 6 inches long, including the base. Remove any dried, wilted, and yellowed leaves. Finely chop the stalk.

Combine the lemongrass, the chopped chilies, and the ground toasted spices with the remaining ingredients in a blender or mini processor and grind them to a fairly smooth purée, stopping often to scrape down the sides and adding a few tablespoons of water as needed to move the blades. Transfer to a jar, seal airtight, and store at room temperature for up to 1 day, or refrigerate for up to 1 month.

MAKES ABOUT 1 CUP.

❦ YELLOW CURRY PASTE ❦

Yellow curry paste is red curry paste with a little less heat and the addition of *pong kah-ree,* which is the standard curry powder we know in the West. It also includes extra turmeric, ginger's most colorful cousin and a regular component of curry powder. Like King Midas, turmeric turns everything it touches gold. Since gold is an auspicious color throughout Asia, turmeric is often used to transform plain food into an inviting dish with a handsome golden sheen. For tips on making the paste, see the chapter introduction on page 196.

15 dried red finger-length chilies such as chiles de árbol or chiles japones

1 tablespoon whole coriander seeds

1 teaspoon whole cumin seeds

10 white or black peppercorns or 1 teaspoon freshly ground pepper

3 stalks lemongrass

¼ cup coarsely chopped fresh cilantro roots, or leaves and stems

¼ cup coarsely chopped shallots

2 tablespoons coarsely chopped garlic (8 to 12 cloves)

1 tablespoon coarsely chopped peeled fresh galanga or fresh ginger

1 teaspoon finely minced fresh wild lime peel or domestic lime peel

1 tablespoon curry powder

1 teaspoon ground turmeric

1 teaspoon salt

Stem the chilies and shake out and discard a lot of the seeds. Break into large pieces. Place the chilies in a small bowl, add warm water to cover, and set aside to soften for about 20 minutes.

In a small skillet over medium heat, dry-fry the coriander seeds until they darken a shade or two, shaking the pan or stirring often, 2 to 3 minutes. Tip out onto a saucer. Toast the cumin seeds in the same way, until they darken and release their rich aroma, 1 to 2 minutes. Add to the saucer along with the peppercorns and then grind the three spices to a fine powder in a mini processor or a Thai-style mortar. Set aside. You can substitute the same amount of ground spices, dry-frying the ground coriander and cumin together for a minute or two, stirring often to prevent burning, and then combining them with the ground pepper.

To prepare the lemongrass, trim away and discard any root section below the bulb base, and cut away the top portion, leaving a stalk about 6 inches long, including the base. Remove any dried, wilted, and yellowed leaves. Finely chop the stalk.

Drain the chilies and combine them with the lemongrass, the ground toasted spices, and the remaining ingredients in a blender or mini processor. Grind everything to a fairly smooth purée, stopping often to scrape down the sides and adding a few tablespoons of water as needed to move the blades. Transfer to a jar, seal airtight, and store at room temperature for up to 1 day, or refrigerate for up to 1 month.

MAKES ABOUT 1 CUP.

∾ MUSSAMUN CURRY PASTE ∾

Mussamun means "Muslim style," and this curry paste is used for making a popular curry that originated in the provinces of southern Thailand where many Thais follow the teachings of Islam. This classic variation on red curry paste includes heavenly spices such as cinnamon, cardamom, nutmeg, and cloves. The finished curry is a luscious, spicy stew of coconut milk seasoned with this curry paste and studded with peanuts, cinnamon sticks, and cardamom pods. For tips on making the paste, see the chapter introduction on page 196.

15 dried red finger-length chilies such as chiles de árbol *or* chiles japones

1 tablespoon whole coriander seeds

1 teaspoon whole cumin seeds

10 white or black peppercorns *or* 1 teaspoon freshly ground pepper

3 stalks lemongrass

¼ cup coarsely chopped fresh cilantro roots, or leaves and stems

¼ cup coarsely chopped shallots

2 tablespoons coarsely chopped garlic (8 to 12 cloves)

1 tablespoon coarsely chopped peeled fresh galanga or fresh ginger

1 teaspoon finely minced fresh wild lime peel or domestic lime peel

1 teaspoon ground cinnamon

1 teaspoon ground cloves

1 teaspoon ground nutmeg

1 teaspoon ground cardamom

1 teaspoon salt

Stem the chilies and shake out and discard a lot of the seeds. Break into large pieces. Place the chilies in a small bowl, add warm water to cover, and set aside to soften for about 20 minutes.

In a small skillet over medium heat, dry-fry the coriander seeds until they darken a shade or two, shaking the pan or stirring often, 2 to 3 minutes. Tip out onto a saucer. Toast the cumin seeds in the same way, until they darken and release their rich aroma, 1 to 2 minutes. Add to the saucer along with the peppercorns and then grind the three spices to a fine powder in a mini processor or a Thai-style mortar. Set aside. You can substitute the same amount of ground spices, dry-frying the ground coriander and cumin together for a minute or two, stirring often to prevent burning, and then combining them with the ground pepper.

To prepare the lemongrass, trim away and discard any root section below the bulb base, and cut away the top portion, leaving a stalk about 6 inches long, including the base. Remove any dried, wilted, and yellowed leaves. Finely chop the stalk.

Drain the chilies and combine them with the lemongrass, the ground toasted spices, and the remaining ingredients in a blender or mini processor. Grind everything to a fairly smooth purée, stopping often to scrape down the sides and adding a few tablespoons of water as needed to move the blades. Transfer to a jar, seal airtight, and store at room temperature for up to 1 day, or refrigerate for up to 1 month.

MAKES ABOUT 1 CUP.

❧ QUICK-AND-SIMPLE CURRY PASTE ❧

Here is my stripped down version of Thai curry paste, using ingredients available in many supermarkets. Make it in a flash and then turn a few spoonfuls of your freshly made paste into tonight's pot of curry. This will work in any recipe calling for a Thai-style paste.

5 fresh serrano chilies, 3 fresh green jalapeño chilies, or 7 long, slender dried red chilies
1 cup coarsely chopped cilantro leaves and stems
½ cup chopped yellow onion
⅓ cup peeled and coarsely chopped fresh ginger

¼ cup chopped garlic (15 to 20 cloves)
1 tablespoon grated lime zest
1 tablespoon ground coriander
1 teaspoon ground cumin
1 teaspoon freshly ground pepper
1 teaspoon salt

Stem the chilies and discard some of the seeds. Chop the fresh chilies coarsely. Soak the dried chilies in hot water to cover for about 10 minutes.

Drain the dried chilies, if using. Combine all the ingredients in a blender or mini processor and grind to a fine, fairly smooth purée, stopping often to scrape down the sides and adding a few tablespoons of water as needed to move the blades. Transfer to a jar, seal airtight, and keep in the refrigerator for up to 2 weeks.

MAKES ABOUT 1 CUP.

✂ EVERYDAY VEGETABLE STOCK ✂

Make up a batch of this simple stock and keep it on hand for Thai soups or any recipe calling for vegetable stock. You can add other vegetables if you like. It is best to avoid sweet peppers, eggplant, celery leaves, and the members of the cabbage family such as broccoli, cauliflower, and kale, as these vegetables do not take well to long simmering. If you have freezer space, make a double batch so that you will have a half gallon or so on hand.

4 large carrots (about 1 pound)	*1 head garlic*
6 celery stalks without leaves	*2½ quarts water*
2 yellow onions	*1 tablespoon soy sauce*
1 bunch fresh parsley	*½ teaspoon salt*

Coarsely chop the carrots, celery, onions, and parsley and combine them in a large stockpot. Cut the garlic head in half crosswise to expose its cloves and add it to the stockpot along with the water. Bring to a rolling boil over medium heat. Boil for about 5 minutes as you skim away and discard any scum that rises to the top. Reduce the heat to maintain a gentle boil and simmer, uncovered, for 1½ hours, stirring occasionally.

Remove from the heat and strain through a fine–mesh sieve into a clean container. Stir in the soy sauce and salt. Let cool to room temperature, cover, and refrigerate for up to 4 days.

MAKES ABOUT 5 CUPS.

NOTE • *You can freeze this stock in airtight containers for 2 months. Freeze in 1- or 2-cup portions so that you can defrost only the amount you need for a given recipe. Freeze some in ice cube trays, too, and then transfer to a lock-top bag. You will then have tablespoon-sized portions available as well.*

✳ ASIAN VEGETABLE STOCK ✳

Here is a vegetable stock fortified with the deep, earthy flavor of dried Chinese mushrooms and a pleasing jolt of fresh ginger. You can use it for Thai vegetarian dishes or for any other recipe calling for vegetable stock. Use other vegetables if you like, but avoid sweet peppers, eggplant, celery leaves, and members of the cabbage family such as broccoli, cauliflower, and kale, as these do not take well to long simmering. For information on freezing this stock, see note on page 204.

4 large carrots (about 1 pound)
6 celery stalks without leaves
2 yellow onions, or 10 shallots
½ bunch fresh cilantro
1 bunch green onions
3 thumb-sized hunks fresh ginger

2 heads garlic
5 dried shiitake mushrooms or Chinese
*   mushrooms*
2½ quarts water
1 tablespoon soy sauce
1 teaspoon salt

Coarsely chop the carrots, celery, onions or shallots, cilantro, and green onions and combine them in a large stockpot. Cut the garlic heads in half crosswise to expose their cloves, and slice the ginger crosswise into coins. Add to the stockpot along with the dried mushrooms and the water. Bring to a rolling boil over medium heat. Boil for about 5 minutes as you skim away and discard any scum that rises to the top. Reduce the heat to maintain a gentle boil and simmer, uncovered, for 1½ hours, stirring occasionally.

Remove from the heat and strain through a fine-mesh sieve into a clean container. Stir in the soy sauce and salt. Let cool to room temperature, cover, and refrigerate for up to 4 days.

Makes 7 to 8 cups.

✦ MUSHROOM MINCE ✦

You will find this delicious mixture used in recipes throughout this book whenever a rich, garlicky filling is needed. I based it on the classic French mushroom concoction called *duxelles*, fortifying it with tofu and revving up the flavors with garlic, cilantro, and Asian seasonings. It keeps well for 2 days in the refrigerator and freezes beautifully for up to 1 month. Double the recipe if you like, and if you have any left over, enjoy it as you would Italian pesto.

2 tablespoons coarsely chopped garlic (8 to 12 cloves)
1 tablespoon coarsely chopped cilantro root, or cilantro stems and leaves
½ teaspoon freshly ground pepper
8 ounces fresh button mushrooms, chopped
4 ounces firm tofu

3 tablespoons vegetable oil
2 tablespoons minced shallots
1 tablespoon palm sugar or brown sugar
1 tablespoon water
2 teaspoons regular soy sauce
½ teaspoon dark soy sauce
½ teaspoon salt

In a mini processor, combine the garlic, cilantro, and pepper and grind to a fairly smooth paste. Set aside. (Or combine the garlic and cilantro in a Thai-style mortar along with ¼ teaspoon whole peppercorns instead of ground pepper. Pound and grind to a fairly smooth paste.)

Chop the mushrooms until they are reduced to a crumbly pile and set aside. Chop the tofu into tiny cubes and set aside as well.

In a skillet over medium heat, warm 2 tablespoons of the oil until a bit of mushroom added to the pan sizzles at once, about 1 minute. Add the garlic-cilantro paste and toss until fragrant and shiny, 2 to 3 minutes.

Add the mushrooms and cook, tossing often, for 5 to 7 minutes. The mushrooms will soften, release their liquid, and brown as they cook. When the liquid has cooked away and mushrooms are shiny and tender, scrape them to the sides of the pan and add the remaining 1 tablespoon oil to the center. Add the tofu and toss until thoroughly combined with the mushrooms and heated through, about 1 minute. Add the sugar, water, both soy sauces, and salt and cook, tossing often, until the mixture is moist, evenly colored, and well combined, 2 to 3 minutes. Remove from the heat, let cool to room temperature, and refrigerate in a tightly covered container until needed.

MAKES ABOUT 1 CUP.

ℰℬ WHEATBALLS ℰℬ

This recipe is my adaptation of Madhur Jaffrey's recipe for wheat gluten balls, which appears in her classic cookbook, *The Art of Vegetarian Cooking*. Wheatballs are terrific little fritters that seem born to enhance Thai stir-frys and curries. You can use almost any wheat flour, keeping in mind that the greater the gluten content, the easier your task of extracting the gluten and the more pleasing your results will be. Gluten flour or bread flour is best for creating chewy-tender little pillows that take on curry flavors with delicious ease. Whole-wheat flour works well and browns beautifully, although like whole-wheat bread, its balls are sturdier and chewier than those made with high-gluten white flour. All-purpose flour is acceptable, but cake flour is too delicate for this task, and flours made from anything other than wheat will not work at all. Plan ahead, as the dough needs to soak overnight before you squeeze out the starch and cook it up into balls.

3 cups flour (see introduction)   *1 cup water*
1 teaspoon salt   *Vegetable oil for deep-frying*

In a large bowl, combine the flour and salt and mix well. Pour the water over the flour and use your hands to combine everything together into a soft dough that pulls cleanly away from the sides of the bowl and is not sticky. Transfer to a lightly floured board and knead for about 10 minutes. Cover with a clean kitchen towel and set aside to rest for about 1 hour.

Knead the dough again for about 1 minute, and then place it in a small, deep bowl and add cold water to cover. Let stand 6 to 8 hours or for up to overnight.

Drain off the water and place the bowl in the sink. Add enough fresh water to cover the dough and work it as you would a sponge, squeezing and wringing it to extract starch and leave behind a rubbery, squishy, slippery, fibrous mass of gluten. Squeeze the dough through 3 batches of water, which will turn milk white with the starch, and then place the ball of gluten in a strainer to rest and drain for about 10 minutes.

Divide the squishy dough into 1-inch lumps and set them aside on a tray. Line a baking sheet with paper towels and place near the stove along with a long-handled Asian-style wire strainer or 2 metal slotted spoons. Fill a small bowl with water to use for keeping your fingers moist while you transfer the sticky dough from the tray to the skillet.

Pour oil into a wok or large, deep skillet to a depth of 3 inches. Place over medium heat until the oil is hot but not smoking. The oil is ready when a bit of dough dropped into it sizzles at once. (The oil should register 325 to 350 degrees F on a cooking thermometer.) Moisten your fingers and then carefully add 5 to 7 balls to the oil. Let them cook, gently stirring to keep them separate and to keep tiny waves of oil flowing over them, for about 3 minutes, turning at least once to brown them evenly. The balls will swell, blister, puff up and out, and begin to darken. When ready, they will be appealingly asymmetrical fritters, crusty and golden brown. Scoop out these little clouds, hold them briefly over the oil to drain, and then transfer them to the towel-lined baking sheet to drain and cool. Continue until all the dough is cooked.

When the balls are cool, use them in recipes as directed, or seal airtight and refrigerate for 3 days, or freeze for about 1 month. Use frozen balls in recipes directly from the freezer; do not thaw first.

Makes about 48 wheatballs.

NOTE • *You will need a gallon or so of clean water in which to rinse the dough, so consider pouring it off into a bucket and anointing your garden with this starchy white water while your gluten relaxes in the strainer.* ❖ *You can bake the wheatballs, rather than fry them. Arrange on a lightly greased baking sheet and bake at 375 degrees F for 15 to 20 minutes, turning once early on to discourage sticking and encourage browning. Use and store as directed for fried wheatballs. I find them inferior to fried ones, however, because they puff less, brown unevenly, and have a tough, hard texture.* ❖ *Check the Asian market or mail-order sources (page 232) for an array of wheat gluten products, from soft wheatballs packed in seasoned oil or broth, to mock duck and other imitation meat products molded into particular shapes and textures, to firm hunks of wheat gluten that you can cut into any shape you desire. You will also find wheat gluten in health food stores, often in the refrigerator case alongside tofu and tempeh.*

‿ FRESH COCONUTS FOR COCONUT MILK AND GRATED COCONUT ‿

This is trouble, in terms of the physical effort you spend to open and grate the coconut and the mess it leaves in its wake. Most days I avail myself of the ease of unsweetened coconut milk in canned or frozen form. Both work well and save a tremendous amount of time and work, and I would seldom enjoy coconut milk if I had to make it from scratch every time. But there is something that I love about fresh coconut, and there are times when it seems like another job that gives back more than takes away. Here is how to handle a coconut, should you be so inspired.

Cracking the coconut: Select a dry, brown hairy coconut heavy with juice that sloshes when you shake the nut. Place it on a baking sheet on a counter or a table, and have a hammer handy. If possible, do this outside so that the inevitable mess of hairy fibers and bits of shell will be a gift to Mother Earth and not a clean-up job for you. Examine the coconut and note its teardrop shape, with three eyes on the rounded bottom of the drop. Note also the faint ridges that run from between this trio of eyes all the way up the coconut, intersecting at the pointed tip. Picture the coconut as a hairy little globe, with a pointy north pole and a triple-eyed south pole, and an equator encircling its fattest part.

Nestle the coconut in your palm with the pointed tip aiming away from you and the three eyes facing toward your tummy. Aim your hammer at the point on the coconut's equator closest to you and strike a mighty blow. Continue giving it whacks around the equator, striking on one of the three aforementioned ridge lines whenever possible, as these are weak points where cracking may occur first.

Listen for a change in the sounds your mighty blows create, and you will know when you have struck home by a deep, ringing thud as the first crack opens. Keep striking until the clear juice gushes out and the coconut shell breaks open or can be separated into two or more pieces. Do not despair if you do not get results at once. It can take one or two blows or several trips around the nut, depending on the particular coconut and your aim and confidence. Practice helps, so do it often if you want to become handy with this everyday Asian task. Thais discard the clear juice from inside the coconut, but

I like to strain it well through a fine-mesh sieve or a coffee filter and use it in cooking sweets or add it to juice drinks.

Once you have opened the coconut, use the hammer to break it into pieces smaller than the palm of your hand. Using a blunt table knife, pry the thick white meat away from the hard, dark brown hairy outer shell; discard the hard shells and retain the chunks of white meat, which have a thin brown skin on the side that was attached to the shell. You can leave this on or peel it off. Left on, it will give the coconut milk a pleasant cream color; peeling it will yield pure white milk. Thais peel it if they feel fancy and leave it if they do not, as taste is not affected either way. To peel it, you need either a special sturdy peeler made for this purpose and found in some Asian markets. Or you can use a paring knife or chef's knife, working carefully on the cutting board.

Grating the coconut: To grate the meat for coconut milk, fit a large food processor with the metal blade. Chop the coconut meat into ½-inch chunks. With the machine running, drop the coconut chunks through the large feed tube onto the blade, stopping to scrape down the sides once or twice, until you have a workbowl full of soft, moist grated coconut. You should have about 4 cups finely grated coconut.

You can also leave the coconut meat in large pieces and grate it by hand on a box grater, taking great care to avoid scraping your knuckles as each piece becomes small. Or leave the coconut in two bowl-shaped halves and use a claw-bladed hand-held grater or stool-mounted coconut grater, both found in Asian markets, to scrape the white meat from the shell.

Making coconut milk: Place the grated coconut in a bowl and add about 3 cups warm water. Squeeze with your hands to mix well, and let stand for about 15 minutes. Then place a fine-mesh sieve over a bowl and pour the coconut mixture through it. Squeeze the grated coconut left behind in the strainer well, to extract as much white coconut milk as you can. Use at once or cover and refrigerate for up to 2 days. You should have about 4 cups unsweetened coconut milk.

NOTE • *When making coconut milk, I like to combine the grated coconut and the water in a blender and blend it for a minute or two before squeezing out the milk, for a somewhat richer yield.* ❖ *Most books instruct you to pierce the coconut, drain out its juice, and then bake it in a hot oven for a while to crack its shell. The coconut-loving people of the world do not traditionally have ovens, and they have cracked coconuts in a straightforward way for* many generations. I not only prefer to omit the oven step for sentimental reasons, but I also find it extra trouble, because you must poke a hole, shake out the juice, and then deal with a hot, hairy coconut, only to arrive at the very same step of having at it with a hammer to crack it open. The hot oven does get the crack started for you, however, if the prospect of striking mighty hammer blows to split open a hard, brown hairy globe is not something you want to do.

⊂ഠ TAMARIND LIQUID ⊂ഠ

Thai cooks make frequent use of this liquid, pressed from the fruit of the tamarind tree. Its flavor is fabulous, sharp and fruity, sweet and smoky, like a marriage of raisins and limes. Tamarind trees are large, graceful hardwoods that flourish throughout Thailand, but particularly in the northern and north-eastern regions. Their trunks are cut crosswise into thick disks to provide the standard cutting board for traditional Thai kitchens. I remember bicycling to the market early in the morning, under a canopy of their generous branches. My neighbors' children often shouted greetings from on high, hidden from my view by the tamarind tree's lacy leaves and the profusion of J-shaped beanlike pods enclosing its tangy, sweet-sour fruit. You can use fresh ripe tamarind pods if you find them in the market, but the mahogany-colored 1-pound bricks of tamarind pulp, minimally processed to remove the tamarind's brittle peel and many of its seeds, work just as well and taste great with less mess. You handle both of them the same way.

½ cup tamarind pulp   *1 cup warm water*

Place the sticky, gooey tamarind pulp in a small bowl and add the warm water. Let stand for 20 to 30 minutes, poking and mashing occasionally with your fingers or a spoon to break the sticky lump into pieces and help it dissolve.

Pour the tamarind pulp and water through a fine-mesh sieve into another bowl. Use your fingers or the back of a spoon to work the tamarind pulp well, pressing the softened pulp against the sieve to extract as much thick brown liquid as you can. Scrape the outside of the sieve often to capture the thick purée that accumulates there. Discard the pulp, fibers, and seeds that have collected in the sieve and thin the tamarind liquid with water as needed until it is about the consistency of pea soup or softly whipped cream.

Use as directed in recipes, or seal airtight and refrigerate for up to 3 days. It sours and sharpens as it stands, so if it has stood for several days, taste it and adjust the flavor with some sugar.

MAKES ABOUT 1 CUP.

NOTE • *If you want to use fresh tamarind rather than prepared tamarind pulp, be sure you have ripe, not young green tamarind. The latter is prized by Southeast Asians for its ferociously sour flavor; it is hard and smooth outside, and a pale cream color with a greenish tinge inside. Fresh ripe tamarind looks tired, with its thin, brittle peel cracking and exposing its raisiny-brown flesh to the world.* ❖ *Some Thai cooks skip the sieve and simply spoon out the liquid from amongst the fibers once the tamarind pulp has been softened and squeezed to mix it with the water. I find straining a simpler way to avoid seeds and fibers, but try the other method if you find the straining process too much of a strain.* ❖ *Several Thai companies now market a prepared tamarind liquid, which is more like a purée in texture and good enough to stand in for the freshly made tamarind liquid if you are short on time. Keep it airtight and refrigerated, just as you would your own batch, for several days. If it becomes too sharp and sour, temper it with a little sugar, molasses, or honey to a pleasing balance.* ❖ *There is no substitute for tamarind, but you can get by using freshly squeezed lime juice, softened with a little and sugar, honey, or molasses, to impart a sweet-sour flavor to your dish.*

GROWING LEMONGRASS IN YOUR HOME GARDEN

Cooking came naturally to me, even as a child. Gardening is another story, yet with a small amount of effort I can root lemongrass in my kitchen and have it flourishing in my garden in a few weeks' time. A patch of lemongrass is gorgeous to behold, and Thai food fans have a plethora of culinary reasons to bring some to life at home. Thais living upcountry often have a stand of lemongrass in the yard; it is usually as big around as a bucket and frequently shared among neighbors. As with sourdough, all you need is a starter, in this case a supply of decent fresh lemongrass stalks, a small tub of water in which to root them, and a pot or patch of good dirt in which to let your lemongrass family put down roots. Lemongrass is hardy and undemanding once it gets a good start, but it will not appreciate a hard frost much less a freeze. If your garden is not in a tropical clime, bring the lemongrass inside for the winter or start all over each spring.

Start with a dozen or more healthy stalks of lemongrass. Chop off and discard their tops, leaving each stalk about 5 inches long, including the bulbous base. Place the stalks in several inches of water and set them in a sunny spot on your kitchen counter for a few weeks, changing the water every few days, until they generate roots and sometimes tiny new stalks around their bases. Look for two kinds of roots: lots of plump, short white ones, and a few that are long, thin, and hairlike. Happy stalks will send new green leaves poking up out of the flat tops of the rooting stalks.

When these mother stalks are ripe with roots, set them in good dirt in clusters of 3 to 5 stalks. Do not plant them too deeply, just an inch or two, so that your crop of baby stalks will eventually be easy to harvest. Arrange them in a circle about 5 inches in diameter, tilting the stalks a little away from the center, like the petals of a tulip that is past its prime. Pat the dirt firmly around them to hold them in place. They love sun, but partial sun will work fine and shady spots will do.

Give them water often until they are well established. Look for tall, slender spearlike leaves shooting up and then bending over in a gentle curl, and baby stalks sprouting out around their moms. Water occasionally, but otherwise this wild herb needs little fussing once it gets a good start. In San Diego, where I live, it grows year-round, but late spring through summer is when it shows off, gloriously fertile and green. To encourage growth, chop off the tender top leaves whenever they are long and curvy. Inside, give it a sunny spot and let it take occasional sunbaths outdoors when you can.

You will need a sharp knife for the harvest. Select each stalk you want, taking out larger central ones and leaving sidekicks behind for your next little harvest. Reach down, push the chosen stalk down toward the ground a little, and maneuver your knife to slice it free just below the bulb, leaving the root and any of its offspring behind in the dirt. The grassy green leaves are spearlike in more ways than one, capable of inflicting tiny cuts not unlike paper cuts if you do not take care. To avoid this prospect, wear long sleeves and gloves. I do not, because I am used to it, and if you move slowly this should not be a problem.

Trim away the spearlike top leaves and use them in Fresh Lemongrass Lemonade (page 193) or in your tea. If you grow your own lemongrass, use the entire stalk once you have cut off these top leaves, as it is so fresh that every inch has more flavor than what you can buy in the store. Even freshly harvested lemongrass is quite fibrous, and its flavor and aroma will begin to fade as soon as it is cut loose from the earth.

NOTE • *You can do a great big patch or two if you have room, either outside or in big pots for bringing indoors. Just follow the principle of circles of stalks, with some space for them to spread out.* ❖ *A few mail-order retailers of fresh herbs carry lemongrass plants if you prefer that route. I suggest you order at least six starter plants at a time, since a single stalk will its take its own sweet time to generate a workable patch, and you could be harvesting and cooking rather than watching it grow if you start with an abundant supply.*

ɷ ROASTED RICE POWDER ɷ

This crunchy, rustic condiment adds a toasty flavor and textural spark to Issahn–style dishes. In the Pahk Issahn region, located in Thailand's northeast, cooks roast a handful of raw sticky rice in a dry wok and then pound it to a sandy powder for the hearty, hot, and spicy salads known as *yum*. Long–grain sticky rice is the standard choice, but any raw white rice will work well. Since their flavor and aroma fade quickly once they are ground, I store the roasted grains whole and grind them as needed. If you like, however, you can grind it all and store the powder in an airtight container away from heat and light.

¼ cup long-grain sticky rice or other white rice

In a small skillet over high heat, dry–fry the rice grains until they are a wheaty golden brown, 3 to 5 minutes. Shake the pan back and forth frequently to turn the grains and color them evenly. Remove from the heat and set aside. When the rice is cool, transfer to a jar, seal tightly, and keep at room temperature until needed.

To use in recipes, transfer the roasted grains to a heavy mortar and pound with a pestle to a fine, sandy powder. Or, using on–off pulses, grind in a coffee grinder or spice grinder, until the rice powder is fairly smooth but still boasts something of a rough texture and an interesting degree of crunch.

MAKES ABOUT ¼ CUP.

❧ TOASTED COCONUT ❧

This condiment is used in traditional salads and snacks such as Lettuce Bites (page 31) and Kao Yum Rice Salad, Southern Style (page 63). In these build-your-own savory dishes, toasted coconut gives a deep, sweet crunch to a rainbow of ingredients bound together with a sweet and tangy sauce. I like to use the easy-to-find sweetened, shredded coconut available in the baking section in supermarkets, since toasted coconut is used in dishes with a strong sweet note. You could also used the unsweetened grated or shredded coconut that is sold in health-food stores, or crack open and grate a coconut (page 209). Note that unsweetened coconut, freshly grated or not, will take a little longer to brown than the sweetened coconut, since the sugar carmelizes more quickly.

1 cup sweetened shredded dried coconut

Set a plate near the stove where the toasted coconut can cool. In a small skillet over medium heat, dry-fry the coconut until it is lightly browned and fragrant, 3 to 5 minutes. Toss it often as it browns, to color it evenly and discourage it from burning. When it is a rich brown with white-to-brown specks remaining, transfer it to the plate and let it cool to room temperature. Use as directed, or seal in an airtight container and store at room temperature away from heat and light for up to 1 week.

MAKES 1 CUP.

✑ PRESSED OR FIRM TOFU ✑

If you have exquisite, silken tofu on hand and need to transform it into something that is sturdy enough to stir-fry or boil without crumbling to mush,
here is a simple, speedy technique. The resulting tofu will lose its straight,
organized shape in the process, along with up to half its weight in water, so
buy twice the amount of tofu you will need after it is pressed. You can use
the pressed tofu in recipes calling for firm tofu, although it will be a good bit
sturdier and flatter than the firm tofu available in grocery stores.

1 pound soft tofu

Cut the block of tofu in half both horizontally and vertically, so that you have
4 smaller blocks. Cover a plate with a clean kitchen towel folded in half. Center a second kitchen towel, unfolded, on top of the first towel and arrange the
tofu blocks in the center. Fold in the towel to enclose the tofu and then put a
second plate of about the same size on top. Place a heavy weight on the plate,
such as a teakettle filled with water or a few heavy cans. Place this makeshift
press in a spot where it will remain balanced and steady. Let stand for a few
minutes or an hour, depending on how sturdy and flat you want the tofu to
be. The longer the time, the firmer and flatter the tofu.

When the tofu is ready, remove the weight and the top plate. Unwrap the
now-damp towel enclosing the tofu (the towel will have absorbed the water
given up by the soft tofu). Transfer the pads of pressed tofu to a plate. Use at
once, or cover and refrigerate, either as is or immersed in water. Use within
2 days.

MAKES 8 OUNCES PRESSED TOFU.

☙ SEASONED TOFU ❧

To me, the everyday tofu sold in upcountry Thai markets is the most beautiful tofu in the world. It is a firm type, with a handsome golden exterior emblazoned with a large, faint red Chinese chop. I imagine that the golden hue comes from turmeric, the natural dye used to color food and the robes of Buddhist monks for thousands of years. This Thai–style tofu is sold in handy pads, about 4 inches square and 1 inch thick. It is the tofu used in *paht Thai* (page 162) and *mee grop* (page 158), sliced into tiny rods and fried crisp before it is mingled with the noodles. Many other forms of tofu are widely available as well, from silken bricks floating in water to very firm soy sauce–seasoned blocks, fried tofu, and dried tofu skin. You can find seasoned or firm baked tofu in most Asian markets; here is a way to make your own at home. The flavor is mild, but the mahogany color is an appealing change from the standard pale product, and it can be used in lieu of firm tofu in any recipe.

2 tablespoons Vegetable Stock (pages 204 and 205)
2 teaspoons regular soy sauce
1 teaspoon dark soy sauce

½ teaspoon sugar
¼ teaspoon salt
8 ounces firm tofu, cut into ½-inch pieces (about 2 cups)

Combine the vegetable stock, both soy sauces, sugar, and salt in a medium skillet and stir to mix well. Add the tofu and place the pan over medium heat. Cook until the tofu is evenly browned and heated through, 2 to 3 minutes.

Remove from the heat and let cool to room temperature. Cover and refrigerate for up to 2 days. Use in recipes as you would plain tofu.

MAKES ABOUT 2 CUPS.

NOTE • *The dark soy sauce provides a depth of color more than flavor, so if you do not have it, you can still make seasoned tofu in a lighter shade of brown.*

⁓ SALTY EGGS ⁓

Thais employ this traditional Chinese method of preserving and flavoring duck and chicken eggs. While salty eggs are widely available in Asian markets, I provide this recipe for those who will need to make their own or will simply enjoy doing so. The eggs shine alongside a hot curry and a tangy dish of Pickled Cabbage (page 67) or pickled garlic.

4 cups water	*1 cup salt*	*9 duck or chicken eggs*

Combine the water and salt in a medium saucepan, stir well, and bring to a rolling boil over medium heat. Boil the brine for 1 minute, stirring often. Remove from the heat and set aside to cool to room temperature.

Meanwhile, wash the eggs gently in cool water and place in a pickling crock or a large jar with a tight-fitting lid. When the salt brine has cooled, pour it over the eggs to immerse them completely. Cover the jar and set it in a cool place for 1 month.

To cook the eggs, remove the number you want from the brine and place them in a small saucepan. Add water to cover and bring to a rolling boil over medium heat. Reduce the heat to maintain a very gentle boil and cook for 9 minutes. Remove from the heat, drain well, rinse in cool water, and then set aside to cool to room temperature. Peel and cut as desired to serve.

MAKES 9 EGGS.

NOTE • *If the eggs float to the top of the crock or jar, place a small, clean stone or other weight on top to hold the eggs down in the brine.* ❖ *You can buy salted eggs in Asian markets. Often you will find them covered with a thick layer of charcoal ash, which is traditionally used to cushion them from one another once they are removed from their salt brine and packed for market in large crocks. Simply soak in cold water for 5 minutes and then rub each egg gently to remove the ash coating without breaking the egg. Cook the eggs as directed in the recipe.* ❖ *You can also fry the eggs and eat them with Dao Jiow Lone Dipping Sauce with Vegetables (page 34).*

CRISPY GARLIC IN OIL

Thais use a dollop of this simple condiment to light up a steaming bowl of rice noodles in broth. You can also try it in salad dressings and marinades for a pleasing garlic note. It will keep refrigerated in an airtight jar for 3 to 5 days, or you can make a fresh batch while your soup simmers. Either way, your kitchen will glow with its garlicky aroma, and your soups will be enhanced with its toasty perfume and tasty, rustic crunch.

¼ cup vegetable oil   *3 tablespoons coarsely chopped garlic*

Heat a small skillet briefly over low heat. Add the oil and heat until a bit of garlic added to the pan sizzles at once, 1 to 2 minutes. Add the garlic and stir to separate any clumps. As the garlic begins to turn golden and release its perfume, stir gently; as soon as half of the garlic is a soft, wheaty color, after 3 to 4 minutes, remove from the heat and set aside to complete the cooking as the mixture cools to room temperature.

Transfer the garlic and fragrant oil to a glass jar with a tight-fitting lid and store in the refrigerator.

MAKES ABOUT ¼ CUP.

NOTE • *Avoid chopping the garlic to a fine mince for this recipe, as that would increase its tendency to burn. Double the recipe if you want a larger batch, but use a larger pan and expect a slight increase in cooking time. The line between heavenly toasting and bitter burning is easy to cross, so stay by the stove as the garlic cooks.*

ᨦ ROASTED CHILI PASTE ᨦ

Nahm prik pao, or "roasted chili paste," is a rustic, spectacularly tasty condiment made from easy–to–find ingredients. The trick to this simple recipe is to keep the herbs on the pleasing side of burnt, while allowing them to blossom into the robust, charred concoction beloved by Thais. Traditionally this preparation is made by roasting the chilies, shallots, and garlic in or over the feisty coals of charcoal stoves used in upcountry kitchens. If you have a lively bed of coals or a good grill, roast or grill the chilies, shallots, and garlic to a handsome darkness, turning with tongs or chopsticks before they incinerate. Use the chili paste in Tome Yum Soup with Mushrooms and Tofu (page 76), Zucchini and Tofu in Roasted Chili Paste (page 130), and Crispy Rice Cakes with Roasted Chili Paste (page 46).

½ *cup small dried red chilies such as chiles de árbol or chiles japones (about 32), stemmed, halved crosswise and loosely packed, about ½ ounce*
A generous ½ cup unpeeled shallots, cut lengthwise into chunks, about 3 ounces
¼ *cup unpeeled garlic cloves (8 to 10 large cloves), about 1½ ounces*
½ *cup vegetable oil*
3 tablespoons palm sugar or brown sugar
3 tablespoons Tamarind Liquid (page 212)
1 tablespoon soy sauce
1 teaspoon salt

In a wok or a small, heavy skillet, dry–fry the chilies over medium–low heat until they darken and become fragrant and brittle, 3 to 5 minutes. Shake the pan and stir frequently as they roast. Remove from the heat and transfer to a plate to cool.

Increase the heat to medium and dry–fry the shallots and garlic, turning them occasionally, until they are softened, wilted, and blistered, about 8 minutes. Remove from the heat and transfer to the plate to cool.

Stem the chilies and shake out and discard most of the seeds. Crumble the chilies into small pieces. Trim the shallots and garlic, discarding the peel and root ends, and chop coarsely. Combine the chilies, shallots, and garlic in a mini processor or blender and pulse to a coarse paste, stopping to scrape down the sides as needed. Add ¼ cup of the vegetable oil and grind to a fairly smooth paste. Transfer to a small bowl and set aside.

Pour the remaining ¼ cup oil into the wok or a skillet. Place over medium heat until a bit of the paste added to the pan sizzles at once, about 1 minute. Add the ground chili paste and cook, stirring occasionally, until the paste gradually darkens and releases a rich fragrance, about 5 minutes. Remove from the heat and set aside to cool to room temperature.

Combine the sugar, tamarind, soy sauce, and salt in a small bowl and stir well. Add this mixture to the cooled chili paste and stir to combine. The paste will be quite oily, and must be well stirred before each use. Transfer to a jar, cap tightly, and refrigerate for up to 1 month. Use at room temperature in recipes or as a condiment.

MAKES ABOUT 1¼ CUPS.

NOTE • *If you have a heavy mortar and pestle, you can bring this sauce together in the traditional way. Coarsely chop the roasted chilies, shallots, and garlic and place in the mortar. Using the pestle, grind and pound them to a coarse mush, using a spoon to scrape down the sides of the mortar as you work. Add a little of the oil and continue pounding and grinding to smooth out the mixture until you have a fairly smooth paste. Continue as directed, frying the paste in the oil and then seasoning it with the sugar, tamarind, soy sauce, and salt.*
❖ *This sauce has two incarnations, one as a pure chili-shallot-garlic paste roasted in oil, and the other as a rich, tangy chili-tamarind paste softened by palm sugar's voluptuous kiss. You can stop after frying the paste and have the former, or complete the recipe and have the latter. Either will work in recipes in which* nahm prik pao *is used.* ❖ *You can purchase this condiment in Southeast Asian grocery stores, but check the ingredients list. In its traditional form, the seasonings added after frying include fish sauce and dried shrimp.* ❖ *If you adore fiery food, add more chilies up to ½ cup. If you want to cut the heat, you can reduce the amount of chilies to about 2 tablespoons coarsely chopped chilies, about ¼ ounce. Handle the chilies with care, avoiding touching your eyes and other tender areas for a few hours after handling them. When you are roasting the chilies, the fragrant smoke from the pan may make you cough a little.*

∽ SWEET AND HOT GARLIC SAUCE ∽

Thais enjoy this simple, delectable sauce with foods that are deep-fried or grilled. Its hot, sharp flavor makes a piquant contrast to the rich crunch of spring rolls and the deep, earthy taste of onions, eggplant, and sweet peppers hot off the grill. My friend Charlisa Cato makes this sauce in gallon-sized batches in her Arkansas kitchen, so she can have it on hand for sharing with friends.

1 cup sugar
½ cup water
½ cup distilled white vinegar
2 tablespoons minced garlic

1 teaspoon salt
1 tablespoon chili garlic sauce or Red Chili Purée (page 227)

In a medium saucepan, combine the sugar, water, vinegar, garlic, and salt. Bring to a boil over medium heat, stirring until the sugar dissolves.

Reduce the heat to medium-low and simmer until the sauce thickens and becomes syrupy, 18 to 25 minutes. Remove from the heat and stir in the chili garlic sauce or Red Chili Purée. Let cool to room temperature, transfer to a jar, and seal airtight. Refrigerate until serving time, then heat gently until thinned to its original consistency. Serve at room temperature. It will keep in the refrigerator for up to 3 weeks.

MAKES ABOUT ¾ CUP.

NOTE • *This sauce keeps well, although it tends to thicken as it stands. Heat it briefly and gently before serving, or add a little water if it is too thick.* ❖ *Chili garlic sauce is a rust-colored paste of dried red chilies studded with seeds and seasoned with garlic and vinegar. It is widely available in supermarkets and Asian grocery stores, often in a clear jar with a parrot-green top. It keeps indefinitely and makes a great addition to your hot-sauce shelf. If you like things hot, increase the amount of chili garlic sauce used in this recipe. If you do not have chili garlic sauce, make Red Chili Purée, or simply add coarsely chopped dried red chilies or another hot sauce to taste.*

Ꮼ TANGY TAMARIND SAUCE Ꮼ

This sauce accentuates the natural dance of sweet and sour flavors in tamarind, the dark, rich fruit of the ubiquitous lacy-leafed tamarind trees that grace the kingdom's upcountry landscape. Use it with any deep-fried or grilled foods, against which its sharp, gingery notes make a perfect foil. Add more chili garlic sauce if you want to fan the culinary flames.

2 tablespoons coarsely chopped garlic (8 to 12 cloves)
2 tablespoons coarsely chopped shallots
1 tablespoon peeled and coarsely chopped fresh ginger
1 cup Tamarind Liquid (page 212)
½ cup palm sugar or brown sugar

½ cup Vegetable Stock (pages 204 and 205)
2 tablespoons freshly squeezed lime or lemon juice
¼ teaspoon chili garlic sauce or Red Chili Purée (page 227)
¼ teaspoon salt

In a mini processor or blender, combine the garlic, shallots, and ginger and grind to a smooth paste, adding a little of the vegetable stock as needed to move the blades. In a small saucepan, combine the tamarind, sugar, and vegetable stock and bring to a gentle boil over medium heat, stirring often to dissolve the sugar and combine everything well. Cook for 1 minute and then add the garlic mixture. Let the sauce return to a boil and then cook, stirring often, for 2 minutes more.

Remove from the heat and stir in the lime or lemon juice, chili garlic sauce or Red Chili Purée, and salt. Taste and adjust the flavors to your liking with a little more lime juice, salt, or hot sauce. Let cool to room temperature and serve. Or cover and refrigerate for up to 3 days.

MAKES ABOUT 1 CUP.

NOTE • *You can substitute another hot sauce or red chili pepper flakes for the chili garlic sauce or Red Chili Purée.*

❧ CHILI-VINEGAR SAUCE ❧

Look for this tangy little explosion of flavor on the tables in Thai restaurants that take pride in their noodle dishes. With luck it will be in a little carousel of seasonings known as *krueng broong*, which every Thai uses to tailor noodles to his or her taste. You will usually find crushed dried red chilies, white sugar, and ground peanuts along with this sauce. Serve with rice and noodle dishes.

½ cup distilled white vinegar
2 tablespoons Vegetable Stock (pages 204
and 205)
½ teaspoon salt

10 fresh green chilies such as serrano,
jalapeño, or Thai bird chilies, thinly
sliced crosswise

Combine the vinegar, vegetable stock, and salt in a small bowl and stir well to dissolve the salt. Stir in the chilies, cover, and store at room temperature for a day or so, or in the refrigerator for 2 to 3 weeks. Pour into small bowls or tiny saucers to serve, so guests can spoon it on to taste.

MAKES ABOUT ½ CUP.

NOTE • *For extra chili heat, finely chop the chilies and/or increase the amount you use.*

↬ RED CHILI PURÉE ↬

Here is a homemade version of chili garlic sauce, the five-alarm condiment used to set noodles, sauces, and other dishes on fire in Southeast Asian cuisine. You will often find it among the table condiments in Asian noodle cafés, along with chilies in white vinegar (page 226), ground dried red chilies, white sugar, and ground peanuts. It is often available in supermarkets that boast a large Asian food section, but you can make your own in a flash. You can use it in marinades and dipping sauces or whenever you want some chili sizzle. A half portion of this recipe will produce enough to spike my Sweet and Hot Garlic Sauce (page 224), and you will have enough left over to fire up a few sandwiches or bowls of Asian noodle soup. You can double or triple this recipe, but since it is so simple to make and a little goes a long way, I like to grind out a fresh batch as needed.

20 dried red finger-length chilies such as 　　*chiles de árbol or chiles japones*	*1 tablespoon water*
	2 teaspoons distilled white vinegar
2 large cloves garlic	*½ teaspoon salt*

Stem the chilies and shake out and discard some of the seeds. Break in half and place the chilies in a small bowl. Add warm water to cover and let soften for 30 minutes.

Drain the chilies and combine them with the garlic, water, vinegar, and salt in a mini processor or a blender. Grind using on-off pulses and stopping to scrape down the sides, until you have a bright red, nubby, coarse purée with some seeds still visible. Transfer to a small bowl and add a little more water if needed soften the sauce, which should be a little thicker than applesauce. Cover or transfer to an airtight jar and refrigerate for up to 3 days.

Makes about ¼ cup.

NOTE • *Leaving in some seeds not only gives this volcanic condiment an appealing look and texture, but it also reminds you not to overgrind the sauce. When it is ready, you should still have some whole seeds visible, so grind in pulses and check often to avoid turning everything into a smooth red mush. What you want is textured red mush with a diminutive confetti of seeds.*

BIBLIOGRAPHY

These cookbooks and other resource books will help you explore the world of Thai food. See Mail-Order Sources (page 232) for information on bookstores that may carry these.

Cookbooks

Ahmed, Lalita. *Vegetarian Cooking*. Surrey, England: Colour Library Books Ltd., 1986.

Aksomboon, Kwanruan, Somchai Aksomboon, and Diana Hiranaga. *Thai Cooking from the Siam Cuisine Restaurant*. Berkeley: North Atlantic Books, 1989.

Bellefontaine, Jacqueline. *The Great Thai Cookbook*. London: Simon & Schuster, 1995.

Bhumichitr, Vatcharin. *Essential Thai Cuisine*. New York: Clarkson N. Potter, 1994.

——. *The Taste of Thailand*. New York: Atheneum, 1988.

——. *Thai Vegetarian Cooking*. New York: Clarkson N. Potter, 1991.

Bounthuy, Sovan. *Cambodian Cooking: Authentic Recipes*. San Jose, CA: Chez Sovan, 1992.

Brennan, Jennifer. *The Original Thai Cookbook*. New York: Times Books, 1981.

Canungmai, Piyatep, and Pierre Chaslin. *Discover Thai Cooking*. Singapore: Times Editions, 1987.

Chinsomboon, Narumol. *Easy Thai Cooking*. Brooklyn, NY: Vasinee Food Corporation/Thai Tennis Magazine, 1989.

Cost, Bruce. *Bruce Cost's Asian Ingredients*. New York: William Morrow & Company, 1990.

Crawford, William, and Kamolmal Pootaraksa. *Thai Home-Cooking from Kamolmal's Kitchen*. New York: New American Library, 1985.

Esbensen, Mogens Bay. *Thai Cuisine*. Melbourne, Australia: Nelson Publishers, 1986.

Gregory, Marnie, and Radee Pooprapand. *Y.W.C.A. (Bangkok) Cookbook*. Bangkok: Krungthep Y.W.C.A., 1988.

Jaffrey, Madhur. *Madhur Jaffrey's World of the East Vegetarian Cooking*. New York: Alfred A. Knopf, 1981.

——. *A Taste of the Far East*. New York: Carol Southern Books, 1993.

Jue, Joyce. *Asian Appetizers*. Emeryville: Harlow & Ratner, 1991.

Jue, Joyce, and Chris Yeo. *The Cooking of Singapore*. Emeryville: Harlow and Ratner, 1993.

Kahrs, Kurt. *Thai Cooking*. New York: W.H. Smith Publishers, 1990.

Kongpan, Srisamon. *The Best of Thai Cuisine*. Bangkok: Sangdad Publications, 1987.

——, and Pinyo Srisawat. *The Elegant Taste of Thailand*. Berkeley: SLG Books, 1989.

Kuo, Irene. *The Key to Chinese Cooking*. New York: Alfred A. Knopf, 1978.

Loha–Unchit, Kasma. *It Rains Fishes: Legends, Traditions, and the Joys of Thai Cooking*. Rohnert Park, CA: Pomegranate Art Books, 1995.

McNair, James. *James McNair Cooks Southeast Asian*. San Francisco: Chronicle Books, 1996.

Na Songkhla, Vandee. *Thai Foods from Thai Literature, Books I and II*. Bangkok: WNS Books, 1988.

Passmore, Jacki. *The Encyclopedia of Asian Food and Cooking.* New York: Hearst Books, 1991.

Pham, Mai. *The Best of Vietnamese and Thai Cooking.* Rocklin, CA: Prima Publishing, 1996.

Pinsuvana, Malulee. *Cooking Thai Food in American Kitchens.* Bangkok: MP Press, 1976.

——, and the National Women's Institute of Thailand. *Thai Cuisine.* Bangkok: Amarin Press, 1985.

Rau, Santha Rama. *The Cooking of India.* New York: Time-Life Books, 1969.

Ross, Rosa Lo San. *Beyond Bok Choy: A Cook's Guide to Asian Vegetables.* New York: Artisan, 1996.

Saiwichian, Prayad. *My Favorite Thai Recipes.* Chiang Mai: c/o P. Saiwichian, Faculty of Education, Chiang Mai University, Chiang Mai 50002, Thailand, 1988.

Sananikone, Keo. *Keo's Thai Cuisine.* Berkeley: Ten Speed Press, 1986.

Schmitz, Puangkram C. *Practical Thai Cooking.* Tokyo: Kodansha International Ltd., 1985.

Simon, Kelly. *Thai Cooking.* Boston: Charles E. Tuttle Co., Inc., 1993.

Sing, Phia. *Traditional Recipes of Laos.* London: Prospect Books, 1981.

Sodsook, Victor. *I Love Thai Food.* Los Angeles: Spice Market Studio, 1989.

——. *True Thai: The Modern Art of Thai Cooking.* New York: William Morrow, 1995.

Solomon, Charmaine. *Charmaine Solomon's Thai Cookbook.* Rutland, VT: Charles E. Tuttle Co., Inc., 1991.

——. *The Complete Asian Cookbook.* New York: McGraw-Hill, 1985.

Thai Snacks. Bangkok: Tuangthip Food Institute of Thailand, 1990.

Vatanapan, Pojanee, and Linda Alexander. *Pojanee Vatanapan's Thai Cookbook.* New York: Harmony Books, 1986.

Warren, William, Sven Krauss, Laurent Ganguillet, and Vira Sanguanwong. *The Food of Thailand: Authentic Recipes from the Golden Kingdom.* Singapore: Periplus Editions (HK), Ltd., 1995.

Other Books

Botan. *Letters from Thailand.* Bangkok: Editions Duang Kamol, 1982.

Clarac, Achille, and Michael Smithies. *Discovering Thailand: A Guidebook.* Bangkok: Siam Communications, 1972.

Cooper, Robert, and Nanthapa. *Thailand/Culture Shock.* Singapore: Times Books International, 1982.

Hollinger, Carol. *Mai Pen Rai Means Never Mind.* Tokyo: John Weatherhill, Inc./ Houghton Mifflin, 1977.

Osborne, Milton. *Southeast Asia: An Illustrated Introductory History.* Sydney: Allen & Unwin, 1987.

Pramoj, Kukrit. *Si Phaendin (Four Reigns),* Volumes 1 and 2. Bangkok: Editions Duang Kamol, 1981.

Segaller, Denis. *Thai Ways.* Bangkok: Thai International, 1982.

Thirabutana, Prajuab. *Little Things.* London: Fontana Books, 1973.

Warren, William. *Jim Thompson: The Legendary American of Thailand.* Boston: Houghton-Mifflin Company, 1970.

SUGGESTED MENUS

Here are ideas to get you started on putting Thai dishes together into menus you will enjoy. An asterisk (*) means the recipe is not included in this book. Vegan menus are noted with a (V).

Traditional Thai Feast (V)
Tome Yum Soup with Mushrooms and Tofu
Panaeng Curry with Wheatballs and Wild Lime Leaves
Pickled Cabbage
Jasmine Rice
A platter of sweet ripe fruit*

Northeastern Thai Barbecue (V)
Green Papaya Salad
Mixed Grill
Sticky Rice
Roasted Eggplant Dip with Thai Flavors, served with vegetables
Fried Peanuts with Green Onions and Chilies

Southern Thai Feast (V)
Mussamun Curry
Brown rice*
Kao Yum Rice Salad, Southern Style
Banana Splits*, made with Coconut Ice Cream and sprinkled with Toasted Coconut

Summertime Barbecue (V)
Satay Peanut Sauce with Fried Bean Curd and Toast
Grilled Japanese Eggplant and Sweet Peppers*
Sweet-and-Sour Cucumber Salad
Yellow Curry Fried Rice with Crispy Potatoes and Peas
Wild Lime Leaf Sorbet

Spicy Dining (V)
Butternut Squash in Fresh Green Curry
Sticky Rice
Pickled Cabbage
Eggplant and Red Sweet Peppers in Roasted Chili Paste
Firecracker Broccoli
Coconut Ice Cream

Cozy Winter Feast (V)
Burmese-Style Curry with Yams, Mushrooms, and Ginger
Garlicky Brussels Sprouts
Jasmine Rice
Coconut Rice Pudding
Sweet and Spicy Nuts

Too Hot to Cook (V)
Muslim-Style Salad with Peanut Dressing
Sticky Rice Balls with Tangy Tamarind Sauce
Orange Salad in Ginger Syrup with Mint
Fresh Lemongrass Lemonade

Do-Ahead Buffet (V)
Oyster Mushroom Salad with Chilies and Lime
Choo Chee New Potatoes with Fresh Basil
Fried Rice
Thai Fruit Salad
Lemongrass-Ginger Sorbet

Your Kids Will Love It
Crispy Spring Rolls with Sweet and Hot Garlic Sauce
Thai Omelet with Sri Racha Sauce
Coconut Rice with Cilantro and Fresh Ginger
Thai Ice Cream Sandwiches

A Finger-Food Feast
Dao Jiow Lone Dipping Sauce with Vegetables
Roasted Eggplant Dip with Thai Flavors, served on Crispy Rice Cakes
Pineapple Bites
Garlicky Mushroom Turnovers
Crispy Spring Rolls with Sweet and Hot Garlic Sauce

Thai Dim Sum Party
Sweet Potato Shiao Mai
Vegetable Curry Puffs
Lettuce Bites
Chewy "Pearl" Dumplings with Mush–
   room Mince and Crispy Garlic
Curried Corncakes with Sweet and Hot
   Garlic Sauce

Patio Supper
Shredded Bamboo Salad, Issahn Style
Son–in–Law Eggs
Thai Fruit Salad
Pasta Salad*
Lemonade*
Thai Coffee Ice Cream

Vegan Delight (V)
Mung Bean Fritters with Tangy
   Tamarind Sauce
Rice Noodles with Spinach in Shiitake
   Mushroom Soup
Speedy Frozen Fruit Sorbet, made with
   mangoes

Speedy Stir-Fry Supper (V)
Mushrooms and Tofu with Fresh Mint
Jasmine Rice
Green Salad with Spicy Thai Citrus
   Dressing
Thai Iced Coffee

Siam Sunday Brunch
Two–Potato Curry Potstickers with Sweet
   and Hot Garlic Sauce
Steamed Eggs with Cilantro and Crispy
   Garlic
Pineapple Fried Rice
Thai Tea Ice Cream
Cookies*

Sunday Night Supper (V)
Jasmine Rice Soup with Mushrooms,
   Green Onions, and Crispy Garlic
Green Papaya Salad
Paht Thai
Cool, Crisp Rubies in Coconut Milk

Sweet and Tangy Dinner (V)
Mee Grop
Zucchini and Tofu in Roasted Chili Paste
Brown rice*
Speedy Frozen Fruit Sorbet, made with
   strawberries

MAIL-ORDER SOURCES

Here is information to put you in touch with vendors who carry everything you need to cook Thai food at home. I have also included several sources for cookbooks and other books about Thailand, and addresses for food newsletters that I enjoy and recommend.

Sources for Ingredients:

Adriana's Caravan
409 Vanderbilt Street, Brooklyn, NY 11218
(800) 316-0820

Gold Mine Natural Food Company
3419 Hancock Street, San Diego,
CA 92110-4307
(800) 475-3663   (619) 296-9756

House of Spices
82-80 Broadway, Jackson Heights, NY
11373
(718) 478-6912

Indian Groceries and Spices
10633 West North Avenue
Wauwatosa, WI 53226
(414) 771-3535

The Oriental Pantry
423 Great Road, Acton, MA 01720
(800) 828-0368   (508) 264-4576
Fax: (617) 275-4506
E-mail: orientalatorientalpantry.com
Website: www.orientalpantry.com

Penzeys, Ltd.
P.O. Box 1448, Waukesha, WI 53187
(414) 574-0277   Fax: (414) 574-0278

Shepherd's Garden Seeds
30 Irene Street, Torrington, CT 06790
(800) 482-3638

Spice Merchant
P.O. Box 524, Jackson Hole, WY 83001
(800) 551-5999   (307) 733-7811

Sultan's Delight
P.O. Box 090302, Brooklyn, NY 11209
(800) 852-5046   (718) 745-6844
Fax: (718) 745-2563

Thai Kitchen/Epicurean International
P.O. Box 13242, Berkeley, CA 94701
(800) 967-THAI   (510) 268-0209
Fax: (510) 834-3102

Walnut Acres Organic Farms
Penns Creek, PA 17862
(800) 433-3998   Fax: (717) 837-1146

Sources for Cookbooks on the Cuisines and Cultures of Southeast Asia:

Kitchen Arts and Letters
1435 Lexington Avenue, New York, NY
10128
(212) 876-5550

Books for Cooks
4 Blenheim Crescent, London W11 1NN
United Kingdom
0171-221-1992   Fax: 0171-221-1517

Suriwong Book Center, Ltd.
54/1-5 Sri Donchai Road
Chiang Mai 50000, Thailand
(053) 281-052;   Fax: (053)-271-902
Contact: Ms. Chompunoot

Food Newsletters Worth Reading:
Each of these three newsletters illuminates the world of food and cooking in a unique and thought-provoking way.

Asian Food Bookery
P.O. Box 15947, Seattle, WA 98115-0947

Just Good Food
1955 West Cornelia Avenue
Chicago, IL 60657-1021
(312) 549-9139

Simple Cooking
P.O. Box 8
Steuben, ME 04680-0008
E-mail: outlawcook@aol.com

GLOSSARY

Asian bean sauce/dao jiow
A pungent condiment made from salted, fermented soybeans. This astoundingly salty seasoning is an ancient Chinese recipe brought to Thailand with the original migration of people out of southern China nearly a thousand years ago. The English name on the label will in most cases read either "brown bean sauce" or "yellow bean sauce." If you buy a brand of Asian bean sauce imported from Thailand, it will probably be called "yellow bean sauce," not because of the color you see but because the Thai name for raw soybeans, which are yellowish, is *tua leuang*, or "yellow bean." Thais use two types of Asian bean sauce. Most common is tall, long-necked bottles of a café au lait brown sauce, with whole dark beans in thick purée. The other is short, fat jars of whole pale yellow beans in a watery brine. Either will work fine in these recipes, and the brown one is the most commonly available in upcountry Thai kitchens. I have used Asian bean sauce extensively in this book, as it works well in combination with salt and soy sauce as a vegetarian replacement for *nahm plah*, the fermented fish sauce that is ubiquitous in Thai cuisine.

Banana leaf/bai gluay; bai tong
Thais use banana leaves to wrap food for steaming, roasting, and boiling, and as a beautiful tool for food presentation. *Bai gluay* means "banana leaf," but the same leaf is called *bai tong*, or "leaf of gold," when used in cooking. Buy the leaves frozen in large packages at Asian markets and defrost at room temperature for about thirty minutes before using. The leaves are huge, so carefully unfold the amount you need, wipe clean with a wet cloth, and cut to the size you like. Wrap extra leaves tightly and refreeze. Substitute fresh corn husks, or dried corn husks from a Hispanic market, soaking the latter in cold water until pliable.

Basil/bai horapah (*Ocinum basilicum*); bai graprao (*Ocinum sanctum*); bai maengluk (*Ocinum carnum*)
Thais use fresh basil extensively, along with cilantro and mint. Whole leaves are tossed into soups, curries, and stir-fries, most often at the end of cooking time so the delicate burst of flavor and aroma shines through in the finished dish. Thais use particular types of basil in certain dishes, but you can substitute fresh Italian basil or sweet basil any time you do not have access to the ideal one, with good results. You can also use mint, since basils are members of the mint family. See *graprao* basil, *horapah* basil, *maengluk* basil, and mint.

Bean curd/dao hoo   *See Tofu.*

Bean sprout/tua gnok
Sprouted from mung beans, these are widely available in supermarkets in the West, but often neglected and allowed to wilt in the produce bin. Look for crisp, firm sprouts with little scent. If beautiful fresh ones aren't available, omit them.

Bean thread noodle/woon sen
Made from mung bean flour, these unusual noodles are also called glass noodles, silver noodles, and cellophane noodles. Names abound, including the Chinese dialect word *saifun*, the Japanese *harusame* that means "spring rain", and the appetite-dulling English moniker "alimentary paste." These skeins of off-white dried noodle are usually wrapped

up into small, oval bundles and enclosed in cellophane. They resemble fishing wire more than food and are about as tough until they are soaked in warm water for fifteen to twenty minutes. Then they are limp and ready to be briefly stir–fried or dropped into soups just before serving. They cook quickly; as soon as they are translucent, they are done. They have no taste, but they have a lovely soft texture and absorb flavors well. When raw, bean thread noodles look a lot like thin rice noodles, so read the ingredients list on the packet; it should mention mung beans or even green beans, since the Thai name for mung bean is *tua kiow*, or "green bean." You can substitute thin rice noodles, noting that they will need a little more cooking time, and turn white rather than clear when cooked. I like big bags of individually wrapped two–ounce packets; the little packets are a handy size and it's almost impossible to separate out a portion from a large package without soaking the whole mass of noodles. To my amazement, they are widely available in supermarkets, as well as in Asian markets and by mail.

Black sticky rice/kao niow dahm   *See Sticky rice.*

Brown bean sauce/dao jiow   *See Asian bean sauce.*

Cardamom/luke gra–wahn
A fragrant seedpod resembling in shape either a small plump garlic clove or a miniscule head of garlic. Thais use it whole in a few dishes of Indian origin, such as mussamun curry (page 102). In their natural state, cardamom pods are an ethereal shade of green, but you will also find white cardamom pods, which are green pods that have been bleached. Green are preferable, but either will work. Avoid black cardamom, which is a different spice, sold in large, dark, woody pods and used in Indian and South Asian cuisine.

Chee fah chili/prik chee fah (*Capsicum annuum*)   *See Chilies.*

Chili garlic sauce/saus prik
An incendiary Vietnamese–style chili sauce made from fresh red chilis, vinegar, garlic, and salt. It is a coarse, thick fire engine–red paste with visible seeds and pulp, and is widely available in Asian markets. Look for small plastic jars with parrot–green lids; the sauce keeps well. Substitute a freshly made purée of hot red chilies, garlic, and a little vinegar, salt, and oil (page 227), or use another chili sauce such as Sri Racha sauce or Tabasco.

Chilies/prik (*Capsicum* sp.)
Thais adore hot chilies, both fresh and dried, whole and ground. Chilies contain oils that sting and burn, so cultivate the Thai cook's habit of not touching your eyes and other tender spots after handling them. ❖ For fresh chilies, use the slender, tiny chilies called *prik kii noo* and *prik kii nok* (*Capsicum frutescens*). They're often labeled "Thai chilies" or "bird pepper" in Asian markets and are usually sold green, although they turn orange and red as they ripen. You can use other fresh chilies, such as serranos or jalapeños, in their place. ❖ Also used frequently in Thai cooking are *chee fah* chilies (*Capsicum annuum*), which are long and slender like fingers and are usually a brilliant red. Although fiery, they are far milder than *kii noo* chilies, and in most cases are sliced on the diagonal into ovals and added to Thai dishes as a garnish. For this reason, strips of red sweet pepper make a good substitute, since *chee fah* chilies are difficult to find in the West. ❖ *Prik leuang* (*Capsicum annuum*), which means "yellow chili," is a long, slender, mildly hot pepper that is extremely rare even in Thailand. It is used in *gaeng leuang*, a southern Thai curry, along

with dried red chilies for heat and turmeric for yellow color. Substitute serrano chilies, or omit altogether if you cannot find either in Asian markets. ❖ *Prik yuak* (*Capsicum annuum*) is a mildly hot chili, pale green to pale yellow, 3 to 5 inches long, fat at the stem, and tapering to a point. It is also called *prik noom* and is used in the northern Thai chili dipping sauce called *nahm prik noom*. It is difficult to locate in Asian markets in the West, but is often found in well-stocked supermarkets under the name banana pepper or Hungarian wax pepper. ❖ For *prik haeng*, or dried red chilies, use any dried red chilies imported from Thailand and sold in plastic bags, or any other dried red chili you like as long as it is hot. For coarsely ground dried red chili or red chili pepper flakes, buy it already ground, with seeds and pieces of red pepper still visible, or grind your own. Dried chilies keep for months but not forever, so check carefully now and then to see if you need a new batch.

Chinese broccoli/pahk ka–nah (*Brassica* sp.)
A leafy, dark green vegetable of the cabbage family, known in Thai as *pahk ka-nah*. It resembles broccoli, though its stems are more tender and slender, and it has large leaves and tiny flowers. When flowering it has beautiful tiny white blossoms, which are also edible. Dim sum parlors serve it blanched and seasoned with oyster sauce. Thais use it extensively for stir-frying and for combining with noodles. Substitute collard greens, Swiss chard, cabbage, Chinese mustard greens, or any leafy Asian green, or use spinach leaves, adding them toward the end of cooking since they're much more tender.

Chinese mustard green/pahk kwahng–toong (*Brassica* sp.)
A leafy, dark green vegetable of the cabbage family. It often has beautiful tiny yellow flowers, which are also edible. Like Chinese broccoli or *pahk ka-nah*, it has sturdy broccoli-like stalks and large, delicious leaves.

Cilantro/pahk chee (*Coriandum sativum*)
Also called coriander and Chinese parsley, a beautiful, soft, leafy herb adored by Thais and used extensively to add its distinctive flavor to dishes and as a garnish. It's often available in supermarkets, as well as in Asian and Hispanic markets. ❖ Cooks in many countries use cilantro leaves, but only Thai and Lao cooks appreciate the unusually fragrant and flavorful roots as a component of seasoning pastes. Increasingly, produce vendors are becoming aware of the benefits of leaving the roots intact, since the herb stays fresh much longer when the roots have not been removed. If you can't find cilantro with roots attached, substitute chopped stems with some leaves.

Cloud ears/heht hoo noo
A thin, black mushroom with no flavor but a pleasing crunch and appearance. Thais use them in a few dishes of Chinese origin. The Thai name means "mouse ear mushroom," since that's what they look like when fresh or softened. Other common names are *mo-er* mushrooms, tree ears, wood ears, and black fungus. They're seldom available fresh here, but dried ones work fine. They must be softened for about thirty minutes in warm water to cover and trimmed of their hard little navels, the spot at which they were attached to the tree or log on which they grew.

Coconut/maprao
Thais use coconuts extensively in cooking, particularly for sweets and to make coconut milk and coconut cream for curries and soups. See page 209 for instructions on opening coconuts and extracting and grinding their meat.

Coconut candy/nahm tahn maprao   *See Palm sugar.*

Coconut cream and coconut milk/nahm ga–ti
Thais grate the sturdy, white flesh of hairy brown coconuts, soak it in water, and then squeeze it through a fine–mesh sieve to make coconut cream and coconut milk. Cream is *hua ga-ti*, or "the head," and milk is *hahng ga-ti*, or "the tail." Unsweetened canned or frozen coconut milk is a good substitute for freshly made. It is such a rich essence that it would more properly be labeled "coconut cream." Throughout this book, I call for this rich coconut milk straight from the can, or from the freezer, simply thawed. When it needs diluting, I have included stock or water as needed among the recipe ingredients. If you encounter Southeast Asian recipes calling for coconut cream and coconut milk, use this formula. For coconut cream, stir the contents of a can well and use it undiluted. For coconut milk, stir the contents of a can of coconut milk well, dilute it by half, adding an equal amount of water to the coconut cream, and then measure out the amount of coconut milk you need. "First pressing" refers to coconut cream, and "second pressing" refers to coconut milk. In all its forms, unsweetened coconut milk is as perishable as the dairy products it resembles, so keep it chilled and use within 1 or 2 days. See page 209 for more on coconuts.

Coconut sugar/nahmn tahn maprao   *See Palm sugar.*

Coriander seed/luke pahk chee
The whole seeds of cilantro, also known as coriander and Chinese parsley. Thais toast them in a dry skillet to bring out the flavor and then grind them for use in curry pastes and herb pastes.

Cucumber/taeng kwah
Use small pickling cucumbers or large hothouse or Japanese cucumbers if you can. Or use the huge, waxy torpedoes from the grocery store, but peel them well and also scrape out the seeds, as they tend to be large, tough, and bitter.

Cumin seed/meht yee–rah
Used extensively in Thai cooking, usually dry–fried to bring out the flavor and then ground for use in fragrant herb pastes and curry pastes.

Curry paste/krueng gaeng
An intensely flavored paste of herbs and spices used to flavor curries, soups, and other dishes. See Basic Recipes (pages 196–203) for how to make your own, or purchase pre-pared curry pastes in Asian markets. Homemade curry pastes take time and effort to prepare, but they taste wonderful and keep well. Store–bought curry pastes are a good alternative, and they enable cooks to make tasty curries fast. In my kitchen I greatly enjoy using both. Please note that commercial Thai and Thai–style curry pastes routinely include shrimp paste, called *ga-pi*. To avoid this, you must make your own curry paste from scratch. ❖ The most common curry pastes are red, made from dried red chilies and known both as *krueng gaeng peht*, the latter word meaning "fiery hot," and as *krueng gaeng daeng*, the latter word meaning "red"; green, made from fresh green chilies and called *gaeng kiow wahn*, which means literally "green and sweet"; *krueng gaeng kah-ree*, a red curry paste enhanced with Indian spices and turmeric for golden color; and *krueng gaeng mus-samun*, a rich, mildly hot red curry paste flavored with cinnamon, cloves, and other spices. Curry pastes come in cans, plastic tubs, and small and large plastic packets.

Dao jiow *See Asian bean sauce.*

Dark soy sauce/si–yu dahm
Available in bottles in Asian markets, dark soy sauce is valued mostly for the rich, deep color it lends to food, and not for its flavor, which is mild.

Dark sweet soy sauce/si–yu wahn
Available in bottles in Thai and Southeast Asian markets, this is a combination of dark soy and molasses, and is the secret of the delicious rice noodle dish with Chinese broccoli on page oo. If unavailable, substitute two parts dark soy sauce and 1 part molasses, honey, or maple syrup.

Dried Chinese mushroom/heht hohm *See Dried shiitake mushroom.*

Dried red chilies/prik haeng *See Chilies.*

Dried shiitake mushrooms/heht hohm
The Thai name means "fragrant mushroom," and shiitake are used along with other varieties of dried Chinese mushrooms in Chinese–Thai cooking. Soak in warm water for about thirty minutes, remove and discard the stem, or use it in stock, and then cook the softened caps whole or sliced, in soups, stir–fries, and stews. The soaking liquid can be strained and used to flavor soups and sauces. You will find acceptable ones in small packages in supermarkets. If you use them often, buy a supply at an Asian market, where you will find excellent buys on a variety of top–quality mushrooms. They keep indefinitely, sealed airtight, at room temperature and away from light. Expect them to be costly, as they are specialty ingredient within Asian cuisine.

Five spice powder/pong pah–lo
Thais enjoy this Chinese import, a ground mixture of cinnamon, cloves, fennel, Sichuan peppercorns, and star anise, which imparts a deep, sweet, and spicy aroma and flavor to the popular Chinese–style stews known in Thai as *pah–lo* dishes. Try *kai pah-lo*, Five–Spice Hard–Boiled Eggs in Sweet Soy Stew (page 139), and see *Star anise* for further information.

Freshly ground pepper/prik thai pohn
Freshly ground white or black pepper has so much more flavor and aroma than pre–ground that I hope you'll buy yourself a good pepper mill. Many Thai cooks use pre–ground pepper, however, except in curry pastes, where there are other spices to grind as well. I specify black or white pepper in some recipes, but either will work fine.

Galanga/kah (*Alpinia galanga siamensis*)
This first cousin of ginger has a wonderful sharp, lemony taste and a similar hotness. Its Vietnamese name is *rieng*, and it is also known as galangal, Java root, Siamese ginger, *laos*, *lengukual*, *languas*, and *galingale*. Galanga is pale and creamy, much lighter than ginger, and encircled with thin, dark rings. It's never eaten straight, but rather used in large, thin pieces to flavor soups, stews, and curries, or chopped fine to be pounded up in curry pastes and herb pastes. Frozen or dried galanga pieces make a reasonable alternative if you can't find fresh. You could also substitute fresh ginger, which has a different flavor from its cousin but makes a delicious, herbaceous alternative. Ground dried galanga powder has no taste and no scent, so leave it on the grocer's shelf.

Garlic/gratiem (*Allium sativum*)

Every recipe I was given in Thailand seemed to begin with *Hohm, gratiem* . . . ("Shallots, garlic . . ."), and it is assumed a good cook knows how much to use and how to cut it up. I had to watch and write it down, so check the recipes for the details. Be sure to look for fresh, shiny heads of garlic that feel heavy in your hand and don't have soft or dusty, moldy cloves. To me there's no substitute for fresh garlic, crushed, peeled, and chopped as I need it. I buy a dozen heads at a time when I find good ones, and keep it handy in a big basket with shallots, plum tomatoes, an onion, a hunk of ginger, and some chilies.

Garlic, pickled/gratiem dong   *See Pickled garlic.*

Garlic chives/tone gooey chai

These flat green chives have a strong smell and taste. Traditionally they're used in Thailand's two noodle classics, *paht Thai* (page 162) and *mee grop* (page 158), but green onions make an excellent substitute.

Ginger/king (*Zingiber officinale*)

A delicious fresh seasoning with an extraordinary flavor— hot and spicy and yet cooling as well. Happily it's now widely available in the West in well-stocked supermarkets as well as Asian markets. Look for shiny, fat lobes that aren't shriveled or wrinkled. Thais don't use ginger as much as they do its cousins, galanga and turmeric, but they like it and it makes a good alternative if the others are hard to come by.

Glutinous rice/kao niow   *See Sticky rice.*

Grachai/grachai (*Kaempferia pandurata; Boesenbergia pandurata*)

This ginger cousin is also called *zerumbet, zeodary*, rhizome, camphor root, *kentjur* or *kencur*, and lesser galanga. It has a thin, medium brown skin over a creamy interior and is shaped like a bunch of long, tapered fingers. Like all members of the ginger family, it's widely used in traditional Asian medicine as well as in food. It's sometimes available frozen, which makes an acceptable substitute, as does fresh ginger. Ground dried grachai, sometimes labeled "rhizome," is tasteless and scentless, so pass it by.

Graprao basil/bai graprao (*Ocinum sanctum*)

This is often called holy basil, and it's my favorite member of the herb family to which all mints and basils belong. Although it's not easy to find outside Thailand, Asian markets in the West are gradually beginning to carry it. You're most likely to find *graprao* basil in Asian markets that cater to a Lao, Cambodian, and Thai clientele, and often only during the spring, summer, and early fall months. The leaves of graprao basil are not shiny like most basils, nor are they textured like mint. They have a smooth, matte finish and a serrated edge, and the color varies from pure green to a green–red–purple mixture, with or without flowers, all depending on the particular variety and the time of year. It's more fragile than other mints and basils, so when you find it, use it fast and use a lot of it. Any variety of fresh basil or mint makes a good substitute; unfortunately, dried mint and basil just don't work— no scent, no flavor.

Green onion/tohn hohm (*Allium fistulosom*)

Also called scallions, these are used extensively for flavor and garnish.

Holy basil/bai graprao (*Ocinum sanctum*)   *See Graprao basil.*

Horapah basil/bai horapah (*Ocinum basilicum*)
The most widely available Asian basil, it's used extensively in Vietnamese cuisine, as well as in the cooking of Cambodia and Laos. Sometime called Thai or Vietnamese basil, it looks and tastes like a basil, with its shiny, pointy leaves and anise flavor. It usually has purple stems, sometimes tipped with lovely purple flowers; the latter are a nice addition to any recipe that calls for the leaves. Thais use *horapah* basil more than the other types of basil, tossing a handful onto curries, soups, and stir-fries just before serving so that its delicate perfume and flavor are released but not extinguished. *Rau hung* is its Vietnamese name.

Hungarian wax pepper/prik yuak; prik noom (*Capsicum annuum*)
See Chilies, Banana pepper.

Jasmine rice/kao hohm mali
A naturally aromatic, long–grain white rice widely available in Asian markets in the West. Its scent is subtle, somewhere between toasty and nutty, and it's wonderful for general cooking as well as for Thai food. It's sometimes called Thai basmati rice, since basmati is another exotic aromatic, long–grain white rice, albeit a bit different in texture, aroma, and taste. I buy jasmine rice in twenty–five pound sacks because it keeps well and I use it often; many Asian grocers break it down into smaller lots. The large sacks will usually have been marked "jasmine rice, imported from Thailand" in English, somewhere beneath the brand name and various inscriptions in Vietnamese, Khmer, Chinese, Lao, and Thai. See page 149 for instructions on cooking jasmine rice.

Kabocha pumpkin/fahk tong (*Curcurbita moschata*)
Beloved by Thais for use in curries and sweets, these chubby, dark green pumpkins are widely available in supermarkets and Asian markets. Any winter squash will make a fine substitute, although I think kabocha has an especially sweet, pleasing taste. Sweet potatoes work, too, but need shorter cooking time.

Kaffir lime leaves/bai makroot   *See Wild lime leaves.*

Kii noo chili/prik kii noo (*Capsicum frutescens*)   *See Chilies.*

Lemongrass/takrai (*Cymbopogon citratus*)
Lemongrass grows in long, pale green stalks with a woody texture and a lovely lemony scent. It is shaped like a green onion but is stiff and quite fibrous. Its Vietnamese name is *xah* (pronounced zah), and it is also called *serai, sereh, zabalin*, citronella, and fever grass. Thais use only the bulbous base, trimmed of roots and any dry outer leaves. If your lemongrass is fresh, you'll see lovely purple concentric rings inside when you cut it crosswise. Like galanga, lemongrass is seldom eaten because it has such a coarse, fibrous texture and delicate flavor and scent. Instead it is used like bay leaves in Western cooking, to infuse a sauce, a soup, or a curry with its delicate flavor and scent. It is sliced very thin and then finely chopped before being pounded with other ingredients in curry pastes. Try to do any cutting and pounding of lemongrass at the very last minute, as its perfume and flavor quickly fade away. You'll find dried lemongrass, chopped and in powder form, in Asian markets, and I strongly suggest you leave it there; it has no

taste and no scent. Soaking it won't help, since there's nothing left once it's dried.
❖ Lemongrass freezes fairly well, so when you find fresh stalks, buy an extra dozen or so, trim away the tops, and wrap tightly before freezing. Don't defrost it; use it straight from the freezer, just about doubling the amount you would use if it were fresh. If you can't find lemongrass, substitute some juice and zest of lime or lemon. See Basic Recipes chapter, page 214, for instructions on growing lemongrass in your garden.

Leuang chili/prik leuang (*Capsicum annuum*)   *See Chilies.*

Lime/manao
Fresh lime juice is a basic ingredient in Thai cooking, but fresh lemon juice is a good substitute.

Lime leaf/bai makroot   *See Wild lime leaf.*

Maengluk basil/bai maengluk (*Ocinum carnum*)
This basil has a heavenly lemon scent and flavor, and it's used in soups, tossed into the classic *gaeng liang* just before serving. It is also used in some curries, and noodle dishes, including the northeastern version of the steamed curried custard called *haw moke*. It's difficult to find in the West and it fades quickly, so if you come across some at a market, enjoy it right away. Substitute another fresh basil or mint if you like, or any lemony herb such as lemon balm.

Maengluck basil seed/meht maengluck (*Ocinum carnum*)
These tiny black seeds resemble sesame seeds in size and shape, and are sold in markets catering to Thai, Lao, Cambodian and Vietnamese cooks. Not only can you plant them to raise a crop of lemony *maengluck* basil, you can use them Asian style in sweets. Soak them in water for about five minutes and watch each seed enclose itself within a bubble of bluish–grey jelly. In this swollen form, *maengluck* basil seeds are used in sweet puddings and cool fruity drinks. The word in the Thai marketplace is that eating basil seeds causes one to *"lote nahm nahk,"* which means "to release unwanted pounds." I cannot vouch for this but I do love the peculiar pillowed crunch these seeds provide in sweets and drinks. Look for small cellophane packets of seeds, which may be labeled "sweet basil" or with the Vietnamese words *"hot e."*

Mint/bai saranae (*Mentha arvensis*)
Thais adore fresh mint, especially in their hot and spicy salads called *yums*. Any type of mint will do nicely in Thai recipes, or you could substitute any form of basil as a second choice.

Mung bean centers/tua tong   *See Yellow mung bean centers.*

Noom chili/prik noom (*Capsicum annuum*)   *See Chilies.*

Oyster mushroom/heht nahng lome
Beautiful clusters of dove–gray mushrooms that resemble oysters in both color and shape. They are increasingly available in Asian markets and some supermarkets here. Substitute any fresh mushroom.

Palm sugar/nahm tahn beep, nahm tahn maprao
An absolutely delicious, robust sugar made from the fruit of the palmyra palm tree

called *toen pahm*, or from the coconut palm, *toen maprao*. *Beep* refers to the tall tin can in which palm sugar is sold in Thailand, so the package doesn't always specify which type of sugar is inside. Whether it is labeled palm sugar, coconut sugar, or coconut candy, it's a wonderful addition to sauces, curries, and sweets. You can substitute brown sugar or white sugar, or jaggery from India.

Peanut/tua lisong
Used more in the south than in other regions. Peanuts are called groundnuts in some Asian cookbooks. Use roasted peanuts, either salted or unsalted, and then salt the dish you're making to taste. Buy small jars and keep them in the freezer, as they quickly go stale.

Pepper/prik thai   *See Freshly ground pepper.*

Peppercorn/luke prik Thai (*Piper nigrum*)
The original Thai hot seasoning. Thais use both white and black whole peppercorns, particularly in curry pastes and herb pastes, and ground pepper to season stir-fries, sauces, and soups.

Pickled garlic/gratiem dong
Thais pickle diminutive heads of garlic in a simple white vinegar, salt, and sugar brine and use slices or whole cloves as a flavorful foil for salty dishes like *kai kem*, or Salty Eggs (page 220). Pickled garlic is sold in jars in many Asian markets. For a classic *mee grop* (page 158) garnish, slice heads crosswise into ¼-inch-thick rounds and drape over the mound of noodles.

Pomelo/soem-oh
A delicious cousin of grapefruit, it has sturdier, drier flesh and much thicker skin. Unlike grapefruit, it has a round shape that is a trifle irregular, distended at the stem end, and its ripe meat is much sweeter. Peel off the skin, separate the sections, gently cut them open to extract the glistening juicy flesh, and enjoy it in chunks out of hand. For a palace-style presentation to a very important guest, a Thai chef might separate the peeled sections of pomelo into individual teardrops of fruit. Look for pomelos in Asian markets, especially around Chinese New Year in January and February. You can substitute a combination of peeled sections of grapefruit and orange.

Pressed tofu/ dao hoo keng
Firm bean curd can be pressed under a heavy weight to extract a portion of its water content. This makes it sturdy enough to hold its shape, for use in recipes where it is vigorously tossed, stirred or stewed. You will find it shrink-wrapped in the refrigerator case in Asian markets and health-food stores, either plain or seasoned with soy sauce and sometimes shredded into long thin strands. You can make it easily at home (page 218).

Rice/kao   *See Jasmine rice.*

Red chili pepper flakes/prik pong
These coarsely ground dried red chilies are widely used in Thai cooking for a fiery blast, particularly in sauces and dips. Look for small flakes of red pepper punctuated with a small proportion of whole seeds. Look for them in cellophane bags in Asian markets, in jars in supermarkets, or grind up your own in a Thai mortar or in a mini-processor or a blender.

Rice flour/baeng kao jow
Ground from long–grain white rice and available in Asian markets, this soft, chalk–white powder is made into the tender white rice noodles used in Asian cuisines. It is also widely used in various sweets and savory snacks, and can be substituted for sticky rice flour in a pinch.

Rice noodles/kwaytiow
Wonderful white noodles, sold fresh in large, soft sheets folded into packets, or dried, cut into various widths from angel–hair size (*sen mee*) used for *mee grop* (page 158), to linguine size (*sen lek*) used for *paht Thai* (page 162), to inch-wide size, my personal favorite, which one Thai restaurant menu translated perfectly as "big fat noodle" (*sen yai*). To prepare dried rice noodles for stir–frying, soak them in warm water to cover until they are limp, pliable, and stark white, fifteen to twenty minutes. Drain and proceed according to recipe.

Roasted chili paste/nahm prik pao
A fiercely delicious amalgam of dried roasted chilies, garlic, and shallots, seasoned with tamarind and palm sugar. Available in small jars and big flat packets in Asian markets, or you can make your own (page 222). Note that commercial *nahm prik pao* usually includes ground dried shrimp and fish sauce, so making your own may be a necessity rather than an option.

Roasted rice powder/kao kua pone
Raw grains of sticky rice are dry–fried until wheaty brown and then ground to a fragrant powder with a pleasing crunch and toasty flavor. A traditional ingredient in *yum*, the hearty salads of the northeastern region. Either make your own (page oo) or omit.

Salty egg/kai kem
Sometimes labeled "salted eggs," this is a traditional way of preserving duck eggs. Buy in Asian markets and hard cook just before using, or preserve your own (page 220). Salty eggs are often sold coated with a cushioning ¼-inch-thick layer of gray ash. Soak these in cold water for about five minutes and then gently rub off the ash with your fingers under running water.

Sataw bean/look sataw (*Parkia* sp.)
These unique fat beans look a lot like peeled, shelled lima beans or fava beans, but they have a peculiar taste and aroma. Sataw beans are immensely popular in southern Thailand, where they grow on trees in huge, ladderlike pods. Often available frozen in Asian markets, and of surprisingly good quality. Or substitute fresh young fava beans, shelled and peeled; fresh lima beans, shelled and peeled, or frozen lima beans, thawed and peeled; fresh sugar snap peas; or fresh snow peas. Nothing tastes quite like sataw beans, though.

Seitan
This traditional Asian form of wheat gluten or wheat protein is widely available in health food stores, sold like tofu in the refrigerator case, sealed in small tubs basted by a spiced soy broth rather than water. Like other types of wheat gluten, it is made from a simple wheat flour dough that is kneaded well and then rinsed to remove the starch and the bran. Sometimes called "wheat meat," the variously shaped hunks of firm, chewy seitan can be cut to your liking into strips or bite–sized pieces and used as a protein source instead of tofu or other forms of wheat gluten in many Asian–style recipes.
See Wheat gluten.

Shallot/hohm daeng or hohm lek (*Allium ascalonicum*)
The first Thai name means "red onion," because the tiny shallots of Thailand have a gorgeous pinkish purple color. Thais also call them *hohm lek*, or "tiny onion," and they use them extensively, usually along with garlic. Look for small, hard, shiny shallots without green shoots. Unfortunately, often the only kind you'll find here are huge, wrinkly shallots with green shoots. But they'll do.

Soy sauce/saus si-yu
Thais use soy sauce as a background seasoning in many dishes, often for color as well as taste. See Dark soy sauce and Dark sweet soy sauce.

Spring roll wrappers/paen boh biah
Square, ivory-colored sheets sold at Asian markets in one pound packets of about thirty or so eight inch-square sheets. They are usually sold frozen. They are made of flour and water and usually do not contain egg. They can dry out quickly, so keep them frozen until shortly before you plan to fill and wrap them. The wrapper package needs about 30 minutes to thaw, and it is best to keep unused raw wrappers covered with a damp kitchen towel or plastic wrap while you work. Rewrap leftover wrappers airtight and freeze. Since quality can vary and the wrappers keep well and use little freezer space, I buy several packages of different brands rather than the one package I need. Then if I encounter the occasional dried out, useless batch, I can go to the freezer rather than back to the Asian market. The doughy refrigerated kind widely available in supermarkets will do, too. Note that these usually contain egg, and have a heavier, oilier texture when cooked.

Sri Racha sauce/saus Sii-Rachaa
A terrific five-alarm chili sauce made in the seaside town of Sri Racha. Thais love it as an accompaniment to egg dishes and seafood. Disregard designations on the slender bottles that say "mild" and "hot"– they are all very, very hot.

Star anise/poy kack bua (Illucium verum)
Used in Thai cooking mostly in dishes of clear Chinese origin, such as Five-Spice Hard-Boiled Eggs in Sweet Soy Stew, (page 139), known in Thai as *kai pah-lo*. This gorgeous spice is a reddish brown star with eight pointy pods, each housing a shiny, pungent seed. Botanically it belongs to the magnolia family. Though unrelated to anise, the two spices share a similar licorice flavor and aroma. Thais commonly make use of it in five-spice powder, but whole star anise are often tossed into *pah-lo* dishes along with cinnamon sticks for an extra spice spark.

Sticky rice/kao niow
In its long-grain form, this opaque, bright-white strain of rice is the daily bread of northeastern and northern Thailand, and of Laos. Soaked for three hours and then steamed until tender, long-grain sticky rice plumps up and easily clings into bite-sized lumps, which Laotians and many Thais eat out of hand along with curries, soups, stir-fries and salads. In English, sticky rice is also called glutinous rice and sweet rice. Gluten, the protein in wheat that gives bread its appealing chewy quality, is not present in this rice, but since sticky rice has a unique chewiness, the name has stuck. Though this rice has no sweet taste, short-grain sticky rice is widely used in sweet snacks and desserts throughout Asia, sometimes ground into flour and sometimes in its whole-grain form. Its importance as an ingredient in sweet treats is probably the source of the term, "sweet

rice." See page 150 for instructions on cooking long-grain sticky rice the Thai way. Some Asian markets and health-food stores also carry black sticky rice, which is a handsome medium-grain rice that is black, brown, and white in a calico pattern. Less sticky than its white cousin, it can be soaked and steamed or cooked as you would cook regular rice. However you cook it, you will enjoy seeing its earthy color transformed into a stunning deep-purple hue. Thais often toss cooked black sticky rice with coconut milk and sugar and serve it with ripe mangoes or custard as a sweet course (page 176).

Sticky rice flour/baeng kao niow
Ground from sticky rice, this velvety white powder is widely used in sweets. Its natural stickiness in whole grain form translates to a thick, chewy texture that is treasured in a rainbow of Asian treats, savory as well as sweet. Available in boxes and cellophane bags in Asian markets. Plain rice flour is an adequate substitute. See Sticky rice.

Straw mushroom/heht fahng
Available fresh in Thailand. Buy whole, peeled canned ones, or substitute any fresh mushroom.

Sweet potato/mun
You can use any kind of sweet potato or yam when cooking the curries and dumplings in this book. You could also substitute potatoes, kabocha pumpkin, or any peeled variety of winter squash.

Sweet rice/kao niow   *See Sticky rice.*

Sweet soy sauce/si-yu wahn   *See Dark sweet soy sauce.*

Tamarind/makahm
The ripe fruit of the tamarind tree, it has a complex, fruity sour taste that recalls a smoky combination of raisins and limes. Buy small blocks of tamarind pulp (*makahm biak*) in Asian markets, soak the pulp in warm water, mash to a thick soft paste, strain, and use the liquid. See page 212 for specific directions for extracting the liquid. Thai cooks sometimes use freshly squeezed lime juice or distilled white vinegar as a substitute; although the flavor is not as wonderful, it will do.

Tapioca flour/baeng mun
Made from the dried tubers of the cassava plant, tapioca flour is found in Asian markets and health-food stores. Valued for its power to thicken sauces in a clear, silken way, it is also used in combination with other flours to lend crispness to batters for deep-fried snacks. If it is unavailable, use an equal amount of rice flour, cornstarch, or wheat flour.

Taro/peuak (*Colocasia antiquorum*)
A chubby tuber with fuzzy brown skin that is something like a potato in appearance and taste. There are many types, ranging in size from as small as a walnut to as large as a coconut. The flesh is ivory to gray and often spiked with purple. In Hawaii, taro is used for making *poi*, and in Thailand it is used mostly in sweets such as *kanome maw gaeng*, the classic custard that is the signature sweet of the coastal town of Hua Hin. Since it is peeled and cut into 2-inch chunks before cooking, any variety and size will do for Thai recipes.

Tempeh
These nubby, rectangular patties are a traditional vegetarian protein source that originated in Indonesia. They are made from soybeans that are partly cooked, infused with a starter and then fermented until they are extremely rich in protein and easy to digest. Made from soybeans only, or soybeans mixed with grains and seasonings, tempeh is widely available in health-food stores, vacuum-packed, and stored in the refrigerator case or the freezer. Its thick chewy texture takes well to frying and simmering in curries, and its yeasty, earthy, mushroom-like flavor works well in Asian-style cooking.

Thai bird chilies/prik kii-noo; prik kii-nok (*Capsicum annum*)   *See Chilies.*

Thai coffee/o-liang powder
Roasted sesame seed and corn kernels give this coffee a wonderful burnt flavor. Thais like their coffee ice cold and sweet with evaporated milk, or hot with sweetened condensed milk.

Thai tea/cha Thai
Cinnamon, vanilla, star anise, and a little food coloring give this finely chopped black tea its pleasing, unusual flavor and terra-cotta color. Brewed strong and served only cold and very sweet, topped off with evaporated milk

Tofu/dao hoo
In Thai cooking, fresh tofu, also called bean curd, is used especially in soups and Chinese dishes. Usually sold in large square or rectangular cakes packed in water and sealed in one pound tubs. Purchase the firm type for use in recipes in this book. Store leftover tofu in water to cover in the refrigerator. Change the water every few days and use it as soon as possible.

Turmeric/kamin (*Curcuma longa termeric; Curcuma domestica*)
A member of the ginger family, turmeric is an underground stem or rhizome. It grows in clusters of small, stubby fingers, with a dull, brown skin hiding its gorgeous fluorescent-orange meat. It has a faint, earthy taste, but the color is the point here, and it's used in many dishes for that reason, particularly in southern Thailand. Today turmeric gives ball-park mustard and curry powder their characteristic yellow color, and it is found with the ground spices on well-stocked supermarket shelves. It has been used extensively in Asian medicines since ancient times and is the natural dye traditionally used to color the robes of Theravada Buddhist monks. Since color is what matters in cooking with this herb, ground dried turmeric works fine.

Vegetarian oyster sauce/saus nahmahn hoy jay   *See Vegetarian stir-fry sauce.*

Vegetarian stir-fry sauce/saus nahmahn hoy jay
This newcomer to the prepared Asian condiment market is a version of Chinese-style oyster sauce, with a rich essence of dried shiitake mushrooms used in place of oyster extract, along with soy sauce, sugar, salt, and thickeners. Lee Kum Kee distributes its version to supermarkets, labeled "vegetarian stir-fry sauce," and Asian markets carry other brands labled "vegetarian oyster sauce." This thick, silky, and salty sauce pairs beautifully with stir-fried greens, mushrooms, bean sprouts, and noodles.

Vinegar/nahm som
Thais use plain white vinegar, like the distilled white vinegar widely available in grocery stores. Japanese rice vinegar or white wine vinegar will work, although they are both more strongly flavored.

Water chestnuts/haew, (*Elocharis dulcis*)
Fresh water chestnuts resemble giant, rustic Hershey kisses, walnut-sized with rounded bottoms and a brittle yet pliable skin. Check Asian markets for firm, plump water chestnuts that are heavy for their size, and keep them loosely wrapped and chilled for about one week. Peeling away the brown outer covering is *lambahk*, a nifty Thai word meaning a bothersome task, but the result is a sweet crunchy nugget that outshines the canned ones. Slice off the tip and the rounded base, and then peel the barrel-like sides with a paring knife. The crunchy white heart is somewhat like jicama in texture, though drier and denser. Peeled whole water chestnuts are widely available in cans and make a very good substitute for fresh. Rinse and drain well before using them, and store any leftovers in water in the refrigerator for a week or so, changing the water every few days.

Water spinach/pahk boong (*Ipomoea aquatica*)
Also called swamp cabbage, water convolvulus, long green, and morning glory, its Cantonese name is *ong choy*, its Vietnamese name is *rau muong*, and its Malay name is *kang kong*. It has distinctive hollow stems with widely spaced, arrowhead-shaped leaves. It resembles watercress in color and spacing of the leaves, although water spinach is much larger. It comes in huge sheaves; don't worry, however, as it cooks down considerably. Substitute spinach, watercress, or Chinese broccoli, adjusting cooking time according to the vegetable you use.

Wheatballs/look baeng sah-lee   *See Wheat gluten, as well as recipe on page 207.*

Wheat gluten/look baeng sah-lee
This traditional Asian vegetarian protein source is a bland, chewy dumpling made by separating the gluten or protein from the starch and bran in wheat flour and cooking this elastic dough into sturdy little protein-packed lumps. Fried brown and crisp, boiled, simmered, or baked, it is used in traditional Chinese vegetarian cooking in many dishes as a substitute for meat. Also known as wheat protein, wheat meat, wheatballs, and seitan, you can buy it canned and sometimes fresh in Asian markets, usually marinating in a seasoned liquid, or you can make your own at home (page 208).

Wheat protein/look baeng sah-lee   *See Wheat gluten.*

Wild lime leaf/bai makroot (*Citrus hystrix*)
Gorgeous emerald leaves of the wild lime tree, used in soups and curries for their unique, citrusy flavor, exquisite aroma, and beauty. Wild lime leaves are also called *djeroek poeroet, limau purut,* and kaffir (or keffir) lime leaves. They grow attached to each other in pairs, end to end. Look for wild lime leaves in small plastic bags in Asian markets, usually in the refrigerator case. They are difficult to find, but the pleasure of their culinary presence makes it well worth the extra effort to track them down. Sealed airtight and chilled, they will keep four or five days. When the recipe calls for slicing them crosswise into thin threads, try to remove the sturdy vein that runs lengthwise through each wild lime leaf. Start at the pointed end rather than the thick stem end, and use a paring knife to lift up the vein. Use fresh ones or omit them, as dried ones have only a

faint memory of their former greatness. They freeze fairly well, so buy a lot and keep them frozen, using twice the amount called for, straight from the freezer. You could also substitute fresh domestic lime or lemon leaves, or a combination of grated lime zest and freshly squeezed lime juice to taste if these little green treasures are unavailable.

Wild lime peel/piew makroot (*Citrus hystrix*)
This extremely fragrant, flavorful peel of the wild lime is an important ingredient in curry pastes. Wild limes, which have a distinctive, knobby texture, are also referred to as kaffir (or keffir) limes. Inside there is only a little rather bitter juice, which has traditionally been used in shampoos and soaps rather than in the kitchen. Substitute domestic lime peel, or use dried wild lime peel, sold in Asian markets in cellophane packets; soften it in a little warm water until pliable, or break it into bits and grind to a powder.

Winged bean/tua poo
A pale green legume with four sharp-edged fins running lengthwise. The fins seem softly serrated along their edges, as if they have been gathered by a seamstress with a green thumb. According to Elizabeth Schneider, in her excellent reference book *Uncommon Fruits and Vegetables*, this delicate tropical vegetable is very nutritious and high in protein, but its fragility in the face of cool temperatures makes it difficult to cultivate outside Southeast Asia and the Pacific Islands. The flavor of the beans is quite mild, but southern Thais adore their raw, starchy, or *faht-faht*, taste. It is difficult to find them in the West, and they wilt quickly, so keep them wrapped and chilled and use as soon as possible. Green beans look mighty plain by comparison, but they make an excellent substitute.

Yam/mun
You can use any variety of yam for the recipes in this book. Or substitute any kind of sweet potato, potato, kabocha pumpkin, or any kind of winter squash.

Yellow bean sauce/dao jiow kao   *See Asian bean sauce.*

Yellow mung bean centers/tua tong
Known in Thai as "golden beans," these flat oval yellow pellets resemble petite, sturdy rolled oats. They are the split hearts of dried green mung beans, which are in turn the source of the big white bean sprouts that are ubiquitous in Asian cooking. Southeast Asian cooks are partial to these pretty little beans, using them whole in sweet coconut puddings and iced beverages, and steamed and ground to fortify the batter for savory Indian-style fritters (page 23), and the crispy Vietnamese-style filled pancakes known in Thai as *kanome bueang*. Look for them in Asian markets in cellophane packets that may bear the Vietnamese name *dau xanh ca.*

Yuak chili/prik yuak (*Capsicum annuum*)   *See Chilies.*

INDEX

TABLE OF EQUIVALENTS

The exact equivalents in the following tables have been rounded for convenience.

US/UK	Metric
oz = ounce	g = gram
lb = pound	kg = kilogram
in = inch	mm = millimeter
ft = foot	cm = centimeter
tbl = tablespoon	ml = milliliter
fl oz = fluid ounce	l = liter
qt = quart	

WEIGHTS

US/UK	Metric
1 oz	30 g
2 oz	60 g
3 oz	90 g
4 oz (¼ lb)	125 g
5 oz (⅓ lb)	155 g
6 oz	185 g
7 oz	220 g
8 oz (½ lb)	250 g
10 oz	315 g
12 oz (¾ lb)	375 g
14 oz	440 g
16 oz (1 lb)	500 g
1½ lb	750 g
2 lb	1 kg
3 lb	1.5 kg

OVEN TEMPERATURES

Fahrenheit	Celsius	Gas
250	120	½
275	140	1
300	150	2
325	160	3
350	180	4
375	190	5
400	200	6
425	220	7
450	230	8
475	240	9
500	260	10

LIQUIDS

US	Metric	UK
2 tbl	30 ml	1 fl oz
¼ cup	60 ml	2 fl oz
⅓ cup	80 ml	3 fl oz
½ cup	125 ml	4 fl oz
⅔ cup	160 ml	5 fl oz
¾ cup	180 ml	6 fl oz
1 cup	250 ml	8 fl oz
1½ cups	375 ml	12 fl oz
2 cups	500 ml	16 fl oz
4 cups/1 qt	1 l	32 fl oz

LENGTH MEASURES

US/UK	Metric
⅛ in	3 mm
¼ in	6 mm
½ in	12 mm
1 in	2.5 cm
2 in	5 cm
3 in	7.5 cm
4 in	10 cm
5 in	13 cm
6 in	15 cm
7 in	18 cm
8 in	20 cm
9 in	23 cm
10 in	25 cm
11 in	28 cm
12 in/1 ft	30 cm